THE IDEOLOGY OF THE BRITISH RIGHT, 1918–1939

THE IDEOLOGY OF THE BRITISH RIGHT 1918-1939

G. C. WEBBER

ST. MARTIN'S PRESS
New York

Library of Congress Cataloging-in-Publication Data

Webber, G.C., 1958-
    The ideology of the British Right.

    Bibliography: p.
    Includes index.
    1. Conservatism — Great Britain — History — 20th
century. 2. Fascism — Great Britain — History — 20th
century. I. Title.
JA84.G7W38   1986   320.5′2′0941   86-17823
ISBN 0-312-00076-6

CONTENTS

For my Mother and Father

ACKNOWLEDGEMENTS

I am particularly grateful to Dr Martin Ceadel of New College, Oxford, for his stimulating criticisms and suggestions, his continued interest and his unfailing support over the past few years; to Nevil Johnson, the late Philip Williams and Vincent Wright, all of Nuffield College, Oxford, for helping me to clarify my ideas; to Michael Brock of Nuffield College, Oxford, Michael Freeden of Mansfield College, Oxford, and Martin Pugh of the University of Newcastle upon Tyne for reading various chapters of the book and the thesis upon which it is based; to Robert Skidelsky of the University of Warwick and Gillian Peele of Lady Margaret Hall, Oxford, for their comments as examiners of my thesis; and to the Fellows of Nuffield College, Oxford, for the grant that enabled me to complete my work so swiftly.

I would like to thank the following for allowing me to quote from documents in their possession: the Bodleian Library, Oxford; Lord Croft; the Masters, Fellows and Scholars of Churchill College in the University of Cambridge; Vice-Admiral Sir Ian Hogg; Mrs D. M. Maxse; Patricia Gill, County Archivist, West Sussex Record Office; the Duke of Northumberland; the Marquess of Salisbury; the Earl of Selborne; and the Syndics of Cambridge University Library. I would also like to thank Stephen Stacey of the Bodleian Library, Oxford, for helping me to find my way through the Conservative Party archives, and Robin Harcourt Williams for his help and hospitality on my visits to Hatfield House.

Finally, but by no means least, I am greatly indebted to all my friends and colleagues, especially to Rhodri Williams of St. Peter's College, Oxford, Chris Collins and Philip Hunt, each of whom influenced my work, and to Christine Morgan who did more than anyone else to keep my academic interests in perspective.

ABBREVIATIONS

The following abbreviations have occasionally been used in the text, notes and bibliography.

(a) Organisations

AGF	Anglo-German Fellowship
ASU	Anti-Socialist Union
BCAEC	British Council Against European Commitments
BCU	British Commonwealth Union
BFs	British Fascists
BPP	British Peoples' Party
BUF	British Union of Fascists
BWL	British Workers' League
CINEF	Centre International d'Etudes sur la Fascisme
EEU	Empire Economic Union
EIA	Empire Industries Association
FBI	Federation of British Industry
IDC	India Defence Committee
IDL	India Defence League
IES	Indian Empire Society
IEUG	Imperial Economic Unity Group
IFL	Imperial Fascist League
ILP	Independent Labour Party
MCU	Middle Classes Union
NCA	National Constitutional Association
OMS	Organisation for the Maintenance of Supplies
UBC	Unionist Business Committee
UBI	Union of Britain and India
UEP	United Empire Party

(b) Publications

APSR	American Political Science Review
EHR	English Historical Review

ER	English Review
HJ	Historical Journal
IER	Indian Empire Review
JBS	Journal of British Studies
JCH	Journal of Contemporary History
JMH	Journal of Modern History
NEW	New English Weekly
PS	Political Studies
PQ	Political Quarterly

(c) Dates

Note that in the abbreviation of dates the British rather than the American system has been employed. For example, 3.8.22 refers to 3 August 1922.

1 INTRODUCTION

This book examines the ideas, and to a lesser extent the activities of dissident Conservatives and of Fascists in Britain between the wars, partly because the topic has been relatively neglected in the existing academic literature, but mainly because it contributes to our understanding of the Conservative Party and of the Fascist movements that existed during these years. It focuses upon the inter-war period because it was at this time that the Conservatives were forced to come to terms with a series of problems that highlighted internal disagreements and revealed features of the party that threatened, but failed to split the organisation on several occasions. It ends in 1939 because the events that culminated in the Second World War disrupted established patterns of right-wing politics and ushered in a period of uncertainty and confusion from which the Right were slow to recover.

Several important assumptions underlay the work. The first is that the study of ideas can and should contribute to our understanding of political behaviour since, although we must be cautious in assessing the role that political thought might play in shaping political practice, beliefs can be regarded as social 'facts' that help to invest political activity with 'meaning'. This is true even of Conservative Party politics. For although it is commonly claimed that British Conservatives are 'pragmatists' rather than 'ideologues', comments of this kind obscure the extent to which Conservative 'pragmatism' was an unintended consequence of attempts to reconcile similar but conflicting ideologies under the common umbrella of anti-radicalism, and they ignore the fact that right-wing Conservatives were characteristically concerned with questions of political principle.

There are, of course, objections to and problems with the study of ideas. One relates to general questions of intention and causality. To put it simply: we know that certain individuals expressed particular ideas because they happen to have left sufficient evidence for us to be able to reconstruct their views, but we can never be entirely sure how far these beliefs were related to their actions, nor how far similar beliefs may be ascribed to groups of people who

1

seem to have been in sympathy with them. Consequently, generalisations about the role of ideas can only be regarded as tentative. Likewise, presumptions about the relative 'importance' of different ideologies need to be considered carefully. To the extent that they failed to determine the legislative programmes even of the two purely Conservative governments between the wars, right-wing ideas can be and often are regarded as 'insignificant', but it would be wrong to dismiss them simply because they did not result in immediate or tangible reforms. Even 'rejected' ideologies are worthy of study, first for their intrinsic interest; secondly for what they reveal about the groups that propounded them; thirdly for what they can tell us about the political culture of which they were a part; and finally for the light that they shed upon related or rival ideologies and the organisations through which they most often sought and occasionally found expression. Just as the study of radical left-wing ideas contributes to our understanding of the Labour Party, so the study of right-wing ideas deepens our understanding of the Conservative Party.

A second assumption of the book is that one of the reasons for the weakness of British Fascism was the inability of the Fascist movement to attract large numbers of right-wing Conservatives away from their 'natural' party. Dissident Conservatives always constituted a potential reservoir of Fascist sympathisers, especially in the early thirties when Fascism was still regarded as a relatively 'respectable' alternative to liberal democracy, and it seems likely that disillusioned Conservatives were, in fact, the single most important source of support both for the small Fascist groups of the 1920s and for the British Union of Fascists (BUF) in the 1930s.[1] But even though a large proportion of Fascist sympathisers were disillusioned Conservatives, few right-wing Conservatives supported the Fascists and this fact appears to have been related, at least in part, to a complex pattern of ideological disagreements which the following chapters seek to explore in some detail.

A third and related assumption is that dissident Conservatives and Fascists can usefully be considered in relation to each other, and in the pages that follow these groups have been referred to collectively as the British Right.[2] This requires a few words of explanation. The vocabulary of Left and Right in politics is as familiar as it is imprecise. Historically, the terms are generally agreed to have originated with the French National Assembly of 1789 in which the nobles took the position of honour to the

President's right and their opponents sat to his left, but the distinction was soon generalised as a way of describing any two groups divided by a central cleavage, and by the 1920s, when the Labour Party had emerged as a major threat to the Conservatives, the language of Left and Right was beginning to gain currency in Britain.[3] Yet there has never been a consensus either about the meaning or about the proper use of these terms, and the result has been confusion. In everyday speech the words Left and Right are often used so loosely that they do not bear close examination; in academic works they are sometimes defined so narrowly that they no longer have much in common with everyday understanding; and even when abstract definitions have been formulated they have invariably proved inadequate as a method of establishing clear but meaningful limits to the subject under discussion.

Definition remains a problem. Self-designation is, at least in this case, a confusing method of definition because the term 'right-wing' has been used so promiscuously, and has so often been used as a term of abuse, that the end result is chaos rather than clarity. Definitions that focus upon institutional structures are also misleading because they tend to assume that parties, movements or pressure groups can be identified with one particular set of values, and although this is a useful piece of academic short-hand it is usually untrue. It is certainly impossible to define the British Right solely by reference to specified organisations (even though their existence and their aims may be useful *indicators* of ideological disagreements),[4] because the Right assumed a multiplicity of distinct but related forms and cut across the established boundaries between poltical parties. The most useful methods of definition are those that focus upon general values and beliefs, but even these have their limitations. Definitions that identify 'common ideological denominators' are necessarily abstract and are usually expressed in such a way that the 'denominators' identified either cease to be exclusive to the group in question, or cease to be useful as tools of empirical research. Furthermore, definitions of this kind tend to reduce ideologies to a list of 'essential' beliefs which disguise the fact that the *meanings* attached to words can and do change over time, and that it is the relationship *between* propositions that most often accounts for the distinctiveness of an ideology.

For all of these reasons, the British Right might best be understood as displaying a kind of 'family resemblance' that is difficult to 'define' in any 'scientific' manner, but which can nevertheless be perceived, described and analysed. In broad terms, the Right can be characterised as a collection of anti-liberals who disliked socialism and despaired of official Conservatism with varying degrees of intensity. Most right-wingers were and remained members or supporters of the Conservative Party (although it follows from what has been said earlier that most Conservatives were not right-wingers). Some were on the fringes of the party. Others still were actively opposed to it, and many of these supported one or other of the fascist movements instead. Institutionally, the British Right were divided by competing loyalties; ideologically they were united by a common dislike of socialism (usually), liberalism (always), and (both invariably and bitterly) the kind of 'liberal conservatism' that was favoured by Baldwin and most of the Conservative Party leadership.

However, the genesis of these 'family resemblances' can only be properly understood in relation to a number of broad social, political and economic changes that affected Britain in the course of the nineteenth and early twentieth centuries, and the impact that these changes had, particularly upon the Conservative Party. The first concerned Britain's position in the world. From the early 1870s onwards, the British Empire became an issue of political importance and an object of ideological controversy. Between them, the unification of Italy and Germany, the emergence of economic rivals, and the renewed burst of imperial expansion in Africa, served to arouse both a pride in and a fear for the Empire. So momentous were the issues and the passions they aroused that these became the basis of a political re-alignment in the years that followed. With Disraeli's commitment to the imperial cause, the clarification of Gladstone's position, the related battles over Irish home rule, and the gradual absorption of the Liberal Unionists within the ranks of the Conservative Party, the re-alignment was complete, and by the turn of the century the major political parties appeared to have established themselves securely in their new roles. But elements of fluidity remained, not only because the Liberal Party (which had become increasingly radical) was soon faced with a challenge from Labour, but also because the new Conservative coalition forged by Disraeli and stabilised by Salisbury was beginning to experience serious internal divisions.

The most immediate, though not the only causes of this schism were the issues thrown up by the war in South Africa. The Boer War (1899–1902) raised doubts not only about the 'morality' of

British imperialism but also about the stability and defensibility of the Empire, the 'efficiency' of the army, and the suitability of the working classes for military service (almost half of all working-class volunteers were found to be physically unfit). In short, the Boer War provided a focus for anxieties about the Empire and the occasion for a break in Conservative ranks. In the years between 1900 and 1914 the creation of Patriotic leagues, the campaign for tariff reform, and the general orchestration of jingoistic sentiment served to identify the cause of imperialism less with the Conservative Party as a whole than with particular groups within and on the fringes of it. As Summers has argued, 'The Leagues' programmes and propaganda articulated a basic vocabulary of nationalism which set the tone for the British Right for decades.'[5]

It is interesting to note that some of the most ardent imperialists to be found amongst the nascent right wing were not originally Conservatives at all but Liberal Unionists such as Joseph Chamberlain and Lord Milner who, having become detached from the Liberals, now found themselves ill at ease with the Conservative Party as well. Like the Liberals from whom they had become divorced and unlike the mainstream Conservatives with whom they disagreed, these men regarded social cohesion as a product of conscious designs rather than a benefit of organic interaction, and this became a common theme of right-wing ideologies. Indeed, Chamberlain and Milner became the very symbols of opposition to official conservatism on a whole range of issues in the turbulent years before the First World War. Chamberlain was the hero of young Social Imperialists such as Leopold Amery and Henry Page Croft who were to continue the battle for tariffs during the 1920s and the early thirties, while Milner emerged as a champion of the Diehard cause in 1911, as a leader of the British Covenanters in the years that followed, as Chairman of the National Service League in 1915, and finally as a member of the War Cabinet that Lloyd George constructed in 1916. Milner's emergence as a man of 'the Right' was symptomatic of the way in which shared fears about the security of the Empire in the years between 1900 and 1914, allied as they were to anxieties about the House of Lords and Ireland, had helped to forge from a number of disparate groups a recognisable body of Conservative dissidents (usually referred to at this time simply as 'Diehards'). But his subsequent experiment with the British Workers' League and the renewed emphasis upon the 'social' aspects of his Social Imperialism after 1918 were a reminder of the fragility of the right-wing 'consensus' since these brought Milner closer to dissident Labour activists such as John Hodge (President of the BWL and Labour MP for Manchester Gorton until 1923) than they did to dissident Conservatives.[6] United more in adversity than in aim, the Right displayed an inherent tendency towards disintegration that paralleled the way in which radical left-wing groups collapsed and divided. Yet this weakness remained obscure for many years because the First World War, the Russian Revolution, the Irish Settlement of 1921, and later the Government of India Act of 1935 continued to provide the basis for a coalition of defensive nationalists.

The Right were not only worried about imperial affairs. They were also concerned about changes in the nature of the domestic economy and about the attitude that the Conservative Party had adopted towards them. In the course of the nineteenth century, the Conservative Party became the party not only of land but also of capital. It sought to represent the interests of *all* property owners whether their wealth was in land or in capital, and in so far as the party was successful in doing this it provided an institution through which new and powerful groups within society could identify their interests with the maintenance of the *status quo*. At the same time, the gradual extension of the franchise meant that the success of the party depended upon its ability to convince those who did not own property that the interests it represented were 'national' rather than 'sectional' ones. The benefit which the party derived from making this transition was that it continued to function as a viable political force at a time when many Liberals hoped and some Conservatives feared that successive Reform Acts would weaken the Conservative cause. However, the cost of making this transition was that it encouraged the party to stress themes of Conservative 'pragmatism' that owed less to the injunctions of Burke than they did to the need to reconcile different and sometimes conflicting interests within the party, and this in turn emphasised the fact that Conservative Party leaders were just as much brokers *between* interests as they were representatives of them.[7]

As a result, Conservative 'principles' became increasingly unclear, and by the turn of the century the party was suffering a crisis of identity that was to reach a climax during the years from 1909 to 1911 when the Lloyd George budget precipitated a constitutional battle which culminated in the Diehard Revolt and in Balfour's resignation as party leader. By 1914, the Conservative

Party had been out of office for eight years, it had lost three consecutive elections, and at least two of the issues that most clearly divided it from the Liberals — the House of Lords and tariff reform — were the same issues that divided Conservatives themselves. In this respect the war was important in diverting attention from some divisive issues and in breaking the deadlock that afflicted others. But it did not solve the fundamental problems that beset the Conservative Party, and it may even have multiplied them. For although it was true that the party recovered its electoral success in the inter-war years, it did so largely because the opposition was divided and only (so the Right believed) at the expense of its principles. Moreover, although the war had submerged some of the 'old' issues such as the Union and the Lords, the extension of the franchise in 1918 had raised new ones that related much more clearly to the state and the economy.

The problems posed by the 'impact of Labour' were exacerbated by political reform. By the end of the nineteenth century the development of industry and the gradual extension of the franchise had combined to make the language of 'class' more usual than the terminology of 'rank' and 'degree'.[8] Even though the process of political reform had begun well before the physical concentration of workers in large factories heightened class consciousness, industrialisation appeared to have divided society into two or three large blocs, and democratisation appeared to have shifted the balance of political power between them. Neither development was welcomed by the Right, although their critiques of the political order (even before 1918, but especially afterwards) tended to take two similar but subtly different forms. One objection was that too much power had been concentrated in the 'wrong' hands; the other objection was that too little power rested with the 'right' people. In the context of a predominantly aristocratic, agrarian society, Tories of the eighteenth and even of the nineteenth centuries (with whom many on the Right identified) had been inclined to extend the power of the state because 'the state' differed little from 'society', and 'society' incorporated only a small number of noble families. However, in the context of a democratic, industrialised society, the political community was gradually extended until by 1918 it encompassed the bulk of the male population, and the state was no longer regarded as automatically beneficial. It now appeared as likely to threaten established interests as it was to protect them, and as a result, the state came to be seen less as an integral part of the social

8 *Introduction*

'organism' than as an impersonal piece of 'machinery' imposed upon it. But the language in which ideological commitments were expressed did not change as rapidly as the problems that they were meant to address, and the consequence of this was that right-wing ideologies often assumed forms that were a curious amalgam of ancient (apparently 'reactionary') and modern (apparently 'progressive') ideas.

The fundamental objection that the Right levelled at the existing order was that society had been divided into antagonistic classes, and that class had become the basis and the focus of political activity. What the Right wanted was a society that was 'classless' but nevertheless highly stratified, in which the state would cease to be an instrument of class interest, and politics would consequently be geared to 'national' rather than 'sectional' demands. However, it was not clear to those on the Right that the Conservative Party was capable of achieving these goals, since the spirit of 'pragmatism' with which the party had become associated weakened the defence of *specific* values and interests. Consequently, in the years after 1918, the Right came to be identified with a series of factional struggles that took place within the Conservative Party and occasionally spilled out beyond it, most notably in the form of support for Fascism.

The relationship between dissident Conservatism and pro-Fascism has rarely been analysed in any depth. Yet Fascist movements in Britain appear to have relied heavily upon disillusioned Conservatives for much of their (always very limited) support, and this is the context within which the present work seeks to analyse various aspects of Fascist ideology. To date this topic has been largely neglected. The lack of detailed knowledge about right-wing Conservatives, and especially about the nature of their beliefs, has inhibited the construction of plausible generalisations about their political behaviour; and the reluctance of authors to accept until relatively recently that those who supported the Fascists may have done so for genuine ideological reasons has obscured an important issue that helped to determine the scope and the nature of the support that the movements received. Until the 1970s, Benewick's judgement of British Fascist ideology as a play-it-by-ear affair in which 'Policy was often manipulated with a callous disregard for principles'[9] remained effectively unchallenged, and although the emphasis has shifted in recent years it still remains difficult to establish a clear perspective. Comparative studies of Fascism soon reveal the British variant to be idiosyncratic; Skidelsky's masterly biography of Mosley inevitably focuses upon 'the leader'; studies of anti-Semitism have tended to distort the overall picture of British Fascism by concentrating exclusively upon a single issue; and Griffith's work on British enthusiasts for Nazi Germany in the 1930s, stimulating though it is, ultimately does the same thing.[10] The most notable recent attempt to redress the balance has perhaps been Neill Nugent's 1977 essay on the ideas of the BUF, but this too has its limitations since Nugent pays more attention to the internal logic of the ideology than he does to its context or its impact.[11]

In short, few books or articles have dealt seriously with the British Right as a whole.[12] This book attempts to fill the gap. In the first place it seeks to clarify and analyse the beliefs that those on the Right held and to demonstrate the fact that, in contrast to the assumptions which are usually made, these ideas were diverse, fluid and often interesting. Secondly, it tries to show how the variety of ideas on the Right contributed to the weakness of the Fascist movement in Britain by creating ideological barriers that limited the support it received from disillusioned Conservatives. Thirdly, it examines the relationship between the right wing and the leadership of the Conservative Party itself and argues that ideology played an important part in the struggle between them. It is also argued that the internal party disputes of the period were not just disagreements about particular questions of policy such as Ireland, tariffs and India, but also arguments about the nature of 'Conservatism' itself, and as a result the discussion of right-wing ideas that follows concentrates mainly upon general themes (namely society, the economy, the state and the international order) rather than specific issues.

The study proceeds at two levels. Chapters 2 and 3 establish the historical context and attempt to show *inter alia* that despite being poorly represented in Parliament, the Right was of considerable importance within the Conservative Party as a whole by virtue of its strength amongst the constituency organisations which, for a number of reasons, had themselves grown in importance and extended their autonomy since the late nineteenth century. Chapters 4 to 7 then analyse the ideologies of the Right as they were revealed in books, journals, newspapers and private correspondence of the period. These chapters focus upon a number of broad themes. Chapter 4 considers perceptions of the social order; Chapter 5 examines attitudes towards property and the economy;

Chapter 6, ideas about the state; and Chapter 7, problems of inter-national relations. Running throughout these chapters are two central questions: first, in what ways were the beliefs of the Con-servative Right related to support for Fascism in Britain? and secondly, in what ways did the right wing of the Conservative Party itself change during this period? The concluding chapter attempts to pull these strands together.

In broad outline the book suggests that the Right drew its support from those on the edges of the constellation of interests usually represented in Britain by the Conservative Party. On the one hand were men and women who belonged to declining or non-elites and felt the fear of 'dispossession' most acutely; on the other, those who belonged to dominant or emergent elites but were insecure despite (or even because of) their success. Between them, these groups generated a number of ideologies which were distinct from 'mainstream' Conservatism and different even from each other, but which nevertheless constituted a perceptible 'family' of related political ideas.

Within this framework, the inter-war years emerge as a period of considerable importance for the Right, and ultimately for the Con-servative Party itself. On the one hand, attempts to invest old-fashioned toryism with 'relevance' sometimes ended in support for Fascism even though the two creeds differed in important respects, but these ideologies were discredited by the fact, if not by the approach of war with the Axis powers and seemed increasingly anachronistic after 1945. On the other hand, most right-wing Con-servatives believed Fascism to be unnecessary or undesirable or both, and their own beliefs were gradually re-defined in such a way that while they remained outspokenly anti-socialist they also became vigorously pro-capitalist and in favour of a 'strong' but, unlike the fascists, a 'minimal' state. However, these transforma-tions bred divisions which were highlighted and multiplied, first by the loss of a common cause (most notably the struggle against the Government of India Act of 1935) and then by the need to tackle questions of European foreign policy about which they disagreed. Consequently, by the end of the 1930s the Right appeared to have lost its corporate identity, and this in turn helped to facilitate a gradual re-alignment of right-wing forces in the years that followed. Until the 1930s the character of the Right was determined primarily by questions of nationalism and imperialism. Gradually, after the 1930s — but not fully until the late 1960s — the character of the Right came instead to mirror sharp economic and constitutional disagreements rather than to reflect a vague social and 'patriotic' consensus.

Notes

1. G. C. Webber, 'Patterns of Membership and Support for the British Union of Fascists', *JCH* (1984), pp. 575–606; G. C. Webber, 'The British Isles' in D. Mühlberger (ed.), *The Social Base of European Fascist Movements* (forthcoming, 1987), ch. 3.
2. The argument that dissident Conservatives and Fascists can usefully be considered in relation to each other does *not*, of course, imply that this is the *only* useful way in which they can be considered. Similarly, the adoption of the label 'the British Right', does not preclude the use of alternative labels such as 'far Right', 'extreme Right', etc. which some may prefer.
3. S. Brittan, *Left or Right: The Bogus Dilemma* (London, 1968), ch. 1.
4. For a brief guide to some of these organisations refer to the Appendix.
5. A. Summers, 'The Character of Edwardian Nationalism' in P. Kennedy and A. Nicholls (eds.), *Nationalist and Racialist Movements in Britain and Germany Before 1914* (London, 1981), p. 85.
6. R. Douglas, 'The National Democratic Party and the British Workers' League', *HJ* (1972), pp. 533–52; J. O. Stubbs, 'Lord Milner and Patriotic Labour, 1914–1918', *EHR* (1972), pp. 717–54.
7. Similar analyses are offered by A. Gamble, *The Conservative Nation* (London, 1974) and N. Harris, *Competition and the Corporate Society* (London, 1972).
8. G. Watson, *The English Ideology* (Allen Lane, London, 1973), ch. 10.
9. R. J. Benewick, *The Fascist Movement in Britain* (1972), p. 133, originally published as *Political Violence and Public Order* (London, 1969).
10. R. Skidelsky, *Oswald Mosley* (London, 1975 and 1981); C. Holmes, *Anti-Semitism in British Society, 1876–1939* (London, 1979); G. C. Lebzelter, *Political Anti-Semitism in England, 1918–1939* (London, 1978); W. F. Mandle, *Anti-Semitism and the British Union of Fascists* (London, 1968); R. Griffiths, *Fellow Travellers of the Right* (London, 1980).
11. N. Nugent, 'The Ideas of the British Union of Fascists' in N. Nugent and R. King (eds.), *The British Right* (Farnborough, 1977), pp. 133–64.
12. The only directly relevant thesis and article not so far mentioned are B. L. Farr, 'The Development and impact of Right-wing Politics in Great Britain, 1903–1932', Ph.D., Univ. of Illinois at Chicago Circle, 1976; and J. R. Jones, 'England' in H. Rogger and E. Weber (eds.), *The European Right* (London, 1965), pp. 29–70.

PART ONE:

THE HISTORICAL SETTING

INTRODUCTION

Chapters 2 and 3 attempt to place the inter-war Right in an historical context, but they are not intended to provide a continuous historical monograph, and they deliberately seek to avoid general
descriptions of Conservative Party politics. Their main objectives
are to introduce the reader to individuals, groups and journals
about which little has been written elsewhere; to say something of
their relationship to each other; and to examine the nature of
dissent within the Conservative Party. Least attention is devoted to
those individuals and organisations (such as Mosley and the BUF)
whose activities have already attracted a large literature, and the
general conclusions which arise from these chapters are outlined in
Chapter 8.

The two chapters are divided into broadly chronological sections
which correspond to changes in the nature or emphasis of right-
wing activism. Chapter 2 deals with the 'Twenties' and is subdivided into two parts: 1918–1922 and 1922–1929. Chapter 3 deals
with the 'Thirties' and consists of two similar subdivisions:
1929–1935 and 1935–1940. Within these parameters the focus
shifts between the parliamentary and the extra-parliamentary Right
according to the relevance of each to our theme, and the approach
varies between different levels of analysis according to their relative
utility. Thus, in the few years prior to 1922 and after 1929 the
emphasis is mainly upon dissent within the Conservative Party, and
the argument is often detailed. At other times the narrative is more
general.

2 THE TWENTIES

1918–1922

For many Conservatives, the years that followed the First World War were ones of anxiety and uncertainty in which, for a number of reasons, political trends seemed not to favour stability. In the first place, the Left were assuming a new importance. The trade union movement had almost doubled in size since 1913; industrial militancy was on the increase; the Labour Party had re-organised itself and adopted a 'socialist' constitution; the franchise had been extended to include large numbers of propertyless adult males; and traditional partisan loyalties had been weakened by wartime co-operation on the one hand and by the influx of new voters on the other. Secondly, the Conservative Party appeared to have become a hesitant and defensive organisation, incapable (some thought) of providing a positive alternative to socialism. Because the Conservative Party had not won a parliamentary majority since the election of 1900, many found it difficult to believe that the Conservatives were still the 'natural' party of government; and because the party leaders had become unusually equivocal in their statements of policy about issues such as tariff reform and after 1914 even Ireland, many were uncertain about what exactly it now meant to be a 'Conservative'. Both were disconcerting. In addition, the Russian Revolution of 1917 and the spate of unrest that subsequently afflicted continental Europe provided pessimistic Conservatives in Britain with a terrifying vision of the fate that could befall the United Kingdom if discontented workers at home or rebellious nationalists in the colonies were somehow to gain the upper hand, and this too heightened Conservative unease.

These fears were not greatly allayed by Bonar Law's decision to shelter behind Lloyd George in the 'Coupon Election' of 1918. From a Conservative point of view, the continuation of the Coalition Government seems in retrospect to have been a prudent move. Lloyd George was a leader whose popularity made him a formidable opponent at the time of the election, but whose lack of support in the Commons (133 MPs to a Conservative total of 383, including the un-couponed Tories) made him a relatively pliable ally in the years that followed. The Conservatives were able to exert a considerable influence over government policy whilst distancing themselves from unpopular measures, and in this respect Lloyd George was a useful partner. He avoided a possible general strike during the unrest of 1919–1920; he introduced the Safeguarding of Industries Act in 1921; and he carried through a policy of retrenchment and de-regulation with less opposition than a purely Conservative government might have expected. But the Coalition was a source of irritation and concern to many Conservative backbenchers who disliked Lloyd George personally and distrusted him politically, especially in the areas of foreign and colonial policy where he carried most weight. Right-wing Conservatives in particular resented his accommodating attitude towards the Soviet Union, were wary of the 1919 Montagu-Chelmsford reforms that established a system of 'dyarchy' in India, and were horrified by the Irish Settlement of 1921.[1]

The Coalition was also unpopular with right-wing Conservatives outside Parliament where the combined impact of political dissatisfaction, industrial tension and social anxiety resulted not merely in a cynical distrust of frontbench politicians but in a wave of anti-Semitic agitation. The reasons for this were many and varied, but two contradictory consequences of the war were of special importance. On the one hand, the war appeared to heighten awareness of national solidarity and to encourage the formation of 'nationalist' organisations hoping to capitalise upon it. So, for example, the tarrif reformer and Conservative MP, Henry Page Croft, created the National Party in 1917; the businessman (and later Conservative MP), Patrick Hannon, helped to establish the Comrades of the Great War in 1918; and journals such as the *Englishman* (which, unusually, championed the cause of specifically English nationalism) appeared soon thereafter.[2] On the other hand, however, the war appeared to witness a sharpening of class consciousness which was evident not only in the growing identification of working-class interests with the Labour Party, but also in the quickening of middle-class activism and the creation of groups such as the Middle Classes Union (established 1919) which were openly pledged to the defence of their class position.[3] As a result, the sense of national solidarity that the Right sought to exploit was often apparent only in opposition to 'out-groups' such as Germans, Russians (Bolsheviks) and Jews.[4] Moreover, the anti-Semitism of this period was subtly different both in substance and in tone from what had come before. For whereas in the past it had usually remained little more than a cultural prejudice, individuals such as George Lane-Fox Pitt-Rivers, groups such as the Britons (established 1919), newspapers such as the *Morning Post*, and journals such as the *Patriot* (established 1922), were seeking to transform it into a conscious ingredient of British political life.[5]

Both inside and outside Parliament, therefore, there was evidence that right-wing Conservatives of all kinds were losing confidence in Conservative Party leaders and so in the organisation that these leaders controlled, but very few options were open to would-be rebels. For even though Conservative leaders had initially been fearful partners in a short-term anti-socialist alliance, the simple fact of survival tempted them towards a new electoral strategy in which a deliberate attempt was made to attract middle-class voters away from the Liberal Party by projecting Labour as the dominant progressive opposition,[6] and the success of this tactic subsequently left Conservative dissidents with little choice but to follow their party leaders. Yet this schematic description of events obscures the fact that the outcome resulted not so much from a process of rational decision-making as from a protracted power-struggle within the Conservative Party in which right-wingers played a prominent part. For although the Carlton Club rebellion (discussed below) was by no means an exclusively right-wing affair, the existence of the Right as an organised 'faction' within the party was of critical importance in shaping the reaction of more moderate Conservatives to the loss of confidence in the Coalition.

The Conservative revolt against the Lloyd George Coalition culminated in the Carlton Club meeting (19 October 1922) at which 187 MPs voted to discontinue the alliance and only 86 MPs voted to maintain it. The reasons for this decision were manifold. The meeting itself came hot on the heels of the 'Chanak Crisis' which appeared to bring Britain close to war with Turkey and which confirmed Conservative prejudices against Lloyd George's foreign policy. It also came on the same day that the result of the Newport by-election was announced — a victory for the independent Conservative in a three-cornered contest which finally convinced the undecided that the party did not need Liberal allies to achieve electoral success in the face of Labour opposition. In addition, a number of junior ministers had felt aggrieved for some time by Austen Chamberlain's magisterial style of leadership and their own relatively limited prospects of promotion, and whole sections of the party (particularly at the constituency level) were dissatisfied with Coalition policies which were thought, if not to be wrong in principle, at least to be an electoral liability in the long-run. Consequently, 'moderate' and 'progressive' Conservatives were, in the end, at least as important as right-wing agitators in determining the fate of the Coalition.[7] But they had never previously taken the initiative in attacking the government, and this was a factor of some significance.

Conservative dissatisfaction with the post-war Coalition had been evident from the start. A number of Tories had stood as 'independent' or 'un-couponed' Conservatives in the election of 1918, and some had abandoned the title altogether, but relatively few of these were returned to Parliament and the ones that were (48 un-couponed Conservatives and a few others) were soon swamped in a sea of coalitionists who commanded an overall majority of 185.[8] Consequently, revolt was slow to surface and in the end it was not until Bonar Law retired from politics in March 1921 and was replaced as party leader by the hapless Austen Chamberlain that the rebels seized their chance. Even then the 'Diehard Revolt' (as this became known, with conscious reference to the events of 1911) was slow to gain momentum.

The initial impetus for a concerted campaign was provided by the 4th Marquis of Salisbury (the eldest son of the famous Prime Minister) who wrote to the press in June 1921 urging the Conservative Party to form an independent government.[9] This was followed in July by a symbolic revolt in the Commons when first Col. Martin Archer-Shee (an ex-Chief Whip) and then Col. John Gretton (Chairman of both the Unionist Business Committee and the Unionist Reconstruction Committee) resigned the party whip in protest at the opening of negotiations with the Irish nationalist leader, De Valera.[10] In October, the 8th Duke of Northumberland, a leading exponent of the Jewish-Bolshevik conspiracy theory who had made a name for himself during the post-war miners' strike, also declared his public opposition to the Coalition.[11] But still the revolt was weak and disorganised. On 31 October 1921, Col. Gretton and Rupert Gwynne (Conservative MP for Eastbourne) forced a division in the House on a motion of censure on the government's handling of the Irish negotiations. The result was a disappointment for the rebels: 43 voted in favour of the censure; 439 voted against.[12] And although they might have expected more success at the party's annual conference in Liverpool in November, their attempts to reverse the government's policy on Ireland once again met with defeat.

However, as so often in Conservative politics, appearance and reality were very different. The Diehards had actually been well received by the delegates at the Liverpool conference and Chamberlain, who was privately worried about the result of the debate, had secured a victory for the government only by using Archibald Salvidge, one of the most important Conservative politicians in Lancashire, to confuse the issue by turning the vote into one of confidence in Chamberlain's leadership and by arguing that the party could only keep its pledges to Ulster so long as it remained intact.[13] As Lindsay and Harrington suggest, 'It was obvious that many, possibly most, delegates had voted against their true convictions, and that the leadership could ignore those convictions only at its own peril.'[14] Yet this was precisely what Chamberlain proceeded to do and within months of the conference the Diehards were once again in open revolt.

Chamberlain seemed to believe that the Irish Settlement of December 1921 would rob the Diehards of an issue around which to rally, but that was not the case since the Diehards were not concerned solely about Ireland. Indeed, the Irish question had been as much an occasion for rebellion as a cause of it. As we noted above, dissatisfaction with coalition government could be traced back a long way (at least as far as 1917 when Henry Page Croft and Richard Cooper had formed the short-lived National Party) and now that Ireland had become merely one issue among many (albeit an issue of great symbolic value) the Diehard movement emerged as a centre of opposition on a whole *range* of issues from public economy to imperial defence.

In February 1922 Gretton resumed the battle by sending letters to the press and delegations to the party leaders,[15] and although it was all to no avail,[16] the other leading rebels followed suit. Salisbury, the supposed 'leader' of the Diehards had been trying to form a parliamentary opposition since December 1921 with the help of Carson, Londonderry and Ronald McNeill (at that time his only link apart from Viscount Wolmer with Gretton and the other Diehard MPs). But he too had limited success. Publicly, Salisbury exploited the propaganda value of his People's Union for Economy (an up-market version of the Anti-Waste League which was controlled by Lord Rothermere together with Lord Northcliffe and

Horatio Bottomley). Privately he sought to exert influence on the party through its trustees and to coax Bonar Law out of retirement as an alternative leader.[17] Meanwhile, Northumberland was promoting his own brand of conservatism, both indirectly through the *Morning Post* (of which he was later to become the Chairman of the Board of Directors) and more explicitly through the medium of the Boswell Press which he established in 1921, and the columns of the *Patriot* which he established in 1922.[18]

Gradually, from the end of 1921 onwards, these three circles of dissent began to overlap (although Salisbury and Gretton remained at arms length from each other and relied heavily upon intermediaries to maintain communications),[19] and in March 1922 a 'Diehard Manifesto' resounding with general commitments to the Throne, to economy, and to firm government, was circulated by H. A. Gwynne (editor of the *Morning Post*) and published in *The Times*.[20] This amounted to a declaration of war, and although Chamberlain commented sarcastically (and correctly) that the document contained nothing to which he could not put his own name,[21] the significance of the manifesto was that by keeping the commitments general it was able to pull the dissidents together. The list of signatories that appeared below the text bore witness to its success: Salisbury, Carson, Northumberland, Finlay, Londonderry, Linlithgow, Sumner, Sydenham, Sir Frederick Banbury, Joynson-Hicks, Sir A. Sprot (MP for East Fife, Asquith's old seat), Col. Gretton, Capt. Foxcroft (MP for Bath), Rupert Gwynne, Esmond Harmsworth and Ronald McNeill. Salisbury's more famous manifesto of 2 June announcing the creation of the Conservative and Unionist Movement was consequently a move away from the other Diehards rather than a move towards them. Significantly, Salisbury's document stressed the importance of party unity and was not signed by anyone who sat in the House of Commons.[22] But even though the document provided an indication of Salisbury's misgivings about the direction that the anti-Coalition revolt was taking, it was not enough to split the Diehards into openly competing groups, and in July 1922 the *Morning Post*'s 'Diehard Fund' (which raised over £20,000 in less than a month and signalled the strength of support that the rebels enjoyed in the constituencies) was publicly put at the disposal of Lord Salisbury.[23]

With a central organisation existing independently of the official party leadership, with activities in the constituencies, with an embryonic programme of its own, and with a source of finance beyond the control of Chamberlain and the party managers, there was little doubt that the Diehard movement was hardening into a fully-fledged 'faction'.[24] Yet there was still little sign of real unanimity on the Right and the most important cleavage was now the least obvious. For the money upon which Salisbury was supposed to rely had actually been raised by a newspaper more closely allied to his rivals than it was to himself, and *control* of the Diehard Fund did not rest with Salisbury but with the three trustees — Gretton, the Duke of Bedford (a Diehard of 1911), and Admiral Hall (Head of Naval Intelligence during the war and later Principal Agent of the Conservative Party). Consequently, as the pace of events quickened in September and October the Diehard movement found itself in a curious position. It was clear from the columns of the *Morning Post* that the fund was actually being used to encourage activists within the constituency parties to act independently of the party leaders and run Conservative rather than Coalition candidates whenever possible.[25] Yet Salisbury, the nominal leader of the Diehards, was desperately trying to back-pedal. Ever since July he had been trying to convince H. A. Gwynne that they should drop the name 'Diehard' because 'other people take it . . . to mean something sectional',[26] whereas 'what we are out for, of course, is to redeem the whole Conservative Party',[27] and in the end he started to refer to his own supporters as the 'Free Conservatives' instead.[28] But the niceties of language only highlighted the awkwardness of his position. The simple fact was that by September 1922 Salisbury had lost control of his own 'followers' and was unable to prevent Free Conservative candidates from opposing Coalition Unionists.[29]

Consequently, when the Coalition collapsed, the Conservative decision to leave it owed more than is usually supposed to the activists on the Right not only because they were the ones who had forced the pace of events, but also (and more importantly) because they were the ones who seemed most likely to gain from prolonged intransigence amongst Conservative leaders.[30] The impression given by Baldwin that the Conservative Party left the Coalition because they feared the 'dynamic force' of Lloyd George is only a half-truth. In fact, as Bonar Law made clear at the Carlton Club meeting on 19 October 1922, many Conservatives were just as concerned about their own right wing:[31]

The feeling against the continuation of the Coalition is so strong that [if we follow Austen Chamberlain's advice] our party will be broken, that a new party will be formed; and . . . on account of those who have gone, who are supposed to be more moderate men, what is left of the Conservative Party will become more reactionary; and I, for one, say that though what you call the reactionary element in our party has always been there, and must always be there, if it is the sole element our party is absolutely lost.

Interestingly, Bonar Law depicted the Conservative Right as a more-or-less homogeneous group of 'reactionaries', and this impression is still conveyed by most historical accounts of the period. Yet the Diehards of 1922 did not conform to any one stereotype and this was clear even at the leadership level.[32] Thus, on the one hand stood established aristocrats such as Salisbury who wanted a return to the traditions of paternal Tory democracy; on the other stood wealthy businessmen such as Gretton who favoured a more aggressive form of capitalism; and somewhere between the two stood the 8th Duke of Northumberland, a major landowner *and* a leading industrialist, who spoke like a reactionary aristocrat but behaved like a hard-headed businessman and on balance had more in common with Gretton than he did with Salisbury. These three formed an uneasy triangular alliance as leaders of the Diehard movement, but the situation remained complicated: Salisbury was the nominal 'leader' of the Diehards but he had few links with dissident Conservative MPs and he positively disliked Gretton who was the leading rebel in the Commons; Gretton, meanwhile, was difficult to work with and was often distrusted even by his closest associates; whilst Northumberland, largely through his association with the *Morning Post*, the Boswell Press, and the *Patriot*, each of which gave him free publicity, became in effect the alternative leader of the Diehards in the country.[33] For much of the time these divisions did not matter, but they became important during 1922. For as dissatisfaction with the Coalition rapidly spread beyond Parliament so within it the balance of power shifted between the Diehard leaders. So long as prestige within the parliamentary party was the most important asset which the rebels possessed, Salisbury remained indispensable. But as soon as the measure of Diehard strength became the degree of support they could muster amongst constituency parties, the initiative passed to Gretton and Northumberland.

This shifting balance of power on the Right also reflected con-temporary developments in the nature and structure of the Con-servative Party, particularly the growing militancy of constituency parties and the semi-formal organisation of backbench opinion in the Commons. Constituency parties had not become the normal unit of organisation until after 1885 when the leaders and managers of the party sought to improve the efficiency of the party's electoral machinery. Initially the constituency organisations had been sub-servient to the centre, but increasingly they became critical of party leaders and willing to assert their independence. This much was already clear before the First World War both during the tariff reform agitation of 1903 and during the successful campaign against Balfour in 1910/11. The development was still more marked after 1918 when the extension of the franchise freed con-stituency organisations from the need to focus their attention upon registration and when the accompanying re-distribution measures created a large number of safe Conservative seats which encour-aged both backbench MPs and their constituency supporters to be more open in their criticism of party leaders. Especially after the 5th Reform Act of 1928, constituency parties were effectively liberated from Central Office control as membership rose, sub-scriptions increased and the right to choose prospective parlia-mentary candidates was consolidated.[34] Partly as a result of these changes, the annual conference also grew in size and importance to the extent (as we shall see in Chapter 3) where the party leaders began to feel obliged not only to attend them regularly but also, when necessary, to manipulate them.

These developments were also related, both as causes and as effects, to changing patterns of behaviour amongst backbench Conservative MPs. Sporadic revolts and occasional organised rebellions were nothing new in Conservative Party politics, but especially during the First World War attempts were made to create structures by means of which backbench opinion could be co-ordinated, and this had unforeseen repercussions. Thus, although organisations such as the Unionist Business Committee (established 1915) and the Unionist War Committee (established 1916) were tolerated and even encouraged by Conservative Party leaders and managers as a method of maintaining partisan loyalties and enthu-siasms whilst participating in a wartime coalition, similar organisa-tions persisted even after 1918. The Unionist War Committee, for example, a barometer of 'rank and file' sentiment during the war which was headed by Sir Frederick Banbury and Ronald McNeill (both of whom were later to sign the 1922 Diehard Manifesto), was replaced after the war by the Unionist Reconstruction Committee, a belligerent anti-Coalition organisation that included both Col. Gretton and Edward Carson (both of whom had previously been leaders of the Unionist Business Committee and both of whom subsequently signed the Diehard Manifesto). Furthermore, after the collapse of the Lloyd George Coalition, frontbench politicians were sufficiently conscious of the problems that disaffected backbench MPs could create to provide a formal structure through which backbench opinions could be channelled in the form of the 1922 Committee.[35]

Consequently, it would be a mistake to think of the Diehard Revolt of 1921/2 as an isolated example of unrepresentative behaviour encouraged by a group of equally unrepresentative reactionary backbenchers. Rather, it was symptomatic of long-term developments in the way that the Conservative Party organised itself in the country and operated within Parliament, and it reflected the fact that organised dissent was becoming a commonplace feature of Conservative Party politics. Moreover, it highlighted the internal diversity and structural peculiarities of the Conservative Right. For although it was represented in Parliament by peripheral figures with profound differences of opinion and little chance of success, it was supported in the country by large numbers of constituency activists who were increasingly independent and critical of Conservative Party leaders, and these features of the British Right were important factors, not only in providing constraints within which disillusioned Conservatives were forced to work but also in providing a backcloth for many right-wing discussions of themes such as leadership, populism and occasionally fascism.

1922–1929

The years from 1918 to 1922 had been important for the Right in a number of ways. Ideologically, the period had seen the emergence of 'anti-Bolshevism' and the resurgence of anti-Semitism as themes that were to distinguish the post-war from the pre-war Right. Anti-Bolshevism was different both in kind and in content from the anti-socialism of the pre-1917 era, and partly as a consequence, anti-Semitism became more clearly political and more often identified with the Right than the Left. Organisationally, the first few years after 1918 had seen the resurgence of the parliamentary 'Diehards' as an important (but internally divided) faction within the Conservative Party. Tactically, the period had confronted the Right at least with the appearance of a choice between continuing to work with, or attempting to work against the Conservative Party. However, when this option was foreclosed after the return of the Conservative Party to office in October 1922 (and when it remained so despite the creation of a short-lived minority Labour government in January 1924), right-wing activism began to atrophy.

From the end of 1922 onwards the drift of external events arrested the development of a coherent grouping of dissident Conservatives since the gradual decline of industrial militancy and the division of their political opponents during elections made radical-Right solutions seem redundant. Even the apparent set-backs and difficulties of the period could be interpreted by those who favoured moderation as signs that the country could be governed without recourse to extreme measures. For example, although it was true that the Labour Party had gained power briefly and tenuously in 1924, their leaders (at least) had shown themselves to be moderate at heart; and even though the General Strike of May 1926 could still be regarded by some alarmists as a prelude to revolution (while it lasted), it seemed to most more like a pathetic postscript to the troubles of the early twenties. Indeed, the General Strike was symptomatic of the problems that the Right faced during this period. For the 'threat' from the Left against which they were organised was obviously weak or non-existent, whilst the 'defence of the state' to which they were committed meant in practice support for the government, and this robbed them of a distinctive position. Thus, although the *British Gazette* was printed on the machines of the *Morning Post* (the principal shareholder of which was the Duke of Northumberland), and although the enterprise was managed by Admiral Hall (one of the trustees of the Diehard Fund in 1922), the publication was under the general control of Winston Churchill (at this time distrusted by the Right) and the main aim of the campaign was not to strengthen the hand of Cabinet 'hawks' such as Neville Chamberlain, Joynson-Hicks or L. S. Amery, but simply to rally support behind Baldwin.[36]

At first glance it seemed as if the pressure of political

circumstances was forcing Conservatives to settle their internal differences in order to meet the challenge posed by Labour, but this
was not really the case. If anything, the apparent success of the
party merely obliged dissidents to repress their criticisms because
they had no real prospect of establishing an independent organisation capable of mounting an electoral challenge to the Conservative
Party (Croft's National Party had already proved the point in 1918)
and little chance of capturing the party itself. There were also
positive reasons for resisting temptations to rock the boat. In
several respects 1927 marked the high-point of right-wing influence
within the party (and the low-point of intra-party intrigue). Apart
from the passage of the Trades Disputes Act, 1927 saw the with-
drawal of the British Trade Mission to Moscow which effectively
revoked the diplomatic recognition of the Soviet Union granted by
the Labour Government of 1924 (and re-affirmed in 1929). It also
saw the announcement of a plan for the long-awaited reform of the
House of Lords which had orginally been a Conservative condition
for the proposed extension of the franchise in 1917, although these
proposals were swiftly abandoned.

The parliamentary success of the Conservative Party after 1922
muted internal criticisms, but it did little to forge unity. Indeed, the
semi-voluntary suppression of dissent created a growing feeling of
resentment on the Right that finally erupted with enormous force
after the electoral defeat of 1929 when Baldwin adopted the characteristic but unsuccessful slogan of 'Safety First'. The problem was
that the Right disliked Baldwin as a leader (although they were
quite unable to produce an alternative), and became increasingly
critical of his policies and his style. They blamed him for losing the
1923 election by not pushing tariff reform hard enough; they disliked the way in which he re-introduced 'coalitionists' such as
Austen Chamberlain and Birkenhead into the Cabinet of 1924; they
were unhappy when he disposed of Admiral Hall as Principal
Agent; they distrusted him when he placed Churchill at the
Exchequer; they disagreed with his progressive attitudes on social
reform; and even though they applauded the introduction of the
Trades Disputes Act of 1927 (which not only outlawed sympathetic
strikes but made it necessary for trade unionists to contract *in* to
the political levy) they did not forget that Baldwin had opposed the
Macquisten Bill of 1925 with his famous peroration: 'Give peace in
our time, O Lord.'[37] In the circumstances, it was hardly surprising
that the Right considered Baldwin's leadership to be not merely

uninspiring but positively dangerous.

Meanwhile, beyond Parliament (but occasionally within it as well), pro-Fascist publications and explicitly Fascist movements inspired by Mussolini's early achievements in Italy, were beginning to arouse the interest of disgruntled and frustrated right-wing Conservatives. True enough, many of the radical-Right organisations and journals established in the wake of the war had gone into decline after 1922 as the Conservative Party had regained its position of electoral hegemony. The Britons, for example, was practically defunct as a political organisation from 1925 onwards even though it continued to operate as an anti-Semitic publishing company; the idiosyncratic journals of Lord Alfred Douglas (*Plain English* and *Plain Speech*) had both ground to a halt by 1922; and the nationalist paper, the *Englishman*, was wound up in February 1920, less than a year after its launch. But those publications which survived such as the *Morning Post*, the *Patriot*, and Leopold Maxse's *National Review*, all showed considerable interest in Fascism — if only because it promised firm 'leadership' in contrast to that supplied by Baldwin. And in place of those organisations which had withered and died during the early years of the 1920s a number of overtly Fascist groups emerged to give old grievances a new twist. Of course, organisations such as the British Fascists (the BFs, established 1923), the Centre International d'Etudes sur la Fascisme (CINEF, founded in Lausanne in 1927 but represented in Britain by James Strachey Barnes), and the Imperial Fascist League (IFL, created in 1929) were of little practical importance, but they did provide an alternative (or perhaps a supplement) to Conservatism.

There seems little doubt that the Fascist movements of the 1920s were predominantly middle- or upper-middle-class organisations whose members wanted a stronger dose of conservatism than the Conservative Party could or would provide.[38] The British Fascists actually urged its supporters to *vote* for the Conservative Party during elections, and in general movements such as the BFs and the IFL gained most of their support from amongst a small group of 'respectable' middle-class rebels (and in the case of the BFs, minor aristocrats) concentrated in and around London. Socially, British Fascism in the 1920s attracted those who had been (or feared that they might become) 'marginalised' by the competing claims of organised capital on the one hand and organised labour on the other. Politically, this was reflected in their fear that the

Conservative Party might not be capable of resisting socialist advances.

The new Fascist movements even appeared to be driving a wedge between the 'militants' and the 'moderates' on the Right, and by the end of the twenties there were few points of contact between the two. Diehards such as Henry Page Croft (whose sister, Lady Pearson, was later to stand as a BUF candidate) occasionally employed BF 'shocktroops' to police public meetings; individuals such as William Sanderson (a friend of Viscount Lymington and Arnold Leese) or Nesta Webster (a colleague of Northumberland's and a member of the BFs) or even Lord Sydenham (a Conservative Peer who belonged to the Britons and CINEF) provided links between the two wings; and publications such as Col. A. H. Lane's book, *The Alien Menace*, which was first published in 1928 and reproduced in five editions over the next six years, attracted attention both within and beyond Parliament.[39] Yet these were exceptions. In general the two strands of the Right inhabited separate spheres, and it was tempting to assume that this division would widen with time. But the events of the 1930s were to show that this was a false expectation.

Notes

1. The best account of the period is K. O. Morgan, *Consensus and Disunity* (Oxford, 1979).
2. Croft MS, Churchill College, Cambridge; Hannon MS, House of Lords. On the National Party refer to Appendix.
3. Founded, according to *The Times*, 7.3.19, in order to 'withstand the rapacity of the manual worker and profiteer'. In 1921 it changed its name to the National Citizens' Council. Baron Askwith was the MCU's President, but some of its leaders such as Sir J. R. Pretyman-Newman MP (Vice-President) had links with early Fascist groups. Refer to R. J. Benewick, *Political Violence and Public Order* (London, 1969), ch. 2.
4. Sometimes Blacks were picked on too. In 1919 there was a series of race riots directed against West Indian seamen as a result of which several people died. See J. Stevenson, *British Society, 1914–1945* (Harmondsworth, 1984), p. 98. On later anti-Black sentiments refer to Michael Pugh, 'Peace with Italy: BUF Reactions to the Abyssinian War', *The Wiener Library Bulletin* (1974), pp. 11–18.
5. G. L-F. Pitt-Rivers, *The World Significance of the Russian Revolution* (Oxford, 1920); the Britons had been founded by H. H. Beamish who left a considerable sum of money to Arnold Leese of the IFL when he died (in Rhodesia) in 1948 (A. S. Leese, *Out of Step* (Guildford, 1951), pp. 72–3). On the topic in general refer to Chapter 4 of this book; G. C. Lebzelter, *Political Anti-Semitism in England, 1918–1939* (London, 1978); and C. Holmes, *Anti-Semitism in British Society, 1876–1939* (London, 1979). On pre-war anti-Semitism see especially K. Lunn, 'Political Anti-Semitism before 1914: Fascism's Heritage?' in K. Lunn and R. C. Thurlow (eds.), *British Fascism* (London, 1980), pp. 20–40.

6. This is the general argument of M. Cowling, *The Impact of Labour* (Cambridge, 1971).

7. R. Blake, 'Baldwin and the Right' in J. Raymond (ed.), *The Baldwin Age* (Eyre and Spottiswoode, London, 1960), ch. 1.

8. Theoretically, it was 258, but 73 Sinn Fein MPs never took their seats.

9. E.g. *Morning Post*, 20.6.21, but see also H. A. Gwynne to Salisbury, 23.2.20, Sal.MS S(4) 91/63 and Salisbury to Wolmer, 24.12.21, 3rd Earl Selborne MS. d.451/33−7 both of which provide evidence of other attempts to resist coalition and 'fusion'.

10. *Morning Post*, 21.7.21, p. 7.

11. *Morning Post*, 6.10.21 and speech delivered to the Northumberland and Newcastle Unionist Association, 29.10.21 (refer to N. Webster, *The Surrender of an Empire* (London, 1931), pp. 168ff). Northumberland had considered splitting from the Coalition and the Conservatives earlier. Refer to St. Loe Strachey to Northumberland, 25.9.20, Strachey MS.S/10/11/15.

12. HC Debs, 31.10.21, Cols. 1367−1480.

13. Conservative Party Archives, Bodleian Library, Oxford. Report on the annual conference.

14. T. Lindsay and M. Harrington, *The Conservative Party, 1918−1979* (London, 1979), pp. 34−5.

15. R. T. Mackenzie, *British Political Parties* (London edn), p. 91. For a full list of those attending see *Austen Chamberlain MS*, AC 33/1/9.

16. J. Ramsden (ed.), *Real Old Tory Politics* (London, 1984) entry for Sunday, 8.2.22.

17. Salisbury to Wolmer, 24.12.21, 3rd Earl Selborne MS.d.451/33−7; Salisbury to Selborne, 15.11.21, 2nd Earl Selborne MS.1/7/112−14; J. Ramsden, *The Age of Balfour and Baldwin, 1902−1940* (London, 1978), pp. 148−9. Gretton was also trying to coax Bonar Law from retirement prior to the Carlton Club meeting. Refer to W. A. S. Hewins, *The Apologia of an Imperialist*, vol. II (London, 1929), ch. XXII.

18. In its early days, the *Patriot* attracted the leading anti-Semites of the period including Lord Sydenham, Nesta Webster and Ian D. Colvin, a leader writer with the *Morning Post*.

19. Londonderry, Carson and H. A. Gwynne were particularly important. Salisbury certainly had contact with Gretton via Carson who had been created Lord of Appeal in 1921. Refer to Gretton to Londonderry, 23.12.21. Londonderry MS, D.3099/3/17/1−13.

20. *The Times*, 8.3.22, and H. A. Gwynne, MS.17.

21. Austen Chamberlain to Lord Derby, 23.3.22, AC 33/1/52.

22. McKenzie, *Political Parties*, p. 94.

23. *Morning Post*, June/July 1922; Gwynne MS.8.

24. On the theoretical distinctions involved refer to R. Rose, 'Parties, Factions and Tendencies in Britain', *PS* (1964), pp. 33−46. Lord Derby even referred to the movement as a 'party'. Refer to Derby to Austen Chamberlain, 1.9.22, AC 33/2/11.

25. Leslie Wilson, the Chief Whip, told Chamberlain at this time that as many as 184 constituencies would insist on running independent Conservative candidates at the next General Election. See Wilson to Chamberlain, Sept. 1922, AC 33/2/26.

26. Salisbury to H. A. Gwynne, 3.8.22, Gwynne MS.8.

27. Salisbury to H. A. Gwynne, 21.7.22, Gwynne MS.8.

28. Salisbury to H. A. Gwynne, 5.8.22, Gwynne MS.8.

29. Salisbury to Selborne, 26.9.22, 2nd Earl Selborne MS. 1/7/129−33: 'I explained to Bonar Law the difficulty we had in holding our own men and in preventing Free Conservative candidates from opposing Coalition Unionists.' Refer also to Wolmer to Salisbury, 26.9.22, 3rd Earl Selborne MS. d.451.

30. On this point see Austen Chamberlain to Steel-Maitland, 23.3.22, AC 33/1/49.

31. Quoted in McKenzie, *Political Parties*, p. 104.

32. The prevailing view of the Diehards as a group of elderly landowners and Ulstermen with safe seats (M. Kinnear, *The Fall of Lloyd George. The Political Crisis of 1922* (Macmillan, London, 1973), pp. 79–85; D. Close, 'Conservatives and Coalition After the First World War', *JMH* (1973), pp. 240–60) is technically correct but misleading. It concentrates too heavily upon a small number of parliamentarians who were probably unrepresentative of the constituency activists whose support they enjoyed, and ignores the fact that the *most prominent* Diehard MP was Gretton, a 54-year-old Brewer from Burton-on-Trent. Besides, an analysis of the 45 MPs who voted in favour of the motion of censure on 31.10.21 shows that 4 were under 40, 12 were in their 40s, 14 in their 50s, 11 in their 60s, and only 3 were 70 or over (1 unknown). The average age was 56, which was only 4 years older than the average for the party as a whole (refer to J. M. McEwen, 'Unionist and Conservative MPs, 1914–1939', Ph.D. London, 1959, p. 162). Refer also to Sanders Diary, 18.12.21 (Ramsden *Real Old Tory Politics*). There were also regional variations to consider. In July 1922 Chamberlain made a note of areas 'content' and 'discontent' with the Coalition. *Content*: Scotland; Newcastle and Birmingham; East Anglia; Cornwall; Devon. *Discontent*: London and the Home Counties; Midlands and Yorkshire; south and south-west; Liverpool 'in spite of Salvidge'. AC 33/2/4.

33. See e.g. McNeill to Londonderry, 31.12.21, Londonderry MS.; and Northumberland to Londonderry, 23.12.21, Londonderry MS. On Northumberland as a possible leader refer to *Evening Standard*, Nov. 1921: 'If the extremists of the Right do feel their position impossible and decide to secede from the Government, we see no more appropriate leader for them than the Duke of Northumberland.' But this is rather a reflection of the intellectual poverty of the "Die Hards" than a tribute to the endowments of the Duke.' (Quoted in *Plain English*, 8.10.21.)

34. Ramsden, *The Age of Balfour and Baldwin*, pp. 248–56 provides a useful outline of Constituency Association history in the inter-war period. See also A. Potter, 'The English Conservative Constituency Association', *Western Political Quarterly* (1956); and M. Pinto-Duschinsky, 'Central Office and "Power" in the Conservative Party', *PS* (1972), pp. 1–16.

35. On the Unionist Business Committee, War Committee and Reconstruction Committee, refer to Appendix. The papers of the 1922 Committee are unavailable, the only available history of the institution is P. Goodhart, *The 1922. The Story of the Conservative Backbenchers' Committee* (Macmillan, London, 1973).

36. One interesting aspect of this episode was that the Home Secretary, William Joynson-Hicks (a rebel of 1921/2 who remained obsessed by the fear of insurrection and had prosecuted a dozen leading Communists in October 1925 under the ancient Incitement to Mutiny Act of 1797), was deliberately using the OMS (refer to Appendix) as a means of weakening and hopefully destroying the British Fascists. See Scarborough to G. Drage, 30.4.26, Drage MS, Christ Church, Oxford, Box VI.

37. See HC Debs, 6.3.25, for Baldwin's famous 'Peace in our time' speech.

38. The author has written elsewhere about these organisations. G. C. Webber, 'The British Isles' in D. Mühlberger (ed.), *The Social Base of European Fascist Movements* (forthcoming, 1987). See also Benewick, *Political Violence and Public Order*, ch. 2; and Lebzelter, *Political Anti-Semitism*, ch. 3.

39. H. P. Croft, *My Life of Strife* (London, 1948); W. Sanderson author of *Statecraft* (London, 1927), member of the English Mistery, and contributor to the *Fascist*; N. Webster, authoress of numerous books including *The French Revolution* (London, 1921), and *The Surrender of an Empire* (London, 1931): Lord Sydenham, *My Working Life* (London, 1927); Col. A. H. Lane was Chairman of the National

Citizens' Union in 1927 (a version of the MCU, refer to note 3) and later founded the Militant Christian Patriots which published a journal entitled the *Free Press* between 1935 and 1940. Also refer to Appendix.

3　THE THIRTIES

1929–1935

During the latter part of the 1920s the Conservative Party had been strong and (apparently) united while the Fascist movement remained weak and divided. During the early part of the 1930s this pattern was less clear-cut. Although the Conservative defeat of 1929 was not a disaster (the Conservative Party actually polled more votes than Labour) it was nevertheless an important psychological blow. The Labour Party had now emerged for the first time as the largest single party in Parliament and this, the Right believed, had been a direct result of Baldwin's *negative* appeal to 'Safety First'. What was required, according to the critics (who had been arguing a similar case for at least twenty years), was a clear commitment to a *positive* programme and a willingness to define and defend Conservative *principles* rather than to run with an anti-Conservative tide. Consequently, the Conservative Party was once again divided by disputes about ideology in general and the questions of tariff reform and Indian self-government in particular. And in the midst of Conservative confusion, the emergence and growth of the BUF seemed, at least for a while, to offer some kind of alternative to Baldwin and the National Government.

The attacks upon Baldwin's leadership of the party in the years after 1929 first surfaced with the row over tariffs, but the pattern of dissent was characteristically diffuse. There were three major centres of agitation: the Empire Economic Union which had been established in July 1929 and which was headed by the ex-minister, L. S. Amery; the United Empire Party (UEP) which Lords Beaverbrook and Rothermere had created in February 1930; and the Imperial Economic Unity Group which was run by Henry Page Croft and which had been set up in July 1930 as an off-shoot of the Empire Industries Association.[1] Together they represented a formidable challenge and it was fortunate for Baldwin that these three groups were not entirely united. The UEP wanted 'Empire Free Trade' and were prepared to act as an independent party; Croft wanted to establish a similar system but (chastened by his experiences with the short-lived National Party) sought to work through rather than against the Conservative organisation; whilst Amery, more loyal to the Conservative Party than either Croft or the press lords, insisted that his scheme of 'scientifically' graduated preferences was altogether distinct from the policy of blanket tariffs favoured by the other dissidents.[2] Nevertheless there was a good deal of co-operation between these groups in practice if only because they all agreed that trade was simply a means towards imperial unity,[3] and as a result, Baldwin had to tread carefully.

As it was the political struggles were reminiscent of the years after 1903 with Amery and Croft vying for the part of Joseph Chamberlain, Beaverbrook and Rothermere playing the part of the tariff reform press, Baldwin taking the role of Balfour, and Salisbury that of Lord Derby. Yet strangely for one who accepted the need for some sort of protection, Baldwin handled the situation little better (perhaps even a little worse) than Balfour had done before him. His initial response was to make concessions to the tariff reformers in order to take the sting out of their attacks. In February 1930 he declared that 'safeguarding' was no longer an experiment but now a necessity; by March he had conceded the possibility of a referendum on food taxes; and by June he had sacrificed J. C. C. Davidson as party Chairman and installed Neville Chamberlain in his place. But this merely provoked Lord Salisbury, a leading free-trader, to resign as leader of the party in the Lords (ostensibly he resigned on the grounds of ill-health but in fact his action was provoked by a series of policy disputes over such issues as reform of the Lords, Egypt, Ireland and tariffs). Furthermore, it did nothing to deflect the challenge from Rothermere and Beaverbrook since their objective was not only to support a cause but also to topple Baldwin.[4]

The relationship between the press and the parties during the inter-war period was unusual.[5] The growth of the popular press in the first few decades after the creation of the halfpenny *Daily Mail* in 1896 had a number of important consequences. In the first place, the rapid expansion of circulation meant that the viability of newspapers came increasingly to depend upon popular appeal rather than direct political patronage as advertising revenue became the prime source of finance. This in turn led to fierce competition, the domination of the local press by the national (London) newspapers, and the concentration of ownership in fewer and fewer hands. As a result, the 'press barons' came to regard their newspapers as constituent parts of a plebiscitary arm of government (a role that was briefly formalised by the creation of the Ministry of Information in 1918), and were increasingly anxious to realise the supposed political potential of their publications. In some cases this assumed the form of direct partisan support, but especially in the case of the *Morning Post* which supported particular factions within the Conservative Party, and the *Daily Mail* and *Daily Express* which were vehicles for the ambitions of their proprietors (Lords Rothermere and Beaverbrook respectively), the press sought to rival, reform or control the established political parties. This was already evident in the early 1920s when the Northcliffe/Rothermere Anti-Waste League fielded candidates who opposed Coalitionists at by-elections and won several 'safe' Conservative seats on a platform of retrenchment. The battles of the 1930s followed a similar pattern. The intention was to 'capture' the Conservative Party by appealing over the heads of the party leaders to the prejudices of the constituency activists.

Consequently, despite Baldwin's attempts to effect a compromise on the question of tariffs, the press lords subsequently stepped up their campaign, and in June 1930 decided to field UEP candidates in by-elections. In August one such candidate amassed over 9,000 votes in Bromley and his Conservative opponent subsequently confided to Sir George Bowyer (of the Conservative Central Office) that this represented a definite vote against Baldwin: 'I found no-one who had not the greatest respect for him, but very few indeed who would wish him to continue to lead the party, as they have lost confidence in his leadership.'[6] Eventually, on 30 October, the UEP won a by-election against Conservative opposition in South Paddington and Baldwin, anticipating the possibility of defeat, was forced to defend his position as leader by calling a special meeting of Conservative Peers, MPs and candidates on the evening of the by-election at which he survived a call for his resignation (sponsored by Gretton and 16 other MPs) by 462 votes to 116.[7]

This seemed, at the time, to have put an end to the revolt, but in retrospect the astonishing thing was not that Baldwin had secured a vote of confidence but that so many members of the Conservative hierarchy had voted against him. It was clear that something like one fifth of all Conservative Peers, MPs and candidates did not want Baldwin to lead the party. Even in Parliament the tariff reformers, led by Croft, had established themselves as an important group.[8] Attitudes at constituency level were still more hostile to Baldwin, and neither Beaverbrook nor Rothermere had any cause to back down since their intention was, of course, not to overthrow Baldwin in Parliament but to undermine his position in the party by capturing the constituencies.

In March 1931 a by-election took place at St Georges, Westminster. This was an extraordinary contest, not only because it was a straight fight between a Conservative and a UEP candidate but also because it developed into a dispute about the nature of the Conservative Party itself and the suitability of Baldwin to lead it. It was significant that the Conservatives decided to field Duff Cooper (MP for Oldham until 1929) who had given up the chance of fighting a safe seat in Winchester specifically to contest the by-election. It was also significant that Baldwin felt the need to take part in the campaign himself and that he used the occasion to deliver his most vitriolic attack upon the press lords. The stakes were exceptionally high. Duff Cooper believed that if he had lost the contest Baldwin would have been forced to resign.[9] The UEP representative, Sir Ernest Petter (a businessman with no previous political experience), was essentially an 'anti-Baldwin' candidate who stood for 'the most uncompromising brand of Toryism',[10] and in the course of the campaign six Conservative MPs who lived within the constituency refused to sign a letter of support for Duff Cooper while one sent a letter of support to his opponent. All seven of these MPs were well to the Right of the party: Col. Gretton (of course); Carlyon Bellairs (a pre-war Liberal who later joined the BUF); Sir Alfred Knox (British Military Attaché to the Russian front at the time of the revolution, MP for Wycombe, and later a member of the India Defence League); Nigel Colman (MP for Brixton and Director of Reckitt and Colman Ltd.); Reginald Purbrick (MP for Liverpool Walton, later associated with the IDL); Sir Basil Peto (previously a member of the Unionist Business Committee and later a member of the IDL); and Sir William Wayland (MP for Canterbury and also a member of the IDL). Somewhat surprisingly, the *Morning Post* did not throw its weight behind the UEP candidate, but this was only because the paper felt that it would be damaging to invest too heavily in a single campaign since a poor performance would inevitably strengthen Baldwin's position; and in the event the fears were justified. Petter's defeat burst the UEP bubble; in the aftermath of the by-election, Neville Chamberlain managed to arrange a truce with Beaverbrook that openly divided him from the arrogant and intransigent Rothermere by exploiting personal and political differences between the two; and these developments finally put paid to the UEP as an effective political force.

However, this did little to dispose of the problem of intra-party dissent and it came only just in time to prevent the question of tariff reform from overlapping directly with the campaign against the Government of India Act. The tariff dispute had lost its edge by mid-1931 when it became apparent that the severity of the financial crisis would demand reforms that were likely to include a degree of protection. These reforms were introduced in the following year when the Import Duties Act and the Ottawa Agreements established a general tariff of between 10 and 20 per cent (with some exceptions) and preference for Empire goods, especially food. But the struggle for tariff reform approached a conclusion just as the campaign against political reform in India was beginning to pose a serious threat to Baldwin's position, and although the two campaigns ran side-by-side for a short time, Conservative discontent after 1931 increasingly focused upon the government's policy in India.

The status of India was a question about which many Conservatives felt very deeply. India was regarded as the keystone of the Empire and as a symbol of British power and prestige. The possibility that it might eventually be granted self-government (as Lord Irwin had suggested in 1929) appalled the large number of Conservatives who continued to regard their party as a guardian of imperial interests. For many it seemed to epitomise the timid, conciliatory brand of conservatism with which Baldwin had become identified, and it was certainly true that the Conservative politicians most closely associated with the government's policy on India — Baldwin, Samuel Hoare, and Lord Irwin (previously Edward Wood) — all shared liberal assumptions about the value and legitimacy of self-government. Consequently, the revolt that ensued within the Conservative Party was much more than a single-issue campaign.[11] India, like Ireland in 1921, provided a powerful symbol around which dissident Conservatives could unite (indeed, the analogy with Ireland was frequently drawn by the rebels themselves).[12] But dissent over India was much more than a technical disagreement about policy. It was also an attack upon Baldwin's leadership of the party and upon the kind of conservatism which Baldwin favoured. Like the rebellion of 1921/2, the overt battle consisted of a number of 'guerilla attacks' upon the party leaders by small groups of Peers and MPs whose real strength lay in the constituencies, but the underlying questions were *ideological*. As newspapers, journals and books of the time testify, the hidden agenda involved a debate about the meaning of conservatism itself,[13] and it was soon clear that Baldwin was in for a rough ride. There was talk of a 'definite split' in the party as early as February 1931.[14] By March it was said to be 'honeycombed with faction and disloyalty'.[15] And already it was proving difficult to constrain Churchill and his Diehard supporters.[16]

Gradually the India rebels were hardening into a faction. Like the rebellion of 1921/2, the revolt over India was a complex affair. There were (as there had been ten years before) three figures of particular importance: Salisbury, Gretton, and on this occasion, Churchill.[17] Of the three, Churchill was regarded as the most formidable critic of the government's policy. His resignation from the Shadow Cabinet in January 1931 gave him a degree of notoriety and status that was hard to match, and his oratorical skills inevitably ensured him a leading place amongst the rebels. But his position was weaker than it looked. Because Churchill had been 'everything in every party'[18] it was difficult for those who agreed with his stand on India to trust him. Prior to 1931 the Right had regarded Churchill as a political enemy second only to Lloyd George. A 'traitor' to his 'natural' party prior to the First World War, Churchill had been an enthusiastic coalitionist after 1918 and a prominent British negotiator in the talks that led to the Irish Settlement of 1921. Moreover, recent disagreements over tariff reform were difficult to forget since Churchill had been a leading advocate of free trade whilst the majority of those on the Right of the Conservative party had been prominent supporters of tariffs.[19] As Beaverbrook recognised, Churchill did not carry conviction as a Diehard.[20] He was, as J. C. C. Davidson put it, 'the heaven born leader of the party — on . . . only one subject, namely India'.[21]

Of course, Churchill remained a figure of great importance in the dispute over India. But his views were more agreeable to his new colleagues than his presence, and Churchill remained distant from the other rebels for a surprisingly long time. His closest allies (Beaverbrook and Rothermere) were press barons rather than MPs, and it was notable that his first approach to the Diehards did not come until March 1932 when he wrote to Lord Salisbury suggesting that they meet, and asked *him* to invite Gretton and 'a few of his friends' to attend as well.[22] This was somewhat ironic. Salisbury and Gretton, as we have already seen, never really saw eye to eye, and the gulf that had separated them in the early twenties had been widened by recent events, since Salisbury, like Churchill, was a free-trader of sorts, whilst Gretton, along with Croft, had led the tariff reformers. Indeed, in April 1930, Gretton and Croft had even threatened to resign the party whip because of Salisbury's public repudiation of tariff reform which they condemned (somewhat richly) as an act of disloyalty to the party's leader.[23]

Salisbury was also regarded as important. Samuel Hoare thought that he was 'by far the most influential member of the House of Lords . . . the most effective and respected leader of the Diehards [who] the rank and file of the Conservative Party trusted . . . more than anyone except Baldwin. He had therefore to be placated at every turn.'[24] But the documentary evidence suggests that Hoare's picture of Salisbury's importance was exaggerated. It was true that Salisbury had been instrumental in the creation of the Indian Empire Society (IES) in 1930. But this had actually been prompted by Lord Sydenham (the veteran anti-semite and ex-Governor of Bombay who was to die in 1933), and the organisation itself was run by Lord Sumner (previously a signatory of the 1922 Diehard Manifesto). Moreover, Salisbury's correspondence suggests that although he kept in close touch with Lord Lloyd (another ex-Governor of Bombay recently ousted from his position as High Commissioner of Egypt and the Sudan), his links with Churchill were sporadic, and those with Gretton were non-existent.[25] When in 1933 the IES (which was based in the Lords) was merged with Henry Page Croft's India Defence Committee (the IDC, which was based in the Commons) to form the more famous India Defence League (IDL), it was notable that Salisbury's name was not amongst the list of members,[26] and it was more notable still that the IDL was now funded largely by the money which the *Morning Post* had collected eleven years earlier to finance the Diehard Revolt of 1922.[27] Even more than in 1922, Salisbury looked like a man who everybody 'supported' but nobody actually followed. And by 1935, when Salisbury believed that the right wing of the party were 'becoming profoundly estranged' from the leaders, he expressed not the relish of a Diehard but the horror of a party notable and urged Baldwin (as earlier he had urged Bonar Law) to find a means of consolidating the party.[28] Others, even amongst the Peers, were far more radical. Lord Lloyd, for example, was soon to be found in the company of Fascist sympathisers such as Douglas Jerrold as well as respectable MPs such as L. S. Amery who were urging the party to adopt a policy of corporatism,[29] and Viscount Wolmer, a member of the Commons who had identified closely with Salisbury in 1922, was now receiving regular circulars from an ultra-reactionary organisation known as the English Mistery, and later sought to broaden the scope of the IDL rather than to close it down when the Government of India Act was finally introduced in 1935.[30]

The character of dissent in the 1930s was complex; more complex than it had been even in 1922. The real and putative leaders of the revolt in Parliament were sometimes at odds and often out of touch with one another. Churchill, the most prominent of the India rebels, had always taken a 'moderate' line on the Indian question before the 1930s (he had welcomed the Montagu-Chelmsford reforms and refused to support General Dyer). Moreover, his views on imperialism had not changed greatly since the late nineteenth century and his stress upon the need to preserve 'democratic freedoms' (but not, of course, by introducing democratic methods of government) was reminiscent of his former liberalism.[31] Most of those with whom he was now associated were more bluntly concerned with economic control (although there was no simple pattern of economic interest underlying their revolt).[32] Beyond Parliament disaffection was widespread at constituency level although the pattern was not uniform. Lancashire, London and the Home Counties were the strongest areas of opposition.[33] Elsewhere the picture was less clear.[34] Everywhere, however, the flames of discontent which existed were fanned by the *Morning Post* and the *Daily Mail*, and by June 1933 when the IDL was established it was difficult not to consider the movement a 'faction'.[35]

The IDL had much in common with the Diehard movement of 1922. Many of the activists were identical; much of the money was from the same source; and most of the issues were similar, although in this case the catalyst was Indian self-government rather than Irish home rule. Even the tactics were reminiscent of the twenties. But there were significant differences. In 1921/2 the Diehard campaign had mainly consisted of a series of public challenges to the party leaders staged with the assistance of the press (particularly the *Morning Post*). In the early thirties, although the press (especially the *Daily Mail*) remained important as a source of publicity, the India rebels more often attempted to exploit structural weaknesses within the Conservative Party organisation. The emphasis was now upon votes within the Central Council and at the annual conferences, in both of which constituency delegates played an important role. Paradoxically, those who resisted the extension of democracy in India became its greatest advocates in the context of the party. And the tactic was sensible. By March 1933 not only Churchill, but Samuel Hoare as well, believed that the India lobby represented three-quarters of the Tory party, and Hoare feared that 'many Conservatives were beginning to move to the extreme Right'.[36]

At the end of February 1933, by which time the rebels were beginning to plan their attacks properly,[37] the policy of the government escaped condemnation at a Central Council meeting by only 24 votes: 189 voted in favour of the policy; 165 against. Another hundred or so (according to the *Morning Post*) did not vote at all.[38] From this point onwards the Conservative leadership determined to organise their own supporters with equal thoroughness. Having failed to persuade Churchill, Croft or Lloyd to serve on the Joint Select Committee which had now been created to discuss the White Paper (but having succeeded in persuading Salisbury), the government created a front organisation known as the Union of Britain and India (UBI) in May 1933 specifically to influence opinion in the constituencies.[39] It was not clear that the organisation had much success,[40] but in the following month, at another (and larger) Central Council meeting, the party leaders fared much better: 838 voted with the leaders; 356 voted against. But they had voted only to 'suspend judgement' on the Indian Question until the Joint Select Committee had reported, and the 356 votes recorded by the rebels was actually the largest so far registered against the government's proposals.[41] Nor were Baldwin and his allies lulled into inactivity since, as Hoare admitted to Lord Willingdon (Viceroy and Governor General of India), the vote, though it was encouraging, remained 'a disappointment'.[42]

By the time of the party conference in October 1933, the party leaders were more concerned to stage-manage the affair than they had been even in 1932.[43] In the event their efforts proved valuable but indecisive. Neville Chamberlain, replying for the government [sic] to a critical but moderate motion sponsored by Wolmer, once again urged the conference to suspend judgement until the Joint Select Committee had reported. There were 737 delegates in favour of Chamberlain's amendment, but 344 voted against and another

122 abstained altogether.[44] Considering the effort which Baldwin, Hoare and the party managers had put into their own campaigns this was hardly an impressive performance. Nor did it quell the revolt. At the 1934 conference (which was allowed to run its natural course) the government's policy on India escaped criticism by only 23 votes with 39 delegates abstaining.[45] Meanwhile, the parliamentary activists were talking of desertion. Wolmer foresaw a definite split in the party if Baldwin did not resign the leadership before the end of 1935,[46] and he later sought to channel the discontent over India into a movement critical of the government's entire policy of imperial defence.[47] But the rebels were caught in a hopeless position. As Wolmer realised, the IDL could not contest by-elections without creating opportunities for the socialists,[48] and the IDC could not possibly hope to defeat the Government of India Bill in Parliament.

In retrospect, Baldwin's most effective move had not been the creation of the UBI nor even the management of party conferences and the astute manipulation of Conservative loyalties, but the decision to constitute a National Government under MacDonald in October 1931. For although the creation of the National Government in August was welcomed by the Conservative Right as a means of enforcing unpopular economies, Baldwin's decision to serve under MacDonald in October (a situation that remained unchanged until June 1935) proved highly unpopular amongst right-wingers once it became clear that the new National Government emasculated the right wing of the Conservative Party just as effectively as it did the left wing of the Labour Party.[49]

But although the Right were in this way consigned to political oblivion, they were not reconciled to defeat, and dissatisfaction with Baldwin and the National Government found expression in a number of ways. One was the abortive attempt by Douglas Jerrold, the right-wing Catholic editor of the *English Review* from 1931 to 1935, and the so-called '*English Review* Circle' (which included Sir Charles Petrie, Arnold Lunn, Viscount Lymington, Sir Arnold Wilson, and less directly both L. S. Amery and Sir Edward Carson) to introduce 'corporatism' into the Conservative Party programme.[50] Another was the growing admiration for Fascism in Italy, not only amongst Catholics such as Jerrold, Social Crediters associated in particular with the *New English Weekly*, disillusioned anti-capitalists such as Lymington and the English Mistery (established 1931), despairing royalists such as Herbert Vivian and the

Royalist International (established 1929), and self-important aesthetes such as Wyndham Lewis, but also in the pages of popular journals like *Everyman* (edited, briefly, by Francis Yeats-Brown) and the *Saturday Review* (dominated from 1933 until 1936 by the eccentric Lady Houston), and even in the columns of the *Morning Post*.[51] This was the current of opinion which the BUF was subsequently able to tap, especially in the early part of 1934 when Lord Rothermere gave the movement the support of the *Daily Mail* and the Fascists created the 'January Club'.[52]

We know very little about the membership of the BUF and most generalisations about the movement still need to be treated with caution, but in so far as the existing evidence permits informed speculation it does not seem unreasonable to argue that upheaval within the Conservative Party was a precondition of success for the Fascist movement, and that the BUF relied heavily (but by no means exclusively) upon the support of disillusioned Conservatives. This argument rests upon a detailed analysis of the number, the geographical distribution and the class composition of BUF membership.[53]

Until the mid-1970s it was generally agreed that the BUF reached a peak of about 40,000 members in 1934 and that this figure gradually dwindled to about 9,000 in 1939, but in 1975, Robert Skidelsky questioned this assumption by pointing out that the figure of 9,000 only represented 'Division 1' or 'active' members of the movement and that the real level of support was probably nearer 40,000 — about the same as the estimate for 1934. However, Skidelsky's assumption that there were three 'passive' to every 'active' member relies upon an estimate of the ratio in 1934 and this year was not typical of the period as a whole since the support of the *Daily Mail* is widely supposed to have temporarily inflated the inactive membership of the movement.

Recently, the present author has argued that it is more plausible to assume a ratio of one 'active' to one-and-a-half 'passive' members as Home Office records at one point suggest, and this, in conjunction with other information, suggests that the pattern of support did not conform to either of the existing theories. It now appears that, having reached a peak of possibly as many as 50,000 members in mid-1934, support for the BUF fell away rapidly thereafter, slumping to a figure of perhaps 6,000 in February 1935 and no more than 5,000 by October of the same year. This was the movement's lowest ebb. Subsequently support revived. By March 1936 the BUF had about 10,000 members; by November 1936, 15,500; by December 1938, 16,500; and by the time that war was declared the movement had an estimated membership of 22,500, a figure that is much lower than Skidelsky's estimate but still undermines the usual assumption that the Fascists found it increasingly difficult to attract support after 1936.

Members of the Fascist movement were not, of course, evenly distributed across the country, but the geographical distribution changed over time. In mid-1934 membership was concentrated mainly in and around London (but *not* in the East End), in Yorkshire (especially Leeds), in the south-east (particularly in the coastal towns), in Lancashire (especially Manchester and Liverpool), in the rural parts of East Anglia, and in towns such as Birmingham, Wolverhampton and Stoke in the Midlands. However, by 1935 it was the East End of London that dominated what was left of the movement. Approximately 50 per cent of members were concentrated in areas such as Stepney, Shoreditch and Bethnal Green. The remainder were divided between northern cities such as Manchester, Liverpool, Leeds and Hull. This pattern remained largely undisturbed from 1935 until mid-1938, although the East End probably accounted for a growing proportion of the total membership and support definitely fell away in Liverpool. But from the time of the Munich agreements (September 1938) onwards, the geographical distribution of members began to alter. Membership in the East End faded rapidly, but London as a whole remained an important focus of support because new recruits were drawn from areas in the north and west of the city. Meanwhile, support in the north of England became concentrated in Manchester, East Lancashire and Leeds (though the total number of supporters may not have fallen significantly), and support in the south and south-east of the country probably remained steady but geographically scattered.

Attempting to synthesise these observations, it is possible to make an informed estimate of the class composition of the BUF, and of the way that this changed over time. At its peak, in mid-1934, the BUF attracted, on the one hand, numerous professional people, ex-officers, public schoolboys, and in rural areas relatively wealthy farmers, whilst on the other hand it found favour with working-class recruits, especially in the north, who were usually non-unionised and often unemployed. By late 1935 many of the middle-class supporters had ceased to be active members (although they may well have remained sympathetic to the movement as the Special Branch suggested at the time, since the sales of *Blackshirt* remained unaffected by the fall in membership). In the north, the BUF relied heavily upon the support of employed and unemployed cotton workers at this time, and in London the movement became popular amongst working-class East End anti-Semites about whom we know surprisingly little. This pattern was not greatly altered in the years that followed although it seems possible that the steady increase in membership between 1935 and 1938 may have concealed a subtle shift in the social composition of the movement due to a revival of 'respectable' middle-class Fascism in the south and south-east of England. However, by 1939 the BUF was without question a predominantly middle-class organisation. In London support came mostly from disgruntled businessmen, independent taxi-drivers and small shopkeepers, and elsewhere in the country the pattern was probably similar. Even in the north we cannot be sure that BUF supporters were still drawn principally from working-class areas.

Consequently, there are good (but not indisputable) empirical reasons for suggesting that support for the BUF was closely related to dissatisfaction with the Conservative Party. When the movement was doing 'well' (in 1934 and 1939) it relied heavily upon the support of 'natural' Conservative voters and benefited from internal Conservative Party disputes, first over India and then over appeasement. And even when the BUF was doing relatively 'badly' and lost the allegiance of middle-class activists, it tended to attract support from working-class areas with strong anti-socialist traditions (such as the East End of London and, briefly, parts of Lancashire), and consistently failed to penetrate the most highly-unionised sections of the working class who were 'natural' Labour voters. As Petrie subsequently noted in his autobiography, many of those who supported Mosley were simply Tories who were 'weary of the drabness of the Baldwin regime',[54] but although the overlap between Conservatives and Fascists was very real the two groups were only in partial agreement.

The claim (made by a Conservative MP) that 'The Blackshirts [had] what the Conservatives need[ed]' was a sentiment to which many Conservatives subscribed, at least for a while.[55] But Conservative enthusiasts for Fascism did not really want the same things that Mosley desired. Even if they were willing to accept the anti-Semitic aspects of BUF Policy (which were *already* clear by

1934 and which Mosley apparently considered to be one of the *reasons* for the increase in support),[56] they did not, as a rule, support Keynesian economic policies and were unhappy about the use of physical violence (although the *Patriot* refused to praise Mosley *until* the Olympia meeting of June 1934). The relationship between Fascism and dissident conservatism was therefore close but by no means flawless. It is certainly misleading to depict the creation of the BUF as a clearly identifiable 'discontinuity' in right-wing politics as Farr does, because the Fascists relied heavily upon the support of disillusioned Conservatives.[57] But this phenomenon masked numerous disagreements, since many of those who supported the BUF regarded Fascism as little more than an alternative means of pursuing old-fashioned *Tory* ends.

1935–1940

The already complex divisions within the ranks of the Right were multiplied, sharpened and exposed in the years after 1935. Until the mid-thirties the Right had at least been united in their desire to resist what they saw as attacks upon, and the 'surrender' of the Empire. Exceptions notwithstanding, the Indian campaign had unified the disparate forces of the Right more effectively than almost any other issue could have done, and during the early part of 1934 it even appeared as if dissatisfaction with the Conservatives was swelling the ranks of the Fascist movement. But the honeymoon quickly gave way to a messy divorce. By the middle of 1934 Fascist violence had frightened many Conservatives away from the BUF and had caused Rothermere to withdraw the support of the *Daily Mail*, whilst within the Conservative Party itself it was already clear that the campaign against the Government of India Act was doomed to failure (the Act was introduced late in 1934 and became law in August 1935). As a result, the Right lost both prestige and coherence. This was particularly damaging for those who had been most closely identified with the Indian campaign (although Churchill and others were later to recover their reputations). But the significance of this defeat was restricted neither to particular individuals nor merely to the one issue. It also marked the beginning of the end of a negative, but nonetheless important right-wing 'consensus' on foreign policy, and this was exacerbated in the years that followed by a number of additional factors. At home, the resignation of Baldwin and the smooth succession of Neville Chamberlain as Prime Minister and party leader in May 1937 robbed the Right of an agreed target.[58] Meanwhile, abroad, the course of events in Europe created new problems. It was clear from the time of the German re-occupation of the Rhineland in March 1936 that the Right, like everyone else, would have to clarify their attitudes towards the central European powers, but the 'German question' tended to sharpen the divisions that already existed on the Right and sometimes opened up new ones. Especially after the German demand for the restoration of the mandated territories had made the claims of 'imperialism' and those of 'isolation' difficult to reconcile (it was hard to resist Hitler's claims *and* remain neutral), the Right appeared to lose its corporate identity, and by September 1939 was in considerable disarray. Domestic issues were pushed further and further into the background by questions of European foreign policy; but the clarification of attitudes towards Germany and Italy chipped away at the tacit 'agreement to differ' that had previously held the Right together.

On the one hand, international tensions produced a renewed burst of political hysteria akin to that which had followed the First World War. The coincidence of the Spanish Civil War (which was in general *less* of an issue for the Right than it was for the Left)[59] and of a Popular Front government in France (led by a Jew) provoked a *new* wave of 'anti-Bolshevik' anti-Semitism amongst men such as Admiral Sir Barry Domvile (who established the Link in 1937) and Captain Ramsay MP (who established the Right Club in 1938). Yet at the same time that men such as these were joining forces with pro-Germans, pro-Nazis and assorted 'enthusiasts' for appeasement, others were moving in the opposite direction.[60] Churchill, Amery and Rothermere, for example (but also men like Wolmer and Lloyd whose right-wing credentials were impeccable) were at the forefront of the campaign *against* appeasement.

At first glance the Right appeared to divide into two mutually-hostile camps, one of which support traditional 'defencist' organisations such as the National Air League (established as early as 1934) and the Army League (created in the autumn of 1936), whilst the other took a multiplicity of forms that included the Anglo-German Fellowship (created in 1935), the National Socialist League (1937), the British Council Against European Commitments (1938), and the British Peoples' Party (1939).[61] But this was a misleading picture because it underestimated the complexity of political divisions on the Right. For one thing there was no simple correlation between pro-Fascism and pro-Nazism (especially amongst Catholics who admired Mussolini — all the more so after the concordat with the Pope in 1929 — but disliked religious persecution in Germany). For another, there was no necessary link between anti-Semitism and pro-Germanism. Many of those who subscribed to the anti-Jewish tradition fostered in the early twenties by individuals such as Northumberland, Sydenham, Webster and Lane, by organisations such as the Britons, and by publications such as the *Patriot*, the *National Review* and the *Morning Post*, were *also* distrustful of Germany as a nation, and even in the East End of London support for the British Union (as the BUF was then popularly known) collapsed when the movement became too closely identified with Hitler. Consequently, as war approached the prevailing mood on the Right was closer to *indecision* than it was to schizophrenic 'enthusiasm' and this resulted in confusion rather than immediate realignment. But it was not without importance in disturbing the fragile coalition of right-wing forces that then existed, and subsequently (though only gradually) it was *economic* rather than *nationalistic* issues that came to shape the character of right-wing politics in Britain.

Notes

1. A body which was not exclusively right-wing but which was nevertheless dominated by its right-wing members. Refer to Baldwin MS. 105/63–7.

2. See e.g. *Bournemouth Echo*, 26.2.30; L. S. Amery, *My Political Life*, vol. II (London, 1953–5).

3. Beaverbrook to Croft 8.7.36 Croft MS. CRFT 1/4; L. S. Amery, *My Political Life*, vol. I (London, 1953), p. 308: 'Imperial preference . . . is simply the principle of imperial unity in its economic aspect'.

4. L. S. Amery, *My Political Life*, vol. III (London, 1955), p. 28; Beaverbrook to Patrick Hannon, Hannon MS. H 17/1; and Harold Nicolson Diaries, 11.12.31.

5. The most recent comprehensive account of the topic is S. E. Koss, *The Rise and Fall of the Political Press in Britain*, 2 vols (London, 1981). But see also D. G. Boyce, J. Curran and P. Wingate (eds.), *Newspaper History from the Seventeenth Century to the present day* (London, 1978), especially Part 1 and ch. 7.

6. E. T. Campbell to Sir George Bowyer, 15.9.30, Baldwin MS. 51/13–15.

7. K. Middlemas and J. Barnes, *Baldwin* (London, 1969), ch. 21.

8. See e.g. *Evening Standard*, 4.11.31; *Manchester Guardian*, 12.11.31; and Harold Laski, 'Sir Henry Page Croft: The Imperialist with a one-way mind', *Daily Herald*, 9.1.32.

9. Duff Cooper, *Old Men Forget* (London, 1953), p. 175. The seat was available because the initial candidate, Lt. Col. J. T. C. Moore-Brabazon, had withdrawn. It was also clear that it was the party leaders, not the local association who decided

that Duff Cooper should contest it and that this was a clear response to disaffection within the party. See Middlemas and Barnes, *Baldwin*, p. 586ff.

10. Ibid., p. 174.

11. Refer to Duff Cooper, *Old Men*, p. 171; G. Lane-Fox to Lord Irwin 28.1.31 '. . . I am afraid that this [the disquiet over India] represents the position in our party on many things. /Many think that SB is weak and woolly, and is letting the Party down . . .'; and Winston Churchill to Clementine 26.2.31 '. . . There is no doubt that the whole spirit of the Conservative Party is with me, and that much of their dissatisfaction with SB turns itself into favour with me.' (Both are quoted in Martin Gilbert, *W. S. Churchill*, vol. V Companion. Documents. 1929–1935 (London, 1981).)

12. See e.g. *Morning Post*, 29.3.32; Lord Lloyd to Stanley Baldwin, 5.3.31, Baldwin MS.104/226–7; and N. Webster, *The Surrender of an Empire* (London, 1931).

13. E.g. Douglas Jerrold, 'What is Conservatism?', *ER*, June 1931; *Morning Post*, 1.10.32, 'The Meaning of Conservatism'; D. Crisp, *The Rebirth of Conservatism* (London, 1931); 'Kim', 'Is it worth losing India in order to keep Mr Baldwin?', *Saturday Review*, 13.5.33. The tone of the *Indian Empire Review* under the editorship of Sir Louis Stuart was also interesting since this recommended works such as Nesta Webster, *The Surrender of an Empire*; Dorothy Crisp, *The Rebirth of Conservatism*, refer to ch. 5 below; and Col. A. H. Lane: *The Alien Menace* (London, 1928) to its readers, and not infrequently contained articles that were openly hostile to liberal democracy in general. Refer especially to, *IER*, June 1932; Aug. 1932; May 1934, etc. and see ch. 7, n. 20, below.

14. Lord Greenway to Baldwin, 4.2.31, SB MS.104/168–71.

15. T. Jones to a friend, 16.3.31 (Gilbert, *Docs.*, p. 303).

16. E.g. G. Lane-Fox to Lord Irwin, 4.3.31 (Gilbert, *Docs.*, p. 289).

17. The 8th Duke of Northumberland, who had been the 'third man' in 1921/2, died in August 1930.

18. Beaverbrook to Garvin, 2.1.31 (Gilbert, *Docs.*, p. 389).

19. The overlap between the campaigns for tariff reform and against the Government of India Act was *not* perfect. Churchill and Salisbury, for example, were free-traders; L. S. Amery was pro-government on the Indian question. Nevertheless, the generalisation remains valid.

20. Beaverbrook to Sir Robert Borden, 7.1.31 (Gilbert, *Docs.*, p. 241).

21. J. C. C. Davidson to Irwin, 6.3.31 (Gilbert, *Docs.*, p. 293).

22. Churchill to Salisbury, 28.3.32 (Gilbert, *Docs.*, p. 408). It was also notable that (with a few exceptions) the Churchill/Diehard coalition collapsed very rapidly once the Indian question was settled. Derek Walker-Smith (refer to Right Book Club in the Appendix), wrote in *ER*, Jan. 1937: 'Mr Churchill . . . had already [i.e. before the abdication crisis] alienated the good-will of the right wing by his advocacy of an international force to sustain what Sir Edward Grigg has described as the vigour of the Covenant.' (p. 7).

23. *Daily Mail*, April 1930, 'Conservative Party Confusion', Cutting (n.d.), Salisbury MS. S(4) 134/144.

24. S. Hoare, *Nine Troubled Years* (Collins, London, 1954), p. 88.

25. As late as March 1934 Gretton was writing to Salisbury as to a stranger. See Gretton to Salisbury, 20.3.34, S(4)205/150.

26. Full list *Morning Post*, 2.6.33. Salisbury probably remained aloof because he had accepted a place on the Joint Select Committee on India.

27. Gretton to Gwynne, 18.4.33, Gwynne, MS.8.

28. Salisbury to Baldwin, 10.2.35, Baldwin MS.107/12–13.

29. D. Jerrold, *Georgian Adventure* (London, 1937), ch. 11. None of them actively supported the BUF.

30. The English Mistery was run by Viscount Lymington. One EM memo had been prepared specially for Wolmer and Lloyd, although it is not clear whether either of them paid much attention to the organisation. On the attempt to broaden the scope of the IDL refer to *IDL Circular*, 3.4.35, Baldwin MS.107/57−8. It is notable that Wolmer, along with Lloyd, was later to be closely associated with the 'anti-appeasement' lobby grouped around Churchill.

31. M. Gilbert, *Churchill's Political Philosophy* (London, 1981), esp. p. 85. However, Churchill *was* also concerned about economic problems. As he wrote to Lord Linlithgow at this time: 'In my view England is now beginning a new period of struggle and fighting for its life, and the crux of it will be not only the retention of India but a much stronger assertion of commercial rights.' Quoted in Gilbert, ibid., p. 86.

32. Refer to J. M. McEwen, 'Unionist and Conservative MPs, 1914−1939', Ph.D., London, 1959, ch. XII and see e.g. *Morning Post*, 3.2.33, Editorial, p. 10.

33. Hoare to Willingdon, 16.2.34 (Gilbert, *Docs.*, p. 723).

34. Refer *Morning Post*, 27.3.33 for a crude geographical breakdown of support for and opposition to the government's policy on India. Compared with the pattern in 1922 (ch. 2, fn. 31 above) the main areas of continuity appear to be London, the Home Counties, and the central southern region, but the evidence is sketchy. However, this picture is broadly supported by evidence contained in the *IER*, May and June 1933, and the Stuart MS, Bodleian Library, Oxford, File 625. For a rather crude analysis of the Indian rebels refer McEwen, 'MPs', ch. XII and Appendix H.

35. The degree of co-ordination was sometimes surprising. Churchill reprimanded the prominent publicist, Sir Michael O'Dwyer (ex-Governor of the Punjab and an associate of the rebels in 1921/2), for not consulting the IDC (i.e. the IDL in the Commons) before publishing an article that departed from the usual formula. See Churchill to O'Dwyer, 1.3.34 (Gilbert, *Docs.*, p. 732).

36. Churchill to D. Margesson, 1.3.33; Hoare to Lord Willingdon, 3.3.33 and 25.2.33 (Gilbert, *Docs.*, p. 532−7).

37. Sir A. Knox to Churchill, 24.2.33 (Gilbert, *Docs.*, p. 531).

38. *Morning Post*, 1.3.32 pp. 10−11.

39. Hoare to Baldwin, 16.5.33, Baldwin MS.106/78−9; 82−4.

40. G. Peele, 'Dissent, Faction and Ideology in the Conservative Party', unpublished MS, B.Phil., Oxford, 1972.

41. *Morning Post*, 29.6.33, p.13.

42. Hoare to Willingdon, 30.6.33 (Gilbert, *Docs.*, p. 621).

43. On 1932 refer to Hoare to Willingdon, 9.9.32 (Gilbert, *Docs.*, p. 471). On 1933 preparations refer to Stonehaven to Baldwin, 27.9.33, Baldwin MS.48.

44. Conservative Party Archives, Bodleian Library, Oxford. Report of Annual Conference.

45. Ibid. The voting was 543 to 520.

46. Wolmer to E. Mackie, 11.12.33, 3rd Earl Selborne MS. c.1013/123−5.

47. In Dec. 1934 Wolmer launched a short-lived 'Imperial Policy Group'. Refer also to Baldwin MS.107/57−8, although Hoare had already suggested that the leaders could use the link to their own advantage: 'a strong foreign policy will help us politically in England with the Indian question', Hoare to Baldwin, 8.9.33, Baldwin MS. 106/129−33.

48. 'Confidential and Secret Memo — The Policy of Contesting Bye-Elections' (undated but c. Spring/Summer 1935), 3rd Earl Selborne MS. c. 1012/71. Randolph Churchill had already run as a 'Conservative' candidate in Wavertree, Liverpool, in February 1935. He came third and was widely seen as a puppet of the Rothermere press.

49. M. Pugh, *The Making of Modern British Politics 1867−1939* (Oxford, 1983, paperback edn), pp. 273−9. As usual, the *Patriot* provides fine examples. In its

edition of 22 October 1931 the journal argued that the formation of a National Government was 'the only possible constitutional defence against disaster' (p. 377). This assessment soon changed, and several years later the paper published a letter which reflected the *Patriot*'s own perception of events: 'the MacDonald-Baldwin partnership is determined . . . to kill the Conservative Party as such . . . Is it any wonder that the youth of both sexes is rallying under the banner of Sir Oswald Mosley . . . ?' (18.4.35, pp. 318–19).

50. Jerrold, *Georgian Adventure*, ch. 11.

51. See especially R. Griffiths, *Fellow Travellers of the Right* (London, 1980); R. F. B. Bosworth, 'The British Press, the Conservative and Mussolini, 1920–34', *JCH* (1970), pp. 163–82. Refer also to *Morning Post*, April/May 1933 during which time the paper carried a series of articles by Mussolini and a number of pro-Fascist contributions such as Lord Baden Powell (the Chief Scout), 'How Mussolini makes man power', 6.4.33, p.10.

52. R. Skidelsky, *Oswald Mosley* (London, 1981 edn), p. 322; see also C. Cross, *The Fascists in Britain* (London, 1961) for a general history of the BUF.

53. What follows is a summary of the main conclusions of a paper published by the author in 1984. Detailed references can be found in the footnotes to: G. C. Webber, 'Patterns of Membership and Support for the BUF', *JCH* (Oct. 1984), pp. 475–606.

54. C. Petrie, *Chapters of Life* (London, 1950) quoted by Cross, *The Fascists*, p. 101.

55. Lt. Col. T. C. R. Moore, 'The Fascists have what the Conservatives need', *Daily Mail*, 25.4.34. The *Saturday Review* also described the BUF at this time (May 1934) as 'a movement of revolt . . . from official Conservatism'.

56. Compton MacKenzie, *My Life and Times. Octave Seven, 1931–1938* (Chatto and Windus, 1968), p. 169. Refer also to W. F. Mandle, *Anti-Semitism and the BUF* (London, 1968), and Webber, 'Patterns of Membership', pp. 596–7 and fn. 78. C. Holmes, *Anti-Semitism in British Society, 1876–1939* (London, 1979), ch. 11 provides what is probably the best overall account of the problem.

57. B. L. Farr, 'The Development and Impact of Right–wing Politics in Great Britain, 1903–1932', Ph.D, Univ. of Illinois at Chicago Circle, 1976.

58. Attitudes towards Neville Chamberlain were mixed, but as a tariff reformer previously associated with groups such as the EIA most right-wingers were prepared to give him an opportunity to *earn* their hostility.

59. N. Thompson, *The Anti-Appeasers, Conservative Opposition to Appeasement in the 1930s* (Oxford, 1971) aptly describes the Spanish Civil War as a 'distraction', ch. 6, esp. p. 116.

60. On these two trends refers to Griffiths, *Fellow Travellers* and Thompson, *Anti-Appeasers*.

61. On these groups refer to Appendix. Note also that the public image of the BPP was better than the private reality. Refer to Philby MS., File on British Politics, D. Duff to Philby, 4.8.39. She reports that the branch secretary in Folkestone had resigned on learning that the BPP had connections with Admiral Domvile's Link and continues: 'The poor egg-head had never heard of the Link before, and it knocked him completely sideways, and he came over all British . . . I felt like doing nasty things to him with a blunt knife.'

PART TWO:

RIGHT-WING IDEOLOGIES

History suggests that of all weapons the idea is the most potent for good or for evil. Sound conceptions of life have made nations great; false conceptions of life have brought them to destruction. . . . A nation acts as one when it is inspired by the unity of a great tradition of duty and of patriotism; it may tear itself to pieces under the influence of a subversive philosophy. . . . If, however, there is danger in false ideas, there is safety in true ideas . . . and in this way . . . the intelligent may defeat the intelligentsia with their own weapons.

'The War Front of Ideas',
Morning Post, Editorial, 16.11.32

INTRODUCTION

It is often assumed that ideology (by which is meant a set of related political ideas) is of no importance in understanding the behaviour of Conservatives, and of little significance even for the Fascists. However, assumptions of this kind over-simplify a complex issue. As we saw in Chapters 2 and 3, conflict within the Conservative Party often took the form of ideological disagreement, and support for the Fascist movement, where we can analyse it, not infrequently sprang from a feeling that the Conservative Party had ceased to represent 'Conservative principles' effectively (although what those principles were remained a matter of dispute). Consequently, even if Conservative leaders remained faithful to the tradition of 'pragmatism', Conservative dissidents did not, and the following chapters are concerned with one obvious (but to date neglected) question: what exactly did such people believe?

The enquiry proceeds thematically and concentrates upon broad issues rather than specific policy recommendations, partly because this allows us to gain a comprehensive overview of different right-wing ideologies, and partly because this was the most characteristic form of right-wing expression. Chapter 4 deals with attitudes towards society, since fear of social disintegration was usually a root cause of right-wing pessimism. Chapter 5 concentrates upon attitudes towards property and the economy, because these expose most clearly the disagreements that shared social fears tended to obscure. Chapter 6 considers different views of the proper role and function of the state within this framework (an area in which simple generalisations about 'democracy' and 'dictatorship' have misled writers in the past). And Chapter 7 examines the ways in which attitudes towards the outside world contributed to the dis-integration of the Right as a distinctive force in British politics in the years after 1935.

4 SOCIETY

It seemed to many on the Right even before, but especially after 1918 that industrial development and the progressive extension of the franchise were between them creating social problems that threatened to destroy the unity and so sap the strength of the nation. The 'British way of life' appeared to be under threat from a number of different directions. Often external 'enemies' such as Germans, Bolsheviks and Jews, or Irish, Indian and Egyptian nationalists were identified as sources of subversion, and 'aliens' of all descriptions were regarded with distrust. Col. A. H. Lane's book, *The Alien Menace* (1928), being careful to insist that it was not an attack upon 'Jews *qua* Jews', provided a characteristic and influential catalogue of such fears:[1]

> It is not an exaggeration to say that the whole fabric of British life and inspiration is being steadily undermined by the effect of the alien presence, his propaganda, and the evil practices which he has brought with him to this country. In many cases — if not in the majority of cases — he is an undesirable or a criminal in his own country, from which he has been forced to flee to avoid punishment there. So he comes here, free to propagate his filthy and immoral species, and by his degrading activities, to deluge the country with a flood of bitterness and class-hatred, and to create industrial unrest, strikes, Socialism and Communism.

But alongside, and in some ways more worrying than these external threats, right-wingers also detected an internal 'malaise' — a lack of national vigour and purpose — that they usually blamed upon the influence of 'liberalism' and upon consequent developments in the economic and social order. As Viscount Lymington put it in 1933, 'liberalism is the philosophy which sets material increase as an end and not as a means, and which sets individual liberty above social duty. The one ends in making man the slave of material, the other in producing spiritual and moral anarchy. Each is the inevitable evangelist of Bolshevism.'[2]

The social weaknesses which the Right identified were difficult to isolate from one another, but broadly they were thought to result from one of three causes: industrial urbanisation, secularism and general cultural decline, each of which represented potentially fatal flaws in the national character. Sometimes the Right responded to these anxieties with hysterical tirades against the Jews. On other occasions they recommended economic and political reforms, or concentrated upon issues such as nationalism and imperialism which were intended to cut across internal divisions of social class.[3] But often, the Right believed that these social problems were the result of an underlying 'spiritual' crisis and that this could not be tackled by conventional reforms alone, but required the inculcation of 'integrating myths' that would contribute something positive to social solidarity.

These 'integrating myths' fell, like the problems to which they were addressed, under three broad headings: ruralism, religion and cultural renaissance, and each of these themes (particularly the first two) represented deliberate attempts to revive the philosophy of nineteenth-century toryism. However, these attempts failed because the values they sought to preserve were progressively weakened by changing patterns of economic and social behaviour, and this failure had important consequences, since those who clung most tenaciously to anachronistic beliefs (and invariably despaired of the modern Conservative Party) were more susceptible than most to the appeal of Fascism even though the BUF was predominantly 'modernist' in its outlook. It was also interesting, not only because it emphasised the variety of reasons that different individuals had for supporting the Fascists, but also because it highlighted the fact (examined more fully in the next chapter) that the *majority* of right-wing Conservatives did *not* follow the same path.

Industrialism and Ruralism

Anxieties about the long-term consequences of industrial development tended to assume one of two forms. Negatively, they found expression in an intense but transient burst of anti-Semitism during the years from 1918 to 1922. Positively, they resulted in philosophies of 'ruralism' that became increasingly popular on the Right during the early thirties as economic difficulties led men of all political colours to question the efficacy of capitalism.

Anti-Semitic conspiracy theories were surprisingly popular in the years after 1918, and especially so in the period between the first publication in English of the (fraudulent) *Protocols of the Learned Elders of Zion* (1920) and their subsequent exposure as a forgery by *The Times* in August 1921.[4] Anti-Jewish sentiments were by no means confined to the lunatic fringe in these years, but were frequently expressed by Members of Parliament, were publicised daily in the columns of the *Morning Post*, and were even to be found in popular works of fiction such as *The Thirty-nine Steps*, and the *Bulldog Drummond* stories.[5]

This wave of anti-Semitism had many different roots. In part it could be seen as one example of a tradition that dated back at least as far as the eighteenth century and perhaps as far as the Middle Ages. In part it was a continuation of Edwardian traditions fostered on the one hand by liberal anti-imperialists (such as Hobson, Chesterton and Belloc) and exploited on the other by tariff reformers in the East End of London (an area that had experienced an influx of immigrants from Eastern Europe in the 1880s and 1890s and was strongly anti-alien).[6] However, several new factors emerged to give the post-war agitation its special flavour, even though, as Kenneth Lunn has pointed out, Jewish conspiracy theories as well as both ethno-centric and racial anti-Semitism were firmly established well before 1914.[7]

In the first place, the understandable popularity of specifically German conspiracy theories during the First World War helped to create an atmosphere that was conducive to more wide-ranging theories after 1918. German conspiracy theories were often and easily modified to incorporate Jews (and this was one of the routes by which the influential anti-Semite, Nesta Webster, arrived at her conclusions). Secondly, the Russian Revolution gave an added impetus to anti-Semitic conspiracy theories since this was a much-feared but little-understood event that many could only make sense of as a pro-German Jewish plot designed to weaken the anti-German alliance in the midst of war. Thirdly, many right-wingers refused to believe that the growing number of nationalist movements within the Empire were genuine expressions of discontent (just as they refused to take industrial unrest in Britain at face value). And fourthly, the fact that Lloyd George (hated by the Right since at least 1909 and implicated in the 'Marconi Scandal' of 1913) had retained the premiership in 1918 inclined many to believe that frontbench collusion was merely the tip of a vast conspiratorial iceberg.[8]

However, the unifying theme of post-war anti-Semitism (if one can be discerned) was that it represented an attack upon industrial and urban development in a way that later bouts of anti-Semitism did not. In the mid-1930s the anti-Semitic campaigns associated with the BUF were more often attacks upon *finance* than industry (even though they often appealed to a simple hatred of aliens in practice), while similar campaigns at the end of the thirties concentrated less upon domestic than upon international issues (and as they shaded off into pro-Germanism lost the support of traditional anti-Semites in the East End).[9] These distinctions, though they have often been noticed by other writers, have rarely been analysed sufficiently. Holmes, for example, makes some very interesting observations but fails to develop them into a sustained argument, while Lebzelter makes the questionable assertion that the difference between the anti-Semitism of the 1920s and that of the 1930s was simply a matter of 'function' and not a question of 'substance'.[10] Lebzelter's contention seems difficult to sustain. In comparison with later manifestations of anti-Semitism, the agitation of the early twenties was distinctly 'reactionary' and intimately linked with a more general fear of the consequences of industrial development. As George Lane-Fox Pitt-Rivers argued in 1920, Britain's real problem was that she had lost touch with her 'simple agricultural existence'.[11]

> Neither is it surprising in view of her cult of unlimited industrialism and its consequences — an ever expanding industrial and urban population — free commercial exploitation by all and sundry middlemen, usurers, Jews; and the translation of all values into money-values, by which alone can be realised that ideal of personal equality, dead-levelness and compulsory mediocrity in which she glories under the name of Liberalism and Democracy.

Of course, this vein of anti-industrialism might easily be dismissed as a political oddity, but this would be a mistake. For rural nostalgia remained a pervasive feature of English culture between the wars, and sentiments of this kind continued to play an important part in British political life, especially in the hands of Stanley Baldwin.[12] Besides, the social consequences of industrial development were often slow to reveal themselves, and sometimes problems with their roots in the nineteenth century did not strike contemporaries as serious until the 1920s and 1930s. For right-wingers this was particularly true of urbanisation.

Although Britain was an industrially advanced nation well before 1918, it was the development of urban housing projects during the inter-war years and the rapid expansion of middle-class suburbs in the 1930s that did most to heighten concern about the social conse-quences of economic growth. Since development was not a uniform process, it often appeared to sharpen the divisions that already existed between regions and classes by isolating different social groups in geographically distinct areas. Moreover, these features were exaggerated by the effects of the depression in the early thirties. For although this was a period of economic difficulty and high unemployment, these problems were greater in the north and west than they were in the south and east, more acute for the working classes than the middle classes, and most severe in particu-lar areas such as Jarrow and Merthyr. Consequently, while many suffered considerable hardship, those who remained in employ-ment enjoyed a *rising* standard of living and *increasing* material comfort. Industrial capitalism was no longer obviously beneficial even in crudely material terms, and many on the Right were more convinced than ever that it positively damaged the social fabric by creating the 'two nations' of which Disraeli had warned.[13]

These difficulties gave right-wing ruralists a new impetus (in 1931, for example, the English Mistery was created), although the themes that they stressed were well-established and often harked back to the traditions of nineteenth-century toryism. Their arguments usually took one (or more) of four basic forms. The strategic argument was that Britain needed to be agriculturally self-sufficient in order to minimise her vulnerability in wartime (and this was often extended into the economic sphere as a justification for agricultural protection and economic 'autarky'). The biological argument was that a return to rural traditions was essential to the 'fitness' of the 'race' which in turn was important as a means of securing a powerful military force and a contented proletariat. The third argument was that 'communion with nature' was a vital ingredient of spiritual health whilst urban lifestyles encouraged geographical, social, mental and moral instability. Finally, the political argument was that a revival of agrarian traditions would weaken the class consciousness of the labour force, 'balance' the social structure by creating a body of peasant proprietors and restore the political power of a 'true' (i.e. not necessarily of the existing) aristocracy.

Sentiments of this kind found expression across the whole political spectrum, not only amongst right-wing 'extremists' but also amongst 'moderate' and 'progressive' politicians such as Baldwin, Lloyd George and Lansbury.[14] They were nevertheless a particularly noticeable ingredient of right-wing ideologies. Sometimes, for example, rural nostalgia played an important part in Fascist ideas, not only in the writings of men such as James Strachey Barnes (a pro-Italian with a romantic view of peasant proprietorship) and Jorian Jenks (the BUF's agricultural expert), but also in the columns of the Fascist press and occasionally, though oddly for one who was committed to economic modernisation, in the works of Mosley himself.[15] More often, however, ruralism was the preserve of consciously reactionary Tories exemplified by those who supported the English Mistery — William Sanderson, Viscount Lymington, Anthony Ludovici, Rolf Gardiner, Michael Beaumont MP, and Reginald Dorman-Smith (who was appointed Minister of Agriculture in 1939).[16]

William Sanderson, for instance, the English Mistery's 'philosophic leader' (who was also associated with the IFL), argued that as industrial development distanced men from their feudal heritage, exaggerated the importance of 'intellect' and encouraged immigration, so the natural instinct for political leadership (traditionally strongest amongst the now-decimated ranks of the aristocracy) fell into decay, and was weakest of all amongst those who currently dominated government — middle-class men drawn from the ranks of the 'liberal professions'.[17] These developments prevented the state from controlling industrial growth, and this, in turn, created a vicious circle of ineptitude and decay. As Anthony Ludovici remarked in 1921, England was in danger of becoming 'one long ugly street, full of ugly toothless people, pretending that their clammy urban passions [were] more exalted than the rut of rats'.[18]

Right-wing ruralists proposed a number of possible solutions to these problems. One was strict immigration control, another the deportation of undesirable aliens, and a third eugenic manipulation (but *not* on the basis proposed by the Eugenics Society which would have increased the strength of the middle classes).[19] Each of these proposals represented a supplement to, rather than a substitute for, a fundamental re-orientation of the economy. However, reforms of this kind assumed access to power and it was never clear how this was to be achieved. According to ruralist theory, parliamentary democracy was inadequate for the tasks at hand (besides which, in practice it guaranteed their exclusion from power). But the existing aristocracy had patently failed to provide the necessary 'leadership'. Consequently, men such as Viscount Lymington could only seek forlornly to create a 'new nobility' that would sweep to power on a wave of support from the uncorrupted (i.e. non-unionised) masses as the capitalist order collapsed,[20] and in this way self-proclaimed 'elitists' were gradually transformed into desperate advocates of 'populism'. As Lymington put it in 1938:[21]

> If the majority of our aristocracy has sold its birth-right for photography without dignity, comfort without responsibility, and meals without payment; if our squires have been wiped out, and if our middle classes have rallied to a money standard, there is among artisans and working men of England the good stock left that makes England the pivot of Western civilisation.

In appearance, this strand of anti-middle-class authoritarianism resembled and reflected old-fashioned theories of Tory democracy. But in practice, the individuals who clung to such ideas despaired of the Conservative Party, and although few of them trusted Mosley enough to throw in their lot with the BUF, most of them drifted hopelessly towards Fascism as the only viable alternative to toryism.[22]

Secularism and Christianity

Industrial development was also a factor that weakened the power of organised religion. Large-scale urbanisation tended to reduce the communal role of the churches; the emergence of class-based politics diluted the traditional function of religion in public affairs; and new patterns of leisure activity contributed to the steady decline in church attendance and the gradual transformation of the traditional 'sabbath' into the secular 'weekend'. Yet, while church attendance in general fell from about 35 per cent to about 13 per cent of the population between 1901 and 1948, the number of practising Catholics steadily *increased*, both as a proportion of the whole and in absolute terms.[23]

One might have expected that this would have unleashed a new wave of right-wing anti-Catholicism, but this was not the case. For although it was still possible to find anti-Catholic books,[24] and to trace the fear of 'Popery' in the columns of the *National Review* and the *Morning Post*, these attitudes had more to do with the problems in Ireland than the decline of Anglicanism, and had largely vanished by the mid-twenties. It was more usual to find anxieties about religious decline expressed in terms of conventional anti-socialism.[25] The British Fascists, for example, were pledged (like the Scouts and Girl Guides, from which they drew much of their inspiration) to uphold the values of Christianity, and Rotha Lintorn-Orman, the movement's leader, was particularly concerned by the spread of Socialist Sunday Schools which, she alleged, met in laundries and cinemas to pervert young minds with 'sex instruction of a demoralising nature'.[26]

One individual for whom religion was a central concern was the Duke of Northumberland. The Duke, a staunch opponent of liberal divorce laws and prayer-book reform, argued that man was, above all else, a religious animal and that every form of political rule consequently had to be grounded in an overarching faith.[27] When that faith had been Christianity (in the Middle Ages) Britain had enjoyed stability, order and good government. But as the theory of Divine Right gave way to the theory that the Monarch should sanction the church, and as the authority of the clergy fell before the right of private judgement, so politically the nation was weakened by the directionless force of liberalism. And this, in turn, paved the way for Bolshevism which was *not*, as many believed, a negation of religion but a substitute for it: 'the exaltation of pure materialism into a religion — the worship of man'.[28]

However, Anglicans who continued to view religion as a crucial mechanism of social integration were increasingly negative and defensive. Even W. R. Inge, the Dean of St Paul's, and a leading ecclesiastical Tory, despaired of turning the Protestant Church to political advantage.[29] Some, especially amongst the ruralists, even pursued the division between old-fashioned toryism and established religion to the point of embracing paganism instead.[30] And numerous clergymen were attracted to Fascism as a form of militant (anti-socialist) Christianity.[31] Consequently, the politically timid Protestant Right were replaced as the leading exponents of religious conservatism during the inter-war years by a group of right-wing Catholics, many of whom had been pre-war progressives, and most of whom subsequently became enthusiasts for Fascism in Italy (but *not* apologists for National Socialism in Germany).[32]

One of the more extreme examples was Major James Strachey Barnes, cousin of John St Loe Strachey (editor of the *Spectator*), who had been brought up in Italy by his grandparents, was converted to Catholicism in 1914, and became both a friend of Mussolini and a member of the Italian National Fascist Party.[33] For Barnes, the task of the Fascist movement was to create an 'ethical State': 'to educate the new generation into one of believers in a Divine Providence, the heralds of an age of faith . . . [in which] . . . God [was] to become once more the central principle of our conscious life'.[34] However, Barnes was atypical of the Catholic Right as a whole since this group had two distinctly *British* roots.

One was the tradition of 'distributism' established by Belloc and Chesterton prior to the First World War, and later resurrected by Douglas Jerrold, Sir Charles Petrie and the *English Review* as a form of 'corporatism' in which admiration for 'Fascism' rubbed shoulders uneasily with a distrust of the 'Fascists'.[35] Nor was this the only example of the way in which distributism and Fascism overlapped in the 1930s. As Kenneth Lunn has pointed out, especially after G. K. Chesterton's death in 1936, the *Weekly Review* also showed a good deal of sympathy for Fascism, while Fascists, both from the BUF and the IFL, began taking part in distributist meetings and finding space in the correspondence columns of the journal.[36]

The other native root of this kind of pro-Fascism was, more strangely, the Guild Socialist movement. Prior to 1918, Guild Socialism boasted two major figures, G. D. H. Cole (the socialist academic) and A. R. Orage (a teacher and journalist later to become famous as the editor of the *New Age*). These men represented different strands of thought within the group, and when, after the war, the Guild Socialist movement collapsed, each followed a different path. Cole and his circle of admirers remained within the Labour Party. But Orage and his followers, influenced by Major C. H. Douglas and Arthur Kitson, adopted the banner of 'Social Credit', embraced Catholicism, and stressed the (medieval) guild aspects of Guild Socialism — a tradition that was carried into the 1930s by the *New English Weekly* under the editorship of Philip Mairet.[37]   ,

Gradually arguments about innovatory schemes of industrial self-government and de-centralisation were subsumed by discussions of the technical economic aspects of Social Credit and ideas about the dignity of labour, which, although they owed something to Socialism, owed more to the influence of Roman Catholicism and seemed to presuppose that capitalism was capable of sustaining a broadly equitable social hierarchy. Similarly, old ideas about the Guild system found a new expression in the language of corporatism which (as we shall see in Chapter 6) tended to favour a concentration of power in the hands either of the employers or of the state, and in these ways Guild Socialists of the Orage School abandoned much of their former radicalism. But few of them became conventional Conservatives since the majority were temperamentally opposed to political moderation and most of them remained wedded to the belief that social harmony could only be achieved by the conscious manipulation of socio-economic structures. Of course, it was far from inevitable that this would drive such men into the arms of Fascism, and their intellectual backgrounds usually ensured that they remained political 'outsiders', but their steady drift to the Right was difficult to conceal. Like Mosley, the fact that their ideas were rejected by the Left meant that they had nowhere else to go.[38] Moreover, Social Credit demanded such sweeping reforms of the economy that many believed a dictatorship would be necessary to implement them, and since this was linked with Catholic principles, admiration for Mussolini was never far away. As one (worried) reader of the *New English Weekly* put it in 1937, Social Credit was 'merely a way of sitting on an extremely strange fence'.[39]

Cultural Decline and Renaissance

The expansion of educational opportunities, the growth of the popular press and the popularity of new forms of entertainment such as the radio and the cinema created another set of anxieties for the Right. One fear, especially in the wake of the First World War and the Russian Revolution, was that society had now become particularly susceptible to manipulation by clever (usually German, Jewish and Bolshevik) propagandists, and this was responsible for the creation of many new (and usually short-lived) organisations such as the Liberty League, National Propaganda and the British Commonwealth Union whose intention was to beat 'the enemy' at their own game.[40] The BCU, for example, spent about £50,000 in the years from 1918 to 1923 on parliamentary lobbying, open-air propaganda, subventions to dissident Conservative and other 'patriotic' parliamentary candidates, the placement of articles in the local and national press and various payments to trade union officials.[41] The Liberty League had a more representative history. Its greatest achievement was to prepare counter-revolutionary leaflets designed for distribution in public lavatories, but even this plan was undermined when the treasurer absconded with the League's funds.[42]

Another, and more profound fear, was that industrialism and democracy would combine to destroy cultural standards and install a 'dictatorship of the uncultured'[43] since, as J. S. Barnes put it, mass production was bound to produce mass ideas — 'culture in tabloid form, which is no culture at all'.[44] This was a theme that was echoed throughout the Right. Douglas Jerrold, for instance, was concerned that 'the old inspirations [of] race, religion and culture . . . [would] . . . have small appeal to the deracinated, urbanised intelligentsia';[45] Anthony Ludovici believed that 'The common culture [had] been replaced by a congeries of pseudo-cultures, all in active conflict';[46] and the artist and author, Wyndham Lewis expressed the fear that Britain was 'going rotten at the bottom and at the top, where the nation ceased to be a nation — the inferior end abutting upon the animal kingdom, the upper end merging in the international abstractness of men — where there [were] no longer . . . English men, but a gathering of individuals who were *nothing*'.[47]

Not surprisingly, these fears were often expressed most eloquently and forcefully by literary men such as Lewis himself, Roy Campbell, T. S. Eliot, Ezra Pound and W. B. Yeats, each of whom (in different ways) wanted 'form in literature and authority in politics'.[48] Lewis identified for some years with the Nazis in a petulant attempt to offend bourgeois sensibilities; Campbell (a friend of Lewis) identified closely with Franco under the influence of medievalism, Catholicism and French neo-classicism; Pound (also friendly with Lewis) was eventually led by his admiration of order and hierarchy to work for the Italians during the Second World War, and Yeats supported Fascism as the best of a bad choice because his esoteric philosophy suggested the need for a cultural aristocracy, the creation of which, he assumed, would require some form of authoritarian dictatorship.[49] In all of these cases, the demand for absolute values in art spilled over into other areas and ended as an attack upon liberal democracy in general.

T. S. Eliot, though he never supported Fascism, followed a

similar path in search of a civilisation based upon ritual and super-
natural authority guaranteed by the institutions of the church and
the Monarch.[50] His loathing for contemporary social and political
conventions, never far from the surface of his writings, found an
unusually blunt, but perfectly representative expression in *The Idea
of a Christian Society* which he published in 1939.[51]

> By destroying traditional social habits of the people, by dis-
> solving their natural collective consciousness into individual con-
> stituents, by licensing the opinions of the most foolish, by substi-
> tuting instruction for education, by encouraging cleverness
> rather than wisdom, the upstart rather than the qualified, by
> fostering a notion of *getting on* to which the alternative is a hope-
> less apathy, Liberalism can prepare the way for that which is its
> own negation: the artificial, mechanised or brutalised control
> which is a desperate remedy for its chaos . . . [for] . . . as its
> movement is controlled rather by its origin than by any goal, it
> loses force after a series of rejections, and with nothing to
> destroy is left with nothing to uphold and with nowhere to go.

Imbued with such a profound distrust of the prevailing political
culture, it was hardly surprising that most of these writers (with the
exception of Eliot who remained a monarchist) supported Fascism
or, in the case of Wyndham Lewis, Nazism. But their relationship
with the world of politics remained tangential. As Barker has
argued, the views expressed by these writers may have had an
affinity with Fascism, 'But this affinity was symptomatic rather
than essential.'[52] Their pro-Fascism was merely symptomatic of a
cultural elitism that could only relate desired ends to possible
means by acquiescing in the extremes of dictatorship.

However, these men belonged to an intellectual elite who were
treated with suspicion and sometimes with contempt by other right-
wingers. Although William Joyce (a former part-time tutor in
English Literature at London University) was an exception,
Fascists were generally hostile to cultural movements and this was
equally true of right-wing Conservatives educated at public
schools,[53] not that this prevented them from deploring the general
decline of cultural standards. Oscar Boulton, for example, the
organiser of the Unity Band (an aggressively Christian, Conserva-
tive-Fascist front) argued in 1934 that modern trends in art were
exercising 'a definite and deleterious influence on the public taste

of the community'. Nor was this merely a cultural difficulty:[54]

> Beauty, harmony, form, above all clarity, are in art and in life supreme and celestial attributes. Discord, ugliness, obscurity, distortion, all these are essentially powers of darkness, and are being used, consciously or unconsciously, to subserve the forces of evil.

Similarly, the *Patriot* often carried articles denouncing jazz music, modernism in the arts and even Einstein's theory of relativity which was alleged to be part of a Jewish plot to undermine Gentile self-assurance. As a contributor to Lord Alfred Douglas's journal, *Plain English* put it in 1921, 'What Lenin or Trotsky is in politics, what Epstein is in art, Einstein aims to be in science.'[55] But comments of this kind should not be taken out of context. For most right-wingers felt the 'synthetic' culture of literature and art to be less important than the 'organic' culture of common lifestyles, and although they found their own cultural heroes in men such as Shakespeare and Kipling, the Right were usually more interested in practical reforms than they were in intellectual crusades.

Conclusions

It was a notable feature of the British Right between the wars that although they were usually united by their fears they were often divided by their responses to them, and this pattern was confirmed by their attitudes towards society. It was common ground on the Right that social change in general, and the consolidation of working-class consciousness in particular, should be minimised or avoided. But it was not clear how this could be achieved. Some argued that industrialism itself was the root cause of social disintegration and that only a reversion to rural traditions could prevent the collapse of society into warring factions. Others believed that social harmony could be restored via the common bonds of faith. Others still argued that this could be achieved only by consciously re-building a unified 'national culture'. These blueprints for national revival invariably looked back to an idealised past which they hoped to restore, but since the proponents of such schemes were increasingly critical of the Conservative Party, many of them saw no hope of achieving their goals except, possibly, through the intervention of a Fascist movement.

The result was paradoxical. For while Fascism appealed in this way most strongly to the most reactionary Tories, the Fascist movement in Britain (at least in so far as it was represented by Mosley) shared few of their views. Despite occasional indications to the contrary, the BUF believed most consistently in industrial renewal, healthy secularism and a break with the past — and most reactionaries were sufficiently conscious of the fact to draw the line at giving the movement their active support. In some respects, therefore, the conflict of goals that existed between the BUF and the right-wing of the Conservative Party limited the appeal of Fascism (in practice) even to the most old-fashioned and disillusioned of Tories. But these particular disagreements were of little or no importance to the majority of right-wing Conservatives who sought to remedy the evils of society through specific economic or constitutional reforms. On the other hand, arguments about the *form* that changes of this latter kind should take generated their own disagreements and created their own barriers to co-operation, especially when they concerned economic issues.

Notes

1. A. H. Lane, *The Alien Menace*, 2nd edn (London, 1929), p. 10.
2. Viscount Lymington, 'Hammer and Sickle', *ER*, Aug. 1933, p. 185.
3. These themes are dealt with in the chapters that follow.
4. The *Protocols* were translated into English by Victor Marsden in 1919 and were first published by Eyre and Spottiswoode in 1920. From 1922 onwards they were published by the Britons. The forgery was exposed by *The Times* 16–18 August 1921.
5. See e.g. H. P. Croft, letter to *Bournemouth Echo*, 16.10.20; H. A. Gwynne MS., Box 7; Gretton to Maxse, 14.1.25, Maxse MS 478; G. Mitchell, 'Caricature of the Bulldog Spirit', *Patterns of Prejudice* (1974), pp. 25–30; and G. Himmelfarb, 'John Buchan', *Encounter* (Sept. 1960), pp. 46–53. Amongst the anti-Semites of the early 20s were Edward Carson, Rudyard Kipling and Basil Thomson (Director of Intelligence, Scotland Yard).
6. The eighteenth-century tradition sprang up in the wake of the French Revolution and found literary expression in J. Robison, *Proofs of a Conspiracy against all the religions and Governments in Europe, carried on in secret meetings of Free Masons, Illuminati, and Reading Societies* (Edinburgh, 1797). This was an important influence upon Nesta Webster (refer to Appendix and Bibliography). See also R. Hofstadter, *The Paranoid Style in American Politics and Other Essays* (New York, 1965), ch. 1. J. A. Garrard, *The English and Immigration* (London, 1971), deals with post-1880 anti-Semitism.
7. K. Lunn, 'Political Anti-Semitism before 1914: Fascism's Heritage?' in K. Lunn and R. C. Thurlow (eds.), *British Fascism* (London, 1980), ch. 2, pp. 20–40. But note Holmes's view that racist anti-Semitism was not prevalent before 1914 and

that even after 1918 it was only found in conjunction with older forms of hostility: C. Holmes, *Anti-Semitism in British Society, 1876–1939* (London, 1979), p. 228.

8. G. C. Lebzelter, *Political Anti-Semitism in England, 1918–1939* (London, 1978). Classic works of this period include: Lord Sydenham, *The Jewish World Problem* (London, 1921); N. Webster, *World Revolution, the Plot Against Civilisation* (London, 1921. Re-issued in 1971 and still influential amongst the far Right); Anon, *The Cause of the World Unrest* (London, 1920), Intro. by H. A. Gwynne. Other contributors included Ian D. Colvin, Nesta Webster and H. Warner Allen.

9. Like any other generalisation about anti-Semitism, this should be considered only as a useful distinction, not as a rigid schema. The author is well aware of the complexities of the subject, refer to G. C. Webber: 'Patterns of Membership and Support for the BUF', *JCH* (1984), pp. 596–7.

10. Holmes, *Anti-Semitism*, chs 10 and 11, esp. pp. 174 and 186; Lebzelter, *Political Anti-Semitism*, p. 171. Lebzelter argues that the difference between the 1920s and the 1930s was that in the 1930s the Jewish question became the central justification for the BUF's claim to power.

11. *The World Significance of the Russian Revolution* (Oxford, 1920), p. 21. On Pitt-Rivers refer to Appendix.

12. M. Wiener, *English Culture and the Decline of the Industrial Spirit, 1850–1980* (Cambridge, 1981), esp. ch. 6; J. Stevenson, *British Society, 1914–45* (Harmondsworth, 1984), p. 29.

13. These points are developed in J. Stevenson and C. Cook, *The Slump* (London, 1977).

14. Wiener, *English Culture* (1981), ch. 6.

15. J. S. Barnes, *Fascism* (London, 1931); J. Jenks, *Spring Comes Again: A Farmer's Philosophy* (London, 1939); A. Raven Thomson, 'The Yeomen of England', *Action*, 21.5.36; O. Mosley, *Fascism, 100 Questions Asked and Answered* (London, 1936), no. 59; *Tomorrow we Live* (London, 1938), p. 46; and 'The Yeomen and the Soil', *Action*, 24.4.37. Refer also to *The People's Post* (Journal of the BPP) July and August 1939; and O. Wilson, 'Back to the Land', *Nineteenth Century and After*, Aug. 1924.

16. On these individuals refer to Appendix.

17. *Statecraft* (London, 1927). Sanderson was a regular contributor to *The Fascist* in the 1930s. The belief that political leadership declined as industrial urbanisation increased was also expressed neatly by C. Petrie, *Monarchy* (London, 1933), p. 269.

18. *The False Assumptions of Democracy* (London, 1921), p. 212.

19. G. R. Searle, 'Eugenics and Politics in Britain in the 1930s', *Annals of Science* (1979), pp. 159–69. The Eugenics Society had trouble attracting those right-wingers (especially Catholics) who saw birth-control and selective sterilisation as a form of 'race suicide'.

20. English Mistery Memo, 12.8.33, 3rd Earl Selborne MS. c.1013/50–4, p. 2.

21. Viscount Lymington, *Famine in England* (London, 1939), pp. 117–18.

22. On this theme refer C. Petrie, *Chapters of Life* (London, 1950), esp. ch. VI.

23. Assuming York to be representative. Stevenson, *British Society*, ch. 13.

24. E.g. H. E. Stutfield, *Priestcraft* (London, 1921), and *Mysticism and Catholicism* (London, 1925).

25. Especially in the columns of *Nineteenth Century and After*: see e.g. H. B. Chapman, 'Christianity and Bolshevism', Sept. 1924; Lord Salisbury, 'An Outline of Christian anti-Socialism', Feb. 1925; and Rev. J. A. Nairn, 'Marx or Christ?', May 1925.

26. *The Red Menace to British Children* (London, n.d. ?1926), p. 3. Issued by the Fascist Children's Club Dept. which was run by Lady Sydenham.

27. This, and most of what follows is based upon *The Passing of Liberalism* (London, 1925) and *The History of World Revolution* (Hayes, 1954 edn). On divorce refer to *Hofls Debs.*, Vol. 45, Col. 98 28.4.21. On the prayer-book controversy refer to the *Patriot*, 1.12.27. Northumberland belonged to a sect known as the Catholic Apostolic Church.

28. The *Patriot*, 19.3.25, pp. 393–4.

29. *Outspoken Essays* (London, 1919), p. 30; *Outspoken Essays II* (London, 1922, 1933 edn), p. 140.

30. A. M. Ludovici, *A Defence of Conservatism* (London, 1927), p. 169: 'From the standpoint of nationality . . . Christianity . . . is a disturbing force, because it is an international force.' Refer also to R. Griffiths, *Fellow Travellers of the Right* (London, 1983 edn), pp. 145–6 on Rolf Gardiner, and note the attitude even of L. S. Amery, 'My heart is with the Gods of Greece, and Pallas Athene is so much more real to me than Mary of Nazareth' (LSA to his wife, 23.6.15, *Diaries*, vol. 1, p. 119). See also fn. 53 below.

31. Griffiths, *Fellow Travellers*, pp. 175–7.

32. The BUF also attempted to attract Catholics. See e.g. *Blackshirt*, 1–7 July 1933, p. 3; and A. K. Chesterton, 'Fascist Principles in the Middle Ages', *Action*, 13.8.36.

33. J. S. Barnes, *Half a Life* (London, 1933); *Half a Life Left* (London, 1937).

34. Barnes, *Fascism* (1934 edn), p. 50.

35. G. R. Searle, 'Critics of Edwardian Society: The Case of the Radical Right' in A. O'Day (ed.), *The Edwardian Age* (London, 1979), ch. 4; and D. Jerrold, *Georgian Adventure* (London, 1937), esp. ch. 11.

36. Lunn, 'Political Anti-Semitism before 1914', p. 34. On Chesterton and Belloc see esp. R. Barker, *Political Ideas in Modern Britain* (London, 1978), pp. 84–91. However, his comment that 'Chesterton, Belloc and the group around them represented the end of a tradition' (p. 90) overstates the case. The old tradition fed several new ones.

37. S. T. Glass, *The Responsible Society: The Ideas of Guild Socialism* (London, 1966); P. Selver, *Orage and the New Age Circle* (London, 1959); C. Sisson (ed.), *Philip Mairet, Autobiographical and Other Papers* (Manchester, 1981). On Kitson see, L. Wise, *Arthur Kitson* (London, 1946), and the Appendix. Also refer to M. Cowling, *Religion and Public Doctrine in Modern England* (Cambridge, 1980), p. 119.

38. See R. Skidelsky, 'Great Britain' in S. J. Woolf (ed.), *European Fascism* (London, 1968), p. 251.

39. E. Wilkins, letter, *NEW*, 25.3.37, p. 478.

40. On these organisations refer to Appendix.

41. Patrick Hannon MS 10/2, 11/2, 11/13, 12/13 and 13/4.

42. D. S. Higgins (ed.), *The Private Diaries of Sir Henry Rider Haggard, 1914–1925* (Jonathan Cape, London, 1980), 28.4.19, 30.1.20, 3.3.20 and May 1920.

43. John Cowper Powys, *The Meaning of Culture* (London, 1930). This was reminiscent of the fears of nineteenth-century liberals such as J. S. Mill, and of European Conservatives such as Ortega y Gasset, *The Revolt of the Masses* (first published in Spanish, Madrid, 1930; first published in English, London, 1932).

44. Barnes, *Fascism* (1934 edn), p. 147.

45. D. Jerrold, *England* (London, 1935; 1936 edn), p. 202. See also his personal history of the war, *The Hawke Battalion* (London, 1925), especially the 'Afterword. A note on Literature and the War.': 'it is at least arguable that the agonies of soul depicted by these modern writers are not the torments of a superior sensibility, but only the exaggerated reaction of a too specialised civilisation which produces whole classes who have lost the aptitude for practical activity'. p. 230.

46. *The False Assumptions of Democracy* (London, 1921), p. 15.

47. *The Revenge For Love* (London, 1937; Harmondsworth, 1983, edn), p. 12.
48. M. Harrison, *The Reactionaries* (London, 1966), p. 30. Also refer to A. Hamilton, *The Appeal of Fascism. A Study of Intellectuals and Fascism, 1919–1945* (London, 1971). In the late 1930s the BUF also attracted Henry Williamson, author of *Tarka the Otter* (G. P. Putnam's and Sons, London and New York, 1927), a 'ruralist' who had previously identified with the Left.
49. On Campbell refer to B. Bergonzi: 'Roy Campbell: Outsider on the Right', *JCH* (1967), pp. 133–48. On Yeats refer to G. Orwell, 'W. B. Yeats' (1943) in *Collected Essays* (London, 1975 edn), pp. 195–201.
50. See esp. S. Spender, *Eliot* (London, 1975).
51. T. S. Eliot, *The Idea of a Christian Society* (London, 1939), p. 16.
52. Barker, *Political Ideas*, p. 153.
53. On Joyce refer to J. A. Cole, *Lord Haw-Haw — and William Joyce* (London, 1964). When he created the NSL in 1937 he also established a front organisation (akin to the BUF's January Club) called the Carlyle Club. See also Prof. C. Sarolea, 'Was Carlyle the First Nazi?', *Anglo-German Review* (Jan. 1938), p. 51. Few other Fascists were so concerned about their intellectual heritage, and most were hostile to culture. See e.g. G. E. de Burgh Wilmot, 'Our first duty to culture is to destroy it', *Blackshirt*, 3.8.34. The flavour of Conservative anti-intellectualism is neatly captured in H. P. Croft, *My Life of Strife* (London, 1948), p. 29ff, where he boasts of being a 'duffer'. This was sometimes carried to the point of occultism e.g. Croft, *My Life*, ch. 17 and Maj. Gen. J. F. C. Fuller, *The First of the League Wars* (London, 1936). Similar veins of anti-rationalism can be found in the works of men such as Ludovici (who translated Nietzsche) and those interested in eastern mysticism such as Philip Mairet and Francis Yeats-Brown (see esp. *Bengal Lancer* (London, 1930)).
54. O. Boulton, *The Way Out* (London, 1934), p. 89.
55. W. Fraser, 'The Einstein Hoax', *Plain English*, 12.11.21.

THE ECONOMY

As we noted in Chapter 1, it was characteristic of the Right that they were concerned about changes in the nature of the domestic economy and about the role of the modern state within it. Consequently, in analysing the attitudes of the Right towards the economy it is most fruitful to classify them according to the views they took both of capitalism and of state intervention in economic affairs. In this way four broad categories emerge: anti-capitalist statists; anti-capitalist anti-statists; capitalist statists; and capitalist anti-statists. This terminology is clumsy and initially it appears confusing because it does not correspond with more familiar distinctions such as those which are often drawn between 'collectivists' and 'libertarians' or 'Tories' and 'neo-liberals'. Nor do these categories relate very easily to popular terms like 'corporatism' or 'planning'. However, even though these popular terms will be used where they seem appropriate, they have been rejected as tools of analysis because they fail to tell us anything very interesting about the British Right. For instance, analyses that depict Conservative Party politics as a struggle between two different groups oversimplify the arguments, and those that treat toryism and neo-liberalism as antithetical ideas fail to explore the ways in which the two interact. Likewise, corporatism and planning are labels that need to be subdivided before they become useful.[1] Consequently, a four-fold classification of ideological 'ideal types' has been employed instead in order to help us understand what might otherwise remain obscure. Success is their only justification.

Anti-capitalist Statists

Negatively, the anti-capitalist statists were identified by a distrust of industrialism that had its roots in a nostalgia for a golden age of settled social and economic relations usually identified with the dominance of a landed aristocracy. Often this deteriorated into a more or less crude form of anti-Semitism, but for most anti-capitalist statists anti-Semitism had less to do with the Jews as such than with industrial and financial capitalism which the Jews were taken to symbolise. Thus, the Jewish immigrant became the symbol of industrialism which was despised because it disrupted traditional patterns of social and economic life whilst the Jewish plutocrat became the symbol of finance which was feared because its interests were defined independently of the interests of the nation.[2] Their real objection was to the dominance of industrial and financial interests over landed ones.[3] But this objection was usually widened into an attack upon bourgeois values in general, the essence of which was that whilst the ownership of land gave men a fixed and permanent stake in the country, mobile wealth was likely to weaken the nation by undermining the practical patriotism which followed from the possession of a geographically limited interest.[4]

More broadly still, capitalism was believed to have divorced power and responsibility within society by widening the gaps between economic, social and political elites.[5] For the anti-capitalist statists the ownership and use of private property was looked upon less as a right than as a privilege justified by the fact that those who owned great wealth should be fit to command society.[6] Their belief was, however, that those who currently dominated the economic life of the country were not so fitted to control its political life or to establish its social values. Property, they insisted, was a *trust* rather than a *commodity*, and this trust was being betrayed. Consequently it was incumbent upon the state to circumscribe the privileges of private ownership more carefully by extending the scope of state influence and control (though never by abolishing the principle of private property itself).[7]

One minor instance of state control might have been the introduction of protective tariffs (especially for agriculture), but this was fairly common ground on the Right.[8] Another was to insist on a balanced budget as a means of minimising the power of 'aliens' who were said to finance the national debt.[9] A more substantial use of state authority would have been found in domestic policy, but ideas about the form that this should take differed. The more extreme statists believed that all property should, in the last resort, belong to the Monarch.[10] Others believed in the need for a new, directive 'nobility'.[11] But many were attracted instead towards some form of corporatism.

Unlike appeals to a revitalised monarchy or a purified nobility, corporatism — loosely defined as a system in which both organised labour and organised business were incorporated within the structure of the state — had the advantage of being both popular and (apparently) 'modern'. Yet the truth of the matter was that the policy was infinitely flexible. In its widest sense corporatism was associated with an enormous variety of thinkers that ranged from continental extremists such as the revolutionary syndicalist, Georges Sorel, and the reactionary nationalist, Charles Maurras, to more moderate (but no less antagonistic) Englishmen such as the Guild Socialist, G. D. H. Cole, and the businessman, Henry Mond (2nd Baron Melchett, a Liberal MP until 1924 and a Conservative MP after 1929, who was later associated with Macmillan). Moreover, whilst some thought of corporatism as a way of extending and rationalising state regulation, others regarded it as a variety of pluralism; whilst some understood it primarily as a species of economic reform, others concentrated instead upon its constitutional implications (considered separately in Chapter 6); and whilst most thought of it as a 'modern' response to 'modern' problems, the corporate schemes proposed by some of the right-wingers in Britain were distinctly old-fashioned. For instance, Arnold Leese consciously attempted to re-establish a form of pre-industrial aristocratic rule in which industrial interests were to be controlled by political appointees and financial interests made the servant of the state by tightening control over investments.[12] Sir Charles Petrie sought to create an 'ethical state' that would secure the position both of the Catholic faith and the monarchy whilst realising the aims of Chamberlainite Social Imperialists.[13] And James Strachey Barnes saw the corporate state as an instrument of moral guidance in which the means of production were to be 'socialised' in such a way that whilst private property was to remain the foundation of society it was simultaneously to be regarded as a public trust rather than a merely personal possession.[14]

Anti-capitalist Anti-statists

The corporate state was also defended by some of the anti-capitalist *anti*-statists who saw this experimental form of government as a means of de-centralising power and (sometimes) of restoring the autonomy of the medieval guilds. Such, for example, was the case with Douglas Jerrold who, like Petrie and Barnes, was also a Catholic.

Prior to the First World War, Jerrold, like many of the Catholic

Right in the 1930s, had been a 'radical' Liberal. As a Catholic, however, he had always sought to resist the growth of uncontrolled capitalism and rampant individualism, and under the combined impact of the war, what Jerrold saw as the 'death' of 'liberalism', and the (related) growth of 'Bolshevism', he had increasingly drifted to the Right.[15] Fundamentally, Jerrold's distrust of capitalism derived from his belief that the ethos of industrialism had subverted the values of society by stressing the importance of materialism to the detriment of spirituality.[16] Moreover, in practice capitalism tended to undermine rather than secure the independence of the citizen which was essential to moral autonomy. Most obviously this was the result of the accumulation of capital which placed the many in bondage to the few and as a consequence made a mockery of democracy.[17] Most perniciously it was the result of a growing statism which was not inimical to capitalism as many believed but essential to its survival. Increasingly the state was forced to intervene in the market as a means of keeping the economy afloat with the consequence that power became more and more concentrated in the hands of 'the new bureaucracy, the professional organisers and administrators'.[18] But, since the logic of state intervention was devoid of any corresponding logic of limitation, an ever-mounting spiral of collectivism was inevitable. Already there was little to separate State capitalism and Communism save that the latter was openly hostile to Christianity whilst the former was only consequentially so:[19]

> Communism is merely capitalism carried to its logical conclusion; when the owners of capital, of the means of production, distribution and exchange, use these means to dictate to us how we shall live and what we shall eat.

Much of this echoed Belloc's concern with the 'servile state' and foreshadowed Hayek's fear of the spiralling logic of planning as the 'road to serfdom'. But whilst Hayek, as a Liberal, rejected all planning, Jerrold, by now a Catholic Tory, looked instead towards an alternative plan that owed much to the distributists but which was couched in the language of corporatism. In short, his Catholic corporatism sought to reconcile the rights of 'personality' (he was loathe to use the phrase 'the individual') with the necessity of social cohesion. In the first instance this demanded an ever-wider distribution of property as a guarantee of liberty and the foundation of character.[20] But it also demanded the abandonment of the present parliamentary system in favour of a corporate State which, by adopting functional rather than regional representation, would 'restore the reality of self-government in the appropriate spheres and enable a strong central government to speak for the nation, and not merely for a class, on national issues'.[21]

Another inversion of the anti-statist theme was to be found in the writings of men like Mairet, Reckitt and Demant who were associated with the *New English Weekly* during the 1930s.[22] Like T. S. Eliot, with whom they were linked, this group sought somewhat self-consciously to create a Christian society. But the mechanism they favoured was that of 'Social Credit' — an economic doctrine associated with Major C. H. Douglas (and briefly adopted by the State of Alberta in Canada) which argued that lack of purchasing power retarded production by limiting demand and that this could be remedied by a form of credit control under which goods would be sold below cost price and retailers would be reimbursed by the Exchequer.[23] This was seen by its exponents as an adaptation of Guild Socialism and distributism which represented an attack upon left-wing theories of under-consumption that sought a remedy in the imposition of a minimum wage. In theory, it was intended to devolve power within society and to undo the evils of 'plutocracy' by making the ownership of 'things' more important than the possession of money.[24] However, in practice, as we noted in the previous chapter, the philosophy of 'Social Credit' often deteriorated into a simple rationalisation of support for Fascism. Once again the corporate state crept in through the vestry door.

Thus, in practice the differences between the statists and the anti-statists amongst those who criticised and opposed capitalism were minimised. Both tended to resolve themselves into justifications of a corporate state and consequently into an admiration of Mussolini's Italy, and sometimes of Hitler's Germany as well. This was both ironic and, in the long-term, counter-productive: ironic because even in Italy the industrialists became more firmly entrenched in the economic and social system under Fascism than they had been when the Fascists came to power;[25] and counter-productive because their association with the European dictatorships eventually made their own ideas appear 'unthinkable'. To some extent, however, this was a problem that the pro-capitalists faced too, particularly Mosley and the BUF.

Capitalist Statists

Although one can find elements of anti-industrialism in BUF litera-ture,[26] and although the movement's policy of anti-Semitism often gave the impression that it was in principle opposed to capitalism, this was (at least at the level of authoritative policy statements)[27] a misleading picture. In fact, as Skidelsky has pointed out, Fascism in Britain attempted to combine two very different impulses, namely: 'the quest for modernisation and the revolt against its con-sequences'.[28] Thus, despite the popular view that Mosley had turned to Fascism because he developed an abstract lust for power, the truth was that Mosley sought power for the specific purpose of solving the economic problems of the time and that his brand of Fascism was as a result peculiarly programmatic from the very beginning. So, in contrast to continental Fascism where the autho-rity of the state was the first concern, 'in the BUF the attack on the political system was an outgrowth of an economic analysis'.[29]

The essence of the purely economic problem had been consis-tently identified by Mosley as one of under-consumption (a standard ILP analysis), and this itself was held to be the result of three major factors. The first was the lack of purchasing power; the second was the 'outdated' system of distribution which was no longer capable of coping with the increased productive capacity of industry; and the third was the increasing intensity of the struggle for foreign markets amongst all nations which led to an ever-diminishing home market for goods produced in Britain.[30] The solutions were held to be the creation of a planned economy on a corporate basis and the adoption of a system of imperial 'autarky'.[31]

The concept of the corporate state, though it was one of the central planks of the BUF's constructive programme, was not, in fact, a very fully developed idea in Mosley's own thinking. For him the essential requirement was to create a system of *managed capitalism* wherein the government could regulate the factors of supply and demand by the manipulation of wage and price levels, and in this he had been influenced more by the theories of Keynes and the examples of Roosevelt than he had been by Mussolini or by Hitler. For Mosley the corporate state remained a rather vague and adaptable system which was to provide the machinery necessary to establish a *completely* planned economy. Despite his claim that the government would merely set the 'limits' within which conventional capitalist economic activity would operate, it seemed clear enough that there could in practice be no toleration of truly autonomous market activity.[32] On the other hand, Mosley's aims were very different from those of the anti-capitalist statists considered earlier. For whilst men like Lymington were concerned to change the nature of the economy, Mosley was concerned only to change its structure: Lymington despised capitalism; Mosley sought to make it more perfect.[33]

Of course, one did not have to be a Fascist to be a capitalist statist. Indeed, in some respects the various governments of the inter-war years could themselves be classified in this way.[34] Yet amongst those on the Right who were out of sympathy with the emerging 'consensus' at the centre it was difficult to combine the elements of support for capitalism *and* of greater control over capitalists without being regarded as a crypto-Fascist. Nevertheless, L. S. Amery achieved a measure of success.

Although much of Amery's thinking was directed primarily towards the problem of creating and maintaining a strong and unified Empire (to which end he campaigned tirelessly for a policy of imperial preference — 'the principle of imperial unity in its economic aspect'),[35] he also wrote extensively about the need to reform the domestic economy. Here Amery rejected both *laissez-faire* individualism which ignored the interests of the 'community' and socialist planning which ignored the importance of individual enterprise. Instead he urged a policy of 'economic nationalism':[36]

> Nationalism accepts individual enterprise as the mainspring of national economic activity. But it does not admit that the indivi-dual interest necessarily and always coincides with the public interest and insists that it is an essential function of the state to ensure by its legislation that the economic activities of the individual citizen are so guided and, if need be, limited as to make the greatest contribution to the public welfare.

In theory this was supposed to avoid the worst 'excesses' of state control by virtue of the fact that the function of the state would be to 'direct' rather than to 'administer' the economy.[37] But since this direction from above was to operate 'irrespective of its convenience to individuals or to sections of the community',[38] this sounded more like a pious hope than a serious guarantee. Indeed, by the mid-thirties Amery, like so many others on the Right, had come to identify his economic theories with the ubiquitous policy of 'corporatism' and to admire its Italian manifestation even though he did not sanction the emulation of fascist, still less of Nazi, *methods* in Britain. But in practice there was no doubt that his own version of corporatism would have concentrated power firmly in the hands of the state.[39]

What was interesting about this was partly the fact that it demonstrated the ease with which tariff reformers could drift into corporatism.[40] Likewise it was interesting as an example of the way in which the pre-1914 traditions of 'efficiency' and 'technocratic managerialism' associated with Lord Milner were capable of being recast in a corporatist mould.[41] Within the context of this chapter, however, its major significance was that it represented a positive and conscious alternative to the policy of capitalist anti-statism.[42]

Capitalist Anti-Statists

Captialist anti-statism is more familiarly known as 'neo-liberalism' and has recently been treated by Greenleaf as an expression of what he calls 'Libertarian Conservatism'.[43] However, both of these labels are inadequate tools of analysis because the distinction which Greenleaf draws between collectivists and libertarians ignores important disagreements about the nature and value of capitalism within these groups, whilst the common distinction that is drawn between Tories and neo-liberals tends to obscure the fact that the two do not really stand in opposition to one another and that there is nothing very 'liberal' about neo-liberals anyway. In fact they disagree with the 'Tories' more about means than they do about ends. Neo-liberals believe, like the Tories, in the need for hierarchy, order and authority. But they also believe what the Tories do not: that these will be the natural result of the free play of market forces.

In the years immediately following the First World War such ideas were most often advanced by groups such as the Anti-Socialist Union and the British Commonwealth Union which tended to represent the interests of insecure capitalists.[44] The BCU, for example, which was run by Patrick Hannon[45] and financed primarily by businesses that feared nationalisation,[46] supported a policy of 'rigid economy in every branch of public administration' and the virtual abolition of the dole.[47] But although it opposed the extension of the state in so far as it implied increased taxation and restrictions upon private enterprise, 'it was in favour of government intervention to organise industry, to guarantee profits, and to protect British industry against foreign competition and domestic social unrest'.[48]

This was very similar to the policy of the National Party.[49] Indeed, Hannon could not see 'a shred of difference' between the two in 1918, although this was probably because the latter did not clarify its economic policies until September 1920.[50] However, once the National Party's industrial policy *was* codified, it became clear that what it really favoured was a form of corporate control in which power was to be vested almost exclusively in the hands of the employers. Labour representation within the scheme was simply designed to ensure that all industrial disputes would be settled by arbitration rather than by strikes.[51] And the Government was implicated only in an 'advisory' capacity. As with Petrie and with Amery this was further evidence of the ease with which tariff reformers could re-define their aims in the language of corporatism. But unlike Petrie the National Party had no animosity towards capitalism, and unlike Amery it had no desire to see the state interfering in the economy.

This was not very surprising. After all, Croft and Cooper (the party's only two MPs) were both prominent businessmen whilst the manifesto of the National Party had itself been written by F. S. Oliver.[52] But it *was* surprising to find the veteran Diehard, Lord Ampthill, as the party's President[53] — still more surprising that the new 'Diehards' of the early twenties were themselves pledged to a policy of capitalist anti-statism.[54] Thus, the 'Diehard Manifesto' which was signed by men like Salisbury, Carson, Northumberland, Sumner and Sydenham, pledged the group to 'economy and relief from excessive taxation', 'freedom for private enterprise instead of state interference', and 'sound finance' coupled with 'careful administration'.[55]

Of course, there were specific historical reasons for the appearance of this kind of rhetoric. With the Liberals (and the Coalition) under Lloyd George becoming more favourable to policies of collectivism, and with the Labour Party, freshly equipped with a 'socialist' constitution, emerging as the main opponents of the Conservatives, 'libertarianism' became attractive as a stick with which to beat them both.[56] But it would be a mistake to treat this as a sufficient 'explanation' of capitalist anti-statism on the Right. After all, the ideas themselves had a long and respectable history within the Conservative Party;[57] the men who espoused the ideas were not living in an ideological vacuum where tactics determined policy;[58] and the policies which they developed were neither abandoned nor forgotten as historical circumstances changed. Consequently, to see this as a prudential *departure* from Toryism would be to misunderstand what was happening. For although it is tempting to view the emergence of ex-Liberals like Ernest Benn amongst the Diehards of the 1930s as evidence that the Right were simply devoid of a distinctive philosophy, the truth was that their conception of capitalist anti-statism represented a redefinition of traditional Tory concerns.

Hence, for example, the 4th Marquis of Salisbury accepted that, although the only sound basis upon which society could rest was one that reflected the values of Christianity, 'until religion transform[ed] society and self-sacrifice obtain[ed] a complete mastery the only available antidote to the poison of indolence [was] reward'.[59] Market forces, in other words, were relied upon to achieve what organised religion as yet could not, though this was not to sanction the overt materialism of liberal individualists. For the accumulation of wealth was legitimised by the existence of the family and it was this which transformed the desire for material gain into a form of 'altruism'.[60] The old-fashioned Tory concept of property as something which was justified by its social utility remained intact. But the concept of social utility itself had been redefined in such a way that it now centred upon the family rather than upon the 'community' or the nation.

The 8th Duke of Northumberland provides a similar example. Thus, in the immediate post-war years Northumberland stands out as an ultra-reactionary who supported a medieval theocracy and attacked liberal individualism, Jews and the 'monied classes'.[61] Yet by 1923 his politics had taken on a new realism well befitting a man who was a major coal-owner as well as a landed aristocrat:[62]

> The only cure for present day evils is to go back to that freedom in private enterprise and to that individual liberty for which our party has always striven. We are far too much afraid on [sic] Conservative principles, far too much afraid of the taunt that this or that measure will help the Capitalist. If the working man is to be helped the Capitalist must be helped too — one cannot get on without the other.

Likewise, W. R. Inge, Dean of St Pauls, and in many ways one of the most old-fashioned of old-fashioned Tories, believed that the Welfare State (such as it was in 1922) had resulted in a 'suspension of natural selection' by subsidising the incompetent at the expense of the industrious.[63] But whilst 'breeding' was, for Inge, the crucial factor in this analysis it was actually the market which was seen as the determinant of fitness.[64]

Nor were these isolated examples of the ways in which a belief in the efficacy of the free-market economy was being interwoven with traditional Tory themes. Indeed, one can find the same process at work in the columns of the *Morning Post*. The editorial of 2 July 1921, for instance, provides a fine example of the way in which even ruralist themes could be taken to a capitalist conclusion.[65]

whereas in the days of the worthy Mr. SAMUEL SMILES the individual was instructed concerning his duty to the State, in this year of grace the State is being instructed concerning its duty to the individual . . . To teach an animal to rely on itself is one of the most bracing instincts in nature. Can man afford to do otherwise? Messrs Smiles and company emphatically said No . . . However, our new teachers have turned down Mr. Smiles. We live in the dole age . . . what the world needs today is discipline, and if the discipline cannot be imposed from within, then it must be imposed from without . . . Character is the foundation of the British Empire . . . The strength of countries like France and Italy in the end depends upon their peasant populations, and the soil is the great disciplinarian of the world. But in an industrial country like ours great masses of the people never get near the soil, and so they have to depend for their soul's health on other teachers.

By the 1930s this kind of capitalist anti-statism was finding systematic expression in the writings of people such as Ernest Benn and Dorothy Crisp.

Until the mid-twenties Ernest Benn had been a Liberal.[66] By the end of the decade Keynes was to describe him as the leader of those 'very extreme Conservatives' who wanted 'to undo all the hardly-won little which we have in the way of conscious and deliberate control of economic forces for the public good, and replace it by a return to chaos'.[67] Nor was this drift to the Right something that Benn denied, for he too came to see himself as a 'full-blooded, die-hard Tory'.[68] It was interesting that he considered himself a disciple of Herbert Spencer whose most famous book, *The Man Versus the State* (first published in 1884), began by proclaiming that 'Most of those who now pass as Liberals are Tories of a new type.'[69] What Spencer meant by this paradox was that contemporary liberalism had become far too receptive to schemes of State intervention. But what Spencer added in the 1892 edition was this; that[70]

> a new species of Tory may arise without disappearance of the original species . . . [for] . . . the laws made by Liberals are so greatly increasing the compulsions and restraints exercised over citizens, that among Conservatives who suffer from this aggressiveness there is growing up a tendency to resist it.

As proof he cited the existence of the Liberty and Property Defence League (with which he was associated), an overwhelmingly Conservative organisation run by Lord Elcho which acted as a 'co-ordinator of threatened interests'.[71]

In many respects, therefore, Benn was merely following in Spencer's footsteps,[72] although he made up in influence what he lacked in originality since the 1920s was a more propitious time to make the journey than the 1880s had been. Many of those on the Right, as we have seen, had already come to believe in the benefits of a free-market economy quite independently of disillusioned Liberals — Benn was simply able to give their ideas greater clarity of expression and a limited degree of intellectual respectability (most of which was borrowed from Spencer).

Moreover, Benn's own 'liberalism' was not entirely 'unreconstructed'. Thus, although he was an individualist, his individualism was a means to another end. As he stated the matter in 1953: 'Every strengthening of the State machine means a weakening of the individual, but every improvement in the individual means a strengthening of the nation.'[73] Individualism, in other words, was actually defended on the grounds that it increased the scope for *patriotism*.[74] And individual success, as Benn described it, had less to do with negative freedoms than with positive obligations to the extent that it became difficult to see where neo-liberalism began and Tory democracy ended:[75]

> Success to be complete embodies the obligation to help failure,

but failure does not carry with it the right to share success. Life is a personal thing. The power to strive, the obligation to serve and the responsibility to move forwards or backwards on your road whatever it may be, are all personal to you alone and single-handed. You have few rights but many duties.

This curious marriage of 'Liberal' and 'Tory' attitudes was found most strikingly in the work of a young Conservative named Dorthy Crisp whose 1931 credo, *The Rebirth of Conservatism*, stands as an exceptional but 'ideal typical' expression of right-wing 'neo-liberalism'.

Britain, she argued, was threatened by both moral and material decay.[76] The mass of the people were now, more than ever, in need of leadership since it was 'less the violence of the few . . . than the muddle of the many' which society had to fear.[77] But those who were actually charged with leadership were 'rooted in the pre-war world' and incapable of providing the necessary guidance.[78] Consequently it was important to reform the political and economic bases of social life in such a way that leaders *could* lead and that the rest would follow.

Constitutionally this involved a restriction of the franchise and the strengthening of the Lords over the Commons and of the King over the Lords.[79] In terms of social policy it meant an end to the Welfare State which was 'levelling down the whole race' by preserving the 'unfit' at the expense of the 'fit', coupled with the imposition of a national code of education.[80] Economically, however, the emphasis was not on direction and control but on freedom and initiative. So, although strikes were to be controlled by means of enforced arbitration,[81] in all other areas individual enterprise was to be valued, partly as a form of self-expression,[82] but mostly as a way of 'allowing the natural leaders perfect freedom, and each man freedom to the degree of his courage and ability'.[83]

At present heavy taxation served to penalise 'the best citizens' whilst legal restrictions served to prevent him bequeathing his property to his family.[84] But conservatism would set no limits whatsoever upon the wealth of an individual and would remove all barriers to inheritance since the transmission of wealth would strengthen the family and since it was *the family* which was the real unit in a state, and that which sanctified the acquisitive instinct of the individual.[85]

For Crisp, as for Lord Salisbury, property was still justified in terms of social utility, but social utility was measured by reference to the family. Nor was the concept of 'the family' any longer confined to 'the nobility' as it had been in nineteenth-century Tory thinking. Instead it was generalised to include *all* family groups whilst the beneficial properties once ascribed exclusively to the ownership of land came to be ascribed also to the ownership of mobile wealth and the employment of capital. The result was a distinctively *Tory* form of 'neo-liberalism' that attempted to reconcile the demands of 'individual freedom' and those of social discipline through the two institutions of the free market and the family.[86]

Conclusions

The variety and fluidity of right-wing attitudes towards the economy provide us with clues both as to the weakness of the BUF in the 1930s and to the ways in which the right-wing of the Conservative Party itself was changing. The BUF attracted very little support and relied for such limited success as it had upon the influx of disillusioned 'Conservatives' who swelled its ranks for a short time in 1934 and again in 1939.[87] In 1939 the drift towards the BUF appeared to have more to do with middle-class support for the policy of appeasement than any attachment to the principles of Fascism, and in 1934 the explanation was similarly negative, namely that many Conservatives were out of sympathy with Baldwin. As we saw in the previous chapter, most traditional Conservatives who flirted with the Fascist movement did so because they saw it as the only viable alternative to the Conservative Party and because they regarded some aspects of its doctrine as a close approximation to their own brand of toryism. But both beliefs were mistaken. For whilst Mosley sought to create a form of state-controlled capitalism most of the erstwhile Conservatives who admired Fascism in Britain were in revolt against the capitalist order itself and some of them were in revolt against the modern state as well. Few of those on the traditional Right accepted Mosley's combination of support both for capitalism *and* for extensive state intervention, and even when they did (as in the case of L. S. Amery) it by no means follow that they would therefore embrace Fascism. Farr's belief that there was a process of 'evolution' at work in which backward-looking Tories of the Edwardian age became forward-looking Fascists of the inter-war period is consequently dubious.[88] Those old-fashioned Tories who did support the Fascists did not change their ideas but merely dressed them up in jackboots; and those whose ideas were susceptible to change did not become Fascists in the first place.

Indeed, the right wing of the Conservative Party became increasingly identified with a policy of capitalist anti-statism that stood at least in partial *opposition* to Fascism. For although both groups accepted capitalism as necessary and (at least potentially) desirable, the Fascists wanted to control the economy through state planning whereas most Conservatives wanted to set it free from state 'interference'. This kind of capitalist anti-statism could easily be confused with certain kinds of liberalism, but it was not a liberal creed. For although these Tories believed, like some Liberals, in the benefits of economic *laissez-faire* they differed from them in what they believed those benefits to be. For *laissez-faire* liberals, the free play of market forces was valued primarily because it resulted in the progressive extension of an abstract liberty; for the capitalist anti-statist Conservatives, it was valued because it served in practice to perpetuate or accentuate existing social inequalities. The *laissez-faire* liberals regarded free enterprise as good in itself; the capitalist anti-statist Conservatives valued free enterprise only for its results. The former were primarily concerned with the rules of the game; the latter wanted to know who would win.[89]

That capitalist anti-statism eventually became the dominant strand of right-wing thinking after World War Two was not inevitable. But it was understandable. For many of the pro-capitalist alternatives were discredited by their association (real or imagined) with Fascism, whilst all of the anti-capitalist alternatives demanded a massive *redistribution* of wealth (albeit in accordance with 'virtue' rather than 'need'). Besides, capitalist anti-statism gained impetus during the inter-war years as a result of the post-1918 drive for de-regulation and reduced taxation; the need to develop a clear 'anti-socialist' position in the 1920s; and (perhaps) the influx of some Gladstonian Liberals into the Conservative Party. But contingent explanations of this kind do not account for the persistence of such attitudes over time. However, what might account for the gradual transformation of right-wing ideologies are the changing patterns of economic interest that appear to underlie them (although what follows does not pretend to be a thorough, systematic analysis).

The anti-capitalist Right were composed primarily of two

groups, both of which hoped to restore some *status quo ante*: landed aristocrats like Lymington who had not diversified their interests beyond agriculture[90] and individuals such as Arnold Leese (a retired vet), Petrie (a freelance historian), or Mairet (a writer and craftsman) who felt that their values and status were indirectly threatened by industrial development because their interests were marginal to the struggle between capital and labour.[91] The Fascists, who sought to alter the *status quo* without simply turning the clock back and hoped to achieve this by unleashing the power of the state rather than that of the market, also fell into different groups. Thus, along with a limited number of anti-capitalists and displaced professionals who supported them by default, the Fascists tended to attract small-businessmen who felt threatened by open competition, unemployed and non-unionised workers who hoped for personal or industrial protection from the vicissitude of the market, and a handful of big industrialists with an interest in formalising their relationship with the state (although this latter group was very small indeed because the FBI and to some extent Parliament itself *already* provided a substantial link between business interests and government policy by the time that the BUF was created).[92] Meanwhile, the pro-capitalist anti-statist Right sought to perpetuate the *existing status quo* in order to secure their already-extensive interests and privileges against attack. Like the anti-capitalists, they also fell broadly into two categories — businessmen such as Croft and Gretton (both of whom were principally, but not exclusively brewers), and aristocrats such as Northumberland and Wolmer whose interests in industry, commerce and finance allowed them to maintain their aristocratic lifestyles.[93] However, unlike the anti-capitalists and the pro-Fascists, the capitalist anti-statists on the Right were fighting from a position of strength rather than one of weakness, and their ideas consequently appealed to a larger and more vigorous constituency.

Notes

1. H. Glickman, 'The Toryness of English Conservatism', *JBS* (Nov. 1961), pp. 111–43 argues for a 'bipolar' view of Conservatism; W. H. Greenleaf, *The British Political Tradition*, vol. II (Methuen, London and New York, 1983), part II, distinguishes between collectivist and libertarian strains of Conservatism; P. C. Schmitter, 'Still the Century of Corporatism?' *Review of Politics* (1974), pp. 85–131 makes some useful distinctions, especially between 'societal' and 'state'

corporatism; A. Marwick, 'Middle Opinion in the Thirties: Planning, Progress and Political "agreement"', *EHR* (1964), pp. 285–98 provides a useful analysis of 'progressives' who were associated with the Next Five Years Group, but he is inclined to treat planning as if it constituted an ideology rather than a method.

2. Finance, like Christianity, was seen as a 'disturbing force' because it was an *international* force. A. M. Ludovici, *A Defence of Conservatism* (London, 1927), p. 169. On anti-Semitic themes in general refer C. Holmes, *Anti-Semitism in British Society, 1876–1939* (London, 1979); G. C. Lebzelter, *Political Anti-Semitism in England, 1918–1939* (London, 1978), and the previous chapter of this book.

3. This was natural for men like Viscount Lymington, see especially *Ich Dien, the Tory Path* (London, 1931), but it was also to be found amongst those with limited interests in the land such as the novelist, Rider Haggard (D. S. Higgins (ed.), *The Private Diaries of Sir Henry Rider Haggard* (London, 1980), entry for 15 July 1918, p. 142, for example), and those with no direct interest at all such as Francis Yeats-Brown, author of *Bengal Lancer*: 'To me the land is holy, I have never owned a foot of it, or anything I could call a home, but I believe in these things, and hate the subvertors of their sanctity.' Quoted in J. E. Wrench, *Francis Yeats-Brown, 1886–1944* (London, 1948), p. 98.

4. See e.g. Viscount Lymington, *Famine in England* (London, 1938), p. 43: 'It should not be forgotten that those aliens who now appear to have a stake in this country have a stake also in many others.'

5. See e.g. C. Petrie, *The British Problem* (London, 1934), ch. 1.

6. E.g. W. Sanderson to F. S. Oliver, 17.12.17: 'Money is not wealth but the power to command others . . . the basis of private property is [i.e. should be] our fitness to command.' F. S. Oliver MS 98/233–4.

7. The institution of private property itself was inviolable. See, for example, A. M. Ludovici, *The False Assumptions of Democracy* (London, 1921), esp. pp. 35–43. The introduction to this book was written by the veteran Diehard, Lord Willoughby de Broke.

8. Free-traders were few and far between on the Right. Apart from the Duke of Devonshire (first President of the Anti-Socialist Union) and St Loe Strachey (editor of the *Spectator*), the only free-trader of note was Lord Salisbury, but even he was not dogmatic on the subject. As he explained to Selborne in 1918: 'I have drawn a fiscal formula which goes a certain distance . . . the critical phrase there is the "protection of key industries". What are key industries? Top [i.e. Viscount Wolmer, Selborne's son] would say they are many . . . [but] . . . there is no *doctrine* which separates us.' 2nd Earl Selborne MS 1/7/49–52.

9. Viscount Lymington, *English Mistery Circular*, no. 1, Sept. 1936, 3rd Earl Selborne MS c.1013/41–9. P. Mairet and other Social Crediters (who were anti-capitalists *and* anti-statists) had similar fears. See e.g. the columns of the *New English Weekly*, 1932–9.

10. Count Potocki, *The Right Review*, no. 1, Oct. 1936, Leader, 'And Like a Thunderbolt . . .'.

11. Hence the English Mistery. Refer to ch. 4.

12. See especially A. S. Leese, *Mightier Yet!* (1935); *The Fascist*, May 1929; March 1932; Sept. 1935; Nov. 1936; and J. Morell, 'The Life and Opinions of A. S. Leese', M.A., University of Sheffield, 1974, ch. 4.

13. See esp. *The British Problem*, pp. 21–3.

14. *Fascism* (London, 1931), esp. ch. 6, 'The Economic Principles of Fascism'.

15. D. Jerrold, *Georgian Adventure* (London, 1937), pp. 313–15.

16. 'What is Conservatism?', *ER*, June 1931, pp. 51–62.

17. *The Necessity of Freedom* (first published London, 1938; Catholic Book Club edition, 1935), esp. chs. 7, 8 and 9.

18. *England* (London, 1935), p. 156–7.

19. *The Necessity of Freedom*, p. 132.

20. Many on the Right highlighted the crucial connection between property and personality which G. K. Chesterton had expressed elegantly in his 1910 credo, *What's Wrong with the World* (1912 edn, pp. 47−8): 'Property is merely the art of the democracy. It means that every man should have something he can shape in his own image, as he is shaped in the image of heaven. But because he is not God, but only a graven image of God, his self-expression must deal with limits; properly with limits that are strict and small.'

21. *Georgian Adventure*, p. 340.

22. P. Mairet, translator, craftsman and author of *Aristocracy and the Meaning of Class Rule* (London, 1931). Editor of the *New English Weekly*, 1934−9. Rev. M. B. Reckitt, author of *The Meaning of National Guilds* (London, 1918), *A Christian Sociology for Today* (London, 1934), *Religion in Social Action* (1937) etc. Rev. V. A. Demant, Regius Professor of Moral and Pastoral Theology at Oxford, 1949−71 and author of *God, Man and Society. An Introduction to Christian Sociology* (London, 1933), *Christian Polity* (Faber and Faber, London, 1936) etc.

23. The best introduction to the 'philosophy' of Social Credit is to be found in M. B. Reckitt, *As it Happened, an Autobiography* (London, 1941), pp. 164−9; but see also the Conservative Research Department file on the subject contained in the Conservative Party Archives, Bodleian Library, Oxford. Social Credit was summed up by the *New English Weekly* as a means of 'creating and distributing purchasing power *pari-passu* with the expanding means of production.' *NEW*, vol. 1, no. 1, 21.4.32, p. 2.

24. E.g. Demant, *God, Man, and Society*, pp. 80−2.

25. R. Sarti, *Fascism and the Industrial Leadership in Italy, 1919−1940: A Study in the Expansion of Private Power under Fascism* (Univ. of California Press, Berkeley and London, 1971).

26. Especially in the writings of Jorian Jenks and in occasional articles such as 'The Yeomen of England' by A. Raven Thomson, *Action*, 21.5.36, p. 7.

27. On this distinction see N. Nugent, 'The ideas of the BUF' in N. Nugent and R. King (eds.), *The British Right* (Farnborough, 1977). As an example of the confusion that can arise when this distinction is ignored see D. M. Geiger, 'British Fascism as Revealed in the BUF's Press', Ph.D., New York Univ., 1963.

28. R. Skidelsky, *Oswald Mosley* (London, 1981 paperback edn), p. 299.

29. N. Nugent, 'Ideas of the BUF', p. 137. This point is also made in R. Benewick, *The Fascist Movement in Britain* (London, 1972 edn), ch. 7, p. 132.

30. O. Mosley, *The Greater Britain* (London, 1932), ch. 4.

31. Refer to Chapter 7 below.

32. Mosley, *Greater Britain*, p. 168: 'There will be no room in Britain for those who do not accept the principle "All for the State and the State for All".'

33. Mosley believed, to use his words, in a combination of 'Science and Caesarism': O. Mosley, *My Life* (London, 1968), p. 316ff.

34. R. K. Middlemas, *Politics in Industrial Society* (London, 1979), describes the emergence of a 'corporate bias' in Britain.

35. L. S. Amery, *My Political Life*, vol. I (London, 1953), p. 308.

36. *National and Imperial Economics* (Westminster, 1923), pp. 9−10.

37. *The Forward View* (London, 1935), p. 333.

38. Amery, *Forward View*, p. 321.

39. L. P. Carpenter, 'Corporatism in Britain, 1930−1945', *JCH* (1976), pp. 3−25, also makes this point.

40. The same was true of Sir Charles Petrie and Henry Page Croft (at least in the early 20s).

41. On the right wing of the efficiency movement refer Searle in A. O'Day (ed.), *The Edwardian Age* (London, 1979), ch. 4. A recent book on corporatism (Otto

Newman, *The Challenge of Corporatism* (1981)) complains that British corporatism was 'singularly undeveloped, derivative, and second-hand' (pp. 13–14), but this was precisely what made it interesting.

42. L. S. Amery, *My Political Life*, vol. II (London, 1953–5), pp. 173–4. Amery wrote to Worthington Evans in October 1918: 'The one thing we must, above all, avoid being committed to in the future is being a party of vested interests and strict economy — the anti-socialist party if you like.'

43. Greenleaf, *British Political Tradition*, vol. II, part II.

44. On the ASU and BCU refer esp. to ch. 2 and Appendix.

45. Patrick Hannon (1874–1963): Irish businessman, Director of HP Sauce and BSA; Gen. Sec. Navy League 1911–18; Vice-President Tariff Reform League 1910–14; joint founder of the Comrades of the Great War (later incorporated in the British Legion); Director BCU 1918–23; Conservative MP 1921–50; Vice-President Empire Industries Association from 1925; Vice-President Federation of British Industries from 1925; President National Union of Manufacturers from 1935.

46. The biggest contributors were Vickers Ltd and the Metropolitan Carriage, Wagon and Finance Co., but shipbuilders, gas companies, electrical supply companies, and British Sugar refineries were also prominent supporters. Hannon MS Box 8. Also refer to J. A. Turner, 'The British Commonwealth Union and The General Election of 1918', *EHR* (1978), pp. 528–59; and B. L. Farr, 'The Development and Inpact of Right-wing Politics in Great Britain, 1903–1932', Ph.D., Univ. of Illinois at Chicago Circle, 1976.

47. BCU Industrial Group, *Draft Policy* (1924). Hannon MS H13/3.

48. Turner, 'The BCU', p. 550.

49. Founded by Henry Page Croft in August/Sept. 1917; renamed the National Constitutional Association in 1921.

50. Hannon to Croft 19.8.18. Hannon MS H11/1; *National Opinion*, Sept. 1920, p. 5. Prior to this the National Party had been more inclined to attack Bolsheviks and Jews than to propose anything very positive; such proposals as they did make stressed protection and agricultural development.

51. The article (see fn. 50 above) was entitled 'How to Stop Strikes'.

52. F. S. Oliver (1864–1934): Scottish businessman and writer who made Debenhams a major firm and wrote extensively on federalism. Although he lost sympathy with tariff reformers like Croft and Amery in the early thirties (see e.g. FSO to Geoffrey Dawson, 29.10.31, FSO MS 85/239) his views were still far from moderate: 'There is much to be said for the early Victorian virtue of thrift . . . Make a great cut in the dole . . . Put a heavy tax . . . on foreign imports.' (FSO to Dawson, 8.8.31, FSO MS 85/197–9).

53. Lord Ampthill: Private Secretary to Joseph Chamberlain at the Colonial Office; Governor of Madras 1889; Viceroy and Governor General 1904; returned to England 1906 and was then associated with the National Service League.

54. In fact the 'National Party' (such as it was) was later incorporated into the new Diehard movement of 1921/2. Refer to 3rd Earl Selborne MS Box c.1012.

55. *The Times* 8.3.32.

56. This negative, tactical consideration is exemplified by an undated, unsigned memo (c. 1919) 2nd Earl Selborne MS. 7, fols. 66–9: 'The conservative-mined rank and file will want a line of resistance which they can clearly realise. They have no sympathy with the despotic employer but they hate the bureaucracy and the price of coal and the exploitation of the country by the triple alliance.'

57. Greenleaf, *British Political Tradition*, vol. II, ch. 8.

58. Indeed, quite the reverse. It was a distinguishing feature of the Right that they despised the 'trimmers' and 'tacticians' who ran the party, for as Petrie pointed out, 'What must never be forgotten is that the Socialists have a scheme, and those who do not believe in it must produce a practicable alternative' (*The British Problem*,

p. 16). The trouble with the centre, as Lord Salisbury saw it, was this: that although 'They are, of course, anti-socialists. . . . I am bothered if any of them know why they are Conservatives.' (Salisbury to Selborne, 18.3.29, 2nd Earl Selborne MS. 7, fols. 203–5). Hence the importance of ideology. Refer also to ch. 6 below.

59. 'An outline of Christian anti-socialism', *Nineteenth Century and After*, Feb. 1925, previously *Christian Anti-Socialism*, Salisbury MS S(4)111/125.

60. Salisbury, *Christian Anti-Socialism*, p. 10.

61. *The History of World Revolution* (published 1954 but written c. 1920/1).

62. *Comments on the Annual Report of the Northumberland County and City of Newcastle Unionist Association April 26th 1923*. Northumberland MSS Miscellaneous Papers (1978) M/3.

63. 'Eugenics' in his *Outspoken Essays II* (first published London, 1922; 1933 edn), esp. pp. 265–6.

64. Indeed, Inge later became a supporter of Sir Ernest Benn (see below) along with men like Sir Herbert Williams and Sir Waldron Smithers (see Greenleaf, *British Political Tradition*, vol. II, p. 306).

65. *Morning Post*, 2.7.21, p. 6. Cf. Chapter 4 above. Another example of the ways in which various, apparently contradictory themes were being interwoven on the Right can be found in the columns of the *British Lion*. This was the journal of an organisation known as the Unity Band which had close links with the British Fascists. In March 1932 it recommended the following books to its readers: the anonymous *The Cause of the World Unrest*; N. Webster's *World Revolution* and *The Surrender of an Empire*; A. H. Lane's *The Alien Menace*; Ernest Benn's *Account Rendered*; F. Fox's *Parliamentary Government: a failure?*; and D. Crisp's *The Rebirth of Conservatism*. All of these books were sold by the Britons (refer to ch. 2 and Appendix).

66. Ernest Benn: published and author who established the Society of Individualists and the Individualist Bookshop with money raised by Lord Emmott and others before formally breaking with the Liberals in 1929.

67. J. M. Keynes, 'Industry, Economics, Currency, and Trade' (c. 1927/28) in D. Moggridge (ed.), *Collected Writings* (London, 1981), p. 640.

68. E. Benn, *Happier Days* (London, 1949), p. 160.

69. *The Man Versus the State* (Harmondsworth, 1969 edn), p. 63.

70. Spencer, *The Man Versus the State*, p. 81.

71. N. Soldon, 'Laissez-Faire as Dogma: The Liberty and Property Defence League, 1882–1914' in K. D. Brown (ed.), *Essays in Anti-Labour History* (London, 1974), p. 232. This may be an over-simplification since Soldon himself suggests that the group was primarily composed of landed aristocrats *and* 'old-Liberal', 'new-model' employers.

72. And like him created an organisation — The Individualist Society — to further his aims.

73. E. Benn, *The State the Enemy* (London, 1953), p. 17.

74. Ibid., p. 20.

75. *The Return to Laisser-Faire* (London, 1928), p. 219.

76. D. Crisp, *The Rebirth of Conservatism* (London, 1931), p. 108. This book has a preface written by John Buchan.

77. Ibid., p. 97.

78. Ibid., p. 13.

79. Ibid., p. 75.

80. Ibid., pp. 83 and 92.

81. Ibid., ch. 2.

82. Refer to n. 20 above.

83. Ibid., p. 52.

84. Ibid., p. 25.

85. Ibid., ch. 2, esp. pp. 24–7.
86. Just as the so-called 'New Right' do today. See e.g. R. Scruton, *The Meaning of Conservatism* (Harmondsworth, 1980), ch. 5.
87. G. C. Webber, 'Patterns of Membership and Support for the BUF', *JCH* (Oct. 1984), pp. 575–606.
88. Farr, 'Right-wing Politics', Ph.D.
89. Again it is worth noting the similarity with the New Right. See e.g. Rhodes Boyson, 'Why I am a Tory and not a Whig', *Swinton Journal* Oct. 1975. R. Boothby, H. Macmillan, J. de V. Loder and O. Stanley, *Industry and the State: A Conservative View* (Macmillan, London, 1927), claimed that the Diehards were 'paradoxically imbued . . . with whig and liberal traditions' (p. 213) but this was a misleading comment since even where they shared liberal prejudices they did so for anti-liberal reasons. Likewise, the claim made by Kingsley Martin in *The British Public and the General Strike* (London, 1926), that the Right was by this time composed of 'class-conscious capitalists' who believed property to be a natural right which need not be justified in terms of social utility is wide of the mark. The concept of utility was retained but re-defined whilst those who used it did not possess a shared consciousness of class so much as a common perception of threat. What was more, the business Right did not usually like to think of themselves merely as businessmen. Thus, for example, the *Morning Post* insisted that Col. Gretton (refer to n. 93) did not have much in common with what they referred to as 'the newer type of industrial member', 21.7.21, whilst Croft placed more emphasis on his ancestry than his interests. See esp. *The Path of Empire* (John Murray, London, 1912), pp. 116–17.
90. Lymington owned around 45,000 acres of land in Hampshire, Devon, Somerset and Co. Wexford (Ireland). A similar example was the 8th Earl of Glasgow who owned about 38,000 acres of land in Scotland and was linked with both the BFs in the 1920s and the BUF in the 1930s. In general this group were in difficulty and could often survive only by selling land and 'abolishing themselves' as a class. The *Morning Post* of 21.7.32, in an article entitled 'Dislanded Gentry: Victims of Social Change', claimed that nearly one-third of the 2,500-odd families recorded in the 1921 edition of *Burke*'s register had had to sell their land.
91. Fritz Stern's book, *The Politics of Cultural Despair; A Study in the Rise of the Germanic Ideology* (Univ. of California Press, Berkeley, and Los Angeles, 1961) deals with a similar theme in relation to Germany. Refer also to the previous chapter.
92. Refer G. C. Webber, 'The British Isles' in D. Mühlberger (ed.), *The Social Base of European Fascist Movements* (forthcoming, 1987). The growth of a 'Corporate bias' in Britain is the theme of Middlemas, *Politics in Industrial Society*. Middlemas argues that this 'new form of harmony in the political system was established with great difficulty in the decade 1916–26' (p. 18), i.e. well *before* the BUF was created.
93. Croft had interests in brewing, chemicals, and coffee. Gretton was chairman of Bass, Ratcliffe, and Gretton (who brewed Worthington Bass). Northumberland had interests in the mining industry and the press (Chairman of the Board of the *Morning Post* after 1924 and proprietor of *The Patriot*). Wolmer (later 3rd Earl Selborne) had interests in Boots Ltd., cement, and banking (his father, the 2nd Earl Selborne, was on the Board of Lloyd's Bank). The best general work on the very wealthy in Britain at this time is W. D. Rubinstein: *Men of Property* (London, 1981).

6   THE STATE

As the previous chapter demonstrated, there were important disagreements on the Right between those who supported and those
who opposed state intervention in the economy. However, these
disagreements skirted two critical questions: What *kind* of state did
right-wingers favour? And why? And these questions prompted
others that related to the democratic process in general and the role
that the parties played in particular. Of course, such questions did
not emerge suddenly in 1918. As we noted in Chapter 1, anxieties
about democracy and the constitutional balance were evident well
before 1914. But accounts of the British Right in *Edwardian*
England have not been able to shed much light on their attitudes
towards the state. J. R. Jones, writing in 1965, argued that the
radical Right (prior to 1914) were primarily distinguished by their
readiness to use the state in pursuance of policies such as tariff
reform or compulsory military training but that they remained
'empiricists and pragmatists' who wanted 'first the conversion of
the Tory Party, and then of the nation'.[1] Geoffrey Searle, writing
in 1979, concluded that the Right were in fact 'populists' who
became increasingly *ambivalent* about the Conservative Party,[2]
although two years later he revised his opinion by admitting that
alongside these radical populists were a group of 'elitists' intent
upon 'a restructuring of the political system'.[3] More recently, Alan
Sykes has argued that there was a 'major realignment of factions
within the Right' after 1909 to such an extent that by 1911 'the
"Radical Right" was all but swamped in a sea of traditional Conservatives defending traditional causes'[4] although he, in turn,
exaggerates the significance of the argument since, as Gregory
Phillips has pointed out, the remarkable feature of the Diehards
was the extent to which they combined traditional ends with unconventional means.[5] If one can conclude anything from these studies
it would seem only to be that the Right did not possess a coherent
attitude towards the state in the years before 1914. In fact, however, it was only that they did not share any *single* view of its role
and limits, and the same was true of the right wing between the
wars.

94

In the years after 1918 there were two waves of right-wing thinking about the state, each of which reflected a particular anxiety. The first wave came in the five years or so after the extension of the franchise in 1918 when the Right were worried that the Conservative Party might not be able to dominate a popularly elected Parliament. The second came in the five years or so after the election of the Labour government in 1929 (a government elected on a franchise extended for the first time to include women over 21 on the same basis as men) when the Right were concerned that parliamentary government might not be capable of managing the affairs of the country, especially now that it was deep in the shadows of financial crisis and world depression. These anxieties found expression in their attacks upon parliamentary democracy, and these attacks represented a synthesis of two arguments that sometimes proceeded in different directions. One was that the system was 'inefficient'; the other that it was 'corrupt'. Neither argument was new. Charges of inefficiency had been popularised in the early part of the century by the cross-party movement for National Efficiency which advocated streamlined government and Bismarckian social reforms.[6] Charges of corruption were older still, and some of these dated back as far as 1832. Furthermore, both of these arguments were extensively deployed prior to the First World War at a time when the Conservatives appeared unable to win an election and incapable (especially after 1911) of preventing the Liberals from introducing 'radical' legislation. Nevertheless, the arguments were given new twists in the years that followed.

Right-wing critics of 'the system' usually began by attacking the Conservative Party on the grounds that its commitment to 'pragmatism' blinded it to the importance of ideology as a means of consolidating electoral support, sustaining political enthusiasm and forging national unity.[7] These had been important themes on the Right even before the extension of the franchise in 1918. After 1918 (and especially after 1928) the demand for ideological purity was more insistent still since now, as one writer put it, 'not only the man in the street but the girl in the cinema [were] the arbiters of the country's destiny, and the issues at stake [had to] be made clear to them if their vote[s were] not to be used against the interests of the country'.[8] Dorothy Crisp reiterated the point in 1931: 'As socialism has been preached and taught, so then Conservatism must be preached and taught, to drive out fire with fire and counteract enthusiasm with an intenser flame.'[9] If it were not, Conservative governments would be deprived of positive goals and power would pass to those who sought to control the nation through the manipulation of the masses and the intimidation of elected representatives — to those such as militant trade unionists, press barons, plutocrats and Jews whose ambitions would not be thwarted by democratic restraints. Worse still, some believed that the Conservative Party might never be elected in the first place because an organisation that defined itself merely in terms of opposition to socialism would only *strengthen* the link between class and party and so be defeated by sheer weight of numbers.[10]

The problem was that 'enthusiasm' could be generated effectively only by a large political organisation and that the Conservative Party was controlled by men such as Baldwin — the 'trimmers' and 'tacticians' who tried to turn the vice of pragmatism into a virtue.[11] To many on the Right it seemed that the Conservative Party had 'ceased to represent any organised principle of government'.[12] But it was not clear exactly what they should do to remedy the situation. For the most part they did nothing more than write letters to the press demanding 'government by men of character' instead of 'clever men devoid of principles'.[13] Some, however, attempted to work within the Conservative Party to overthrow the leadership, *not*, as a rule, because they were inordinately hungry for office, but rather because they believed that it was only through a change of leader that one might secure a change of policy. This, indeed, was the logic of the revolt over India.[14] As Viscount Wolmer wrote in 1933, 'it is time for Conservatives to ask themselves whether they and Mr. Baldwin really mean the same thing . . . [for] . . . Mr. Baldwin appears to have no conception of a positive Tory policy'.[15]

Some went further still in their attempt to purify conservatism and sought to work outside the established party system altogether. Criticisms of the existing parties had been common since at least 1910 when Hilaire Belloc and Cecil Chesterton published *The Party System*. After 1911 right-wing distrust of the Conservative Party was more pronounced still,[16] and in 1917 Henry Page Croft created an alternative organisation — the National Party — which displayed an aggressively patriotic contempt for existing political forms. The manifesto of the National Party (which was written by F. S. Oliver) stated the problem clearly:[17]

In our view the chief cause of incompetency in British

Government of late years was a worn out party system which had ceased to correspond with any vital distinction of principles, and which, so far as it marked any real division, marked the very worst by which a nation can possibly be divided — *the conflicting interests of classes.*

Of course, parties as such were necessary, but the established parties, since they were no longer united or divided by principles, relied upon the electoral appeal of individuals and the corrupt machinations of a caucus. Standards of public life deteriorated; public respect for politicians evaporated; apathy became the keynote of democracy; and the state itself seemed in danger of collapse or defeat. It seemed to Croft that there were only two alternatives: 'National Unity or Bolshevism'.[18]

Croft's attempt to reconstruct the party system was, of course, a failure. But his desire to 'cleanse' it was common on the Right and he was not alone in wanting to galvanise support for right-wing policies independently of the Conservative Party.[19] The problem was that those who were already inside the party saw only too clearly the dangers of secession,[20] whilst those who were outside the organisation had no idea how they might achieve power. Thus, for example, the Imperial Fascist League could only hope that democracy would collapse through apathy; the British Fascists ceased even to think of themselves as an embryonic government; and the BUF, uncertain whether they ought to prepare for a revolution or a general election, ended up being ready for neither.[21] It was characteristic of the Fascist movement in Britain that the result of the 1935 election was greeted by *Blackshirt* with a headline that read, 'NEARLY TEN MILLION DID NOT VOTE . . . The future is with us.'[22] It was always 'fascism next time'.[23]

Appeals to 'principle' and attempts to 'cleanse' the party system were intended to sever the link between class and political representation, but they were not expected to achieve much on their own. To succeed they required 'leadership', although what this entailed was a matter of dispute. At its most extreme the concept of leadership was indistinguishable from the *Fuhrerprinzip* and inevitably entailed the replacement of parliamentary democracy with some form of dictatorship, though Fascists were rarely keen to admit it. Mosley, for instance, insisted that Fascist dictatorship was *more* democratic than parliamentary democracy because the existing system prevented governments from realising any plans they might have and so installed a 'dictatorship of vested interests' by default.[24] Moreover, although it was possible that power might have rested in the hands of one man alone in a Fascist Britain, it was more likely to be shared between the members of a small 'cabinet' who would also have been the heads of the national corporations.[25] Besides, in much of what Mosley wrote, the advocacy of emergency powers akin to those assumed by the state during wartime was more central to his argument than the construction of an elaborate system of corporate control. Nevertheless, it is difficult not to conclude that the BUF was seeking to construct a conventional dictatorship.[26] As William Joyce (later and better known as Lord Haw-Haw) put it in 1933:[27]

> The supreme function of government is to determine the conduct of the governed. Determination implies a superiority of some element within the system politic, and this element is to be identified with dictatorship . . .

This kind of analysis was, of course, common amongst the Fascists, even though the need for dictatorship was justified in different ways. Arnold Leese of the IFL, for example, wanted to prevent Jewish domination and establish control by a racial elite, while J. S. Barnes of CINEF saw the corporate state as a means of re-integrating society through the imposition of Catholic values.[28] Dictatorship also appealed to those who occupied the grey area between Fascism and conservatism such as the author and journalist, Francis Yeats-Brown, who believed in the need for 'the same sort of dictatorship that exists in a business' which, he believed, would encourage both 'efficiency' and 'stability'.[29]

For others, however, the need to tighten control at the top of the political system did not seem to require the creation of a formal dictatorship so much as the consolidation of 'leadership' within the framework of the existing institutions. Lord Lloyd, for example, an ex-Governor of Bombay and an enthusiast for corporatism 'carried away by the executive desire to get things done',[30] wanted to see more *Leadership in Democracy*.[31] In this respect he was very similar to L. S. Amery who believed that the problem was neither the existence of parliamentary government nor that of democracy *as such*, but the lack of 'direction' which accompanied them.[32] Consequently, Amery proposed the creation of a special 'policy cabinet', of not more than six members, which was to operate independently of the administrative departments of government and so provide the 'leadership' which the existing system was alleged to lack.[33] For Amery, as for Mosley, the ultimate goal was the re-creation of an 'organic' society, but the first requirement was the existence of an 'organised' state.

The more reactionary elements on the Right interpreted the need for leadership differently. Thus, although Anthony Ludovici, for example, was attracted by the idea of a Nietzschean Super-Man (which J. S. Barnes derided as the apotheosis of individualism),[34] his first concern was to restore the constitutional 'balance' that was supposed to have been destroyed by the Parliament Act of 1911.[35] Indeed, reform of the House of Lords was a favourite right-wing hobby-horse that found support amongst all sections of the Conservative Party. But it was a difficult subject around which to generate enthusiasm, and the party leaders preferred to let sleeping dogs lie. Consequently, demands for Second Chamber reform became a regular, but purely decorative feature of Conservative Party conferences. Every year eminent figures such as Lord Selborne or Arthur Steel-Maitland (the former party Chairman) sponsored a resolution in favour of immediate reform; every year it was passed unanimously; and every year (with the partial exception of 1927) it was ceremoniously ignored. But continual rebuffs did little to dampen right-wing ardour for a return to old traditions of aristocratic rule. Viscount Lymington, for example, wanted to see the Lords (reconstituted on a functional basis) providing a small 'cabinet', the Commons reduced to the status of a 'safety valve' shorn of real power, and the crown revived as the focus of loyalty towards which 'leaders might permanently turn'.[36]

Ideas about the restoration of the powers of the monarchy were, in fact, symptomatic of the way in which traditional concerns and radical proposals became hopelessly entangled on the Right. Thus, Sir Charles Petrie believed that monarchy was the best form of government but that the corporate state should be 'worked into the old order';[37] Herbert Vivian saw dictatorship as 'a variety of the idea of Tory Democracy . . . [and] . . . kingship';[38] Lady Houston (during the prelude to the abdication crisis) called upon the King to adopt the role of dictator;[39] the very first principle of the British Fascists was to uphold the King in time of crisis;[40] and even the BUF toyed with the idea of monarchism for a while.[41] The fineness of the line that separated traditional royalism from pro-Fascism was exemplified in the writings of Oscar Boulton (the founder member of the Unity Band). For although he regarded the most desirable form of government as one that revolved around an hereditary Monarch assisted by a small, nominated Parliament, he did not dislike either Italian Fascism or German National Socialism (except in so far as the Nazis were hostile to Christianity). As he put it in 1934:[42]

> they are both based upon the necessity of substituting for a vicious and visibly degenerating political theory of misrule, based on an appeal to the lowest instincts of humanity, a revised and regenerate regime founded on the lively recognition by all citizens, not of their rights, but of their duties, both to each other and to the corporate community of which they are members.

However, making sure that there were 'leaders' who could lead was only one half of the problem. The other difficulty was to ensure that the 'followers' would follow. For the Fascists this was a difficulty that was unlikely to arise. Had Mosley ever gained power on his own terms the new government could have been removed only by an adverse result in a five-yearly 'plebiscite' in which those who were considered 'hostile' to the state would not have been allowed to vote.[43] And although the power to appoint new ministers would then have fallen to the Monarch (in theory restoring his prerogative) no one other than a small clique of Fascist leaders could ever have been chosen as replacements.[44] Meanwhile, the expression of dissent would have been made virtually impossible because the press would have been subject to crippling litigation if it failed to report what the Fascists regarded as the truth.[45] Nor would Parliament any longer have been a forum for criticism. Both Houses were there only to 'advise' the government: the Upper House would have been composed of 'non-technical experts' appointed by the government; the Lower House of representatives elected by members of the various 'corporations'.[46] In theory, the machinery of the corporate state was designed to create a society that was 'vertically integrated' rather than 'horizontally divided'. The class struggle would thus be replaced by a consciousness of 'national' identity, and 'political' disputes would consequently disappear to be replaced by the simple 'administration of things'.[47] In practice, the corporations would have provided a system of authoritative command.

In essence, the Fascist solution was to control the 'electorate' by limiting their ability to partake of government. The government was to be 'of the people' and 'for the people' but not 'by the people'. Others sought to control the electorate in different ways. One obvious and popular solution on the Right was to restrict the franchise, either by introducing an educational requirement or by devising some more complicated scheme, but rarely by reverting directly to a pre-1918 *status quo*.[48] Another solution was eugenic control. Dean Inge, for example, thought that democracy was a disaster. Democracy, he argued, dissolved communities into individuals and collected them again into mobs; it was inherently 'corrupt' because one class imposed the taxes whilst another had to pay them; and it created a situation in which 'the leaders are led, the legislators are delegates, and the electors are ignorant and indolent. The government being weak, inefficient, and . . . corrupt, it is very amenable to pressure.'[49] But there was no obvious alternative to the system since dictatorships were merely temporary expedients that led to fierce reactions.[50] Consequently it was important to create the right kind of electorate by preventing 'the multiplication of undesirable types'.[51] As an article in the *English Review* explained in March 1930, democracy could function properly only when eugenics had ensured that there was 'an aristocracy almost as big as, and almost co-extensive with, the nation'.[52]

However, making sure that the 'right' people would have enough power was not the only problem. It was also important to make sure that this power should not fall into the 'wrong' hands. Indeed, from the Liberal landslide of 1906, through the 1909 Budget, the 1911 Parliament Act, the extension of the franchise in 1918, and the subsequent success (relative though it was) of the Labour Party, the immediate problem was to *set limits* to the power of Parliament. This was true even of those who wanted to strengthen the executive. Thus, alongside his plans for the creation of a small 'directive' cabinet, L. S. Amery proposed to supplement the existing Houses of Parliament with a 'house of Industry' elected on the basis of a 'functional' franchise. In part, this was intended to break the link between class and party by loosening the connection between the ownership and the control of industry. But it was also of 'strategic' importance. For, when democratic leaders were pursuing 'national' ends the corporations would provide a chain of command. When they were pursuing 'anti-national' ends the corporations would protect the economy from socialist interference.

This was what Amery meant when he claimed that the corporate system took the 'politics' out of economic questions.[53]

Corporatism was also favoured by Douglas Jerrold who had at one time been interested in Guild Socialism but later became a Catholic convert and an apologist for Mussolini. For Jerrold, the problem was that as men in secular society were driven by desires rather than guided by beliefs so politics ceased to be a matter of 'principle' and became instead a 'struggle between interests for the control of the machinery of government'.[54] This, in turn, had paradoxical results. On the one hand it produced governments which were incapable of 'governing' the country; on the other, it installed a vast bureaucracy intent upon 'controlling' it.[55] To the extent that the country required 'leadership' the solution might involve the installation of a dictator, since Conservatives, Jerrold argued, were indifferent to the means required to achieve their ends. As he argued in December 1933, 'unless parliament . . . under universal franchise can fulfill the indispensable task of leadership, a dictatorship is not only inevitable, but necessary'.[56] Yet, to the extent that Jerrold believed in *The Necessity of Freedom*,[57] he wanted to restrict the scope of the state by introducing a system of corporate control that would *circumvent* the institutions of parliamentary democracy:[58]

the Conservative Party must turn its back upon the present Parliamentary system in favour of a system which will restore the reality of self-government in the appropriate spheres and enable a strong central government to speak for the nation, and not merely for a class, on national issues.

Corporatism was one way of restricting the political agenda and limiting the freedom of an unreconstructed Parliament. It was not, of course, the only way. Lord Sydenham, for example, was in favour of introducing a written constitution designed to safeguard carefully proscribed rights, although he too was interested in Fascism as an alternative to parliamentary democracy.[59] More popular still (amongst the Right), particularly in the years before and after the First World War, were apparently radical plans to introduce the referendum and to re-organise the state on a federal basis.

Both of these reforms appealed to the second Earl of Selborne. As a result of the crisis that came to a head in 1911, Selborne believed that the constitution had been thrown out of 'balance' and that, unless the crown were to intervene decisively, the best method of avoiding a tyrannical majoritarianism was to introduce the referendum.[60] In appearance this was radically 'democratic'. In fact, it was nothing of the sort. Selborne was a 'democrat' only to the extent that he believed popular participation might present *obstacles* to 'radical' change.[61] The same was true of federalism, a scheme defended primarily on the grounds of 'efficiency' and 'stability'. As he wrote in 1918:[62]

I regard the introduction of the federal system as in my judgement by far the most Conservative thing that can now be done, far the greatest stabilizing force possible to our Constitution as it now exists. I know of no other means of making so secure what I most love and prize in the institutions and customs of my country. Further, it would enable questions affecting the Empire and the whole U.K., which are of the first importance, to be properly considered for the first time by a body elected for that special purpose, instead of being very ill-considered, or constantly shelved, by a body principally elected for other purposes . . . Also I regard it as the only way by which the problem of reconstruction in domestic affairs can possibly be dealt with and, therefore, as the greatest safeguard against revolution . . . Lastly I consider Federalism as contributing that balance and check in a purely democratic system of government that is otherwise applied in the non-democratic systems . . . and I believe that these checks and balances can be obtained without reducing the power of the central executive authority beyond the point that is essential for good government.

This was the crux of the problem for the Right: that the state had to be strong but that its strength was to be available only for certain purposes. What exactly these purposes were was a matter of dispute, although it was usually clear that the one thing the state should *not* be able to interfere with was the institution of private property. However, as right-wing attitudes towards the economy became more favourable to capitalism, so proposed reforms of the state seemed less concerned to *avert* the struggle between classes than to *stabilise* it.

Dorothy Crisp, for example, writing in 1931, sought to combine an appeal for unrestricted capitalism with a demand for:[63]

The abolition of the pauper vote, the universal raising of the age at which a vote may be claimed to twenty-five, the Commons as the expression of, and safety valve for, public opinion, but not the complete controller of all government, the reformed Upper House, the creation of whose new members rests in the hands of the most politically experienced person in the realm, His Majesty the King — in short, the revival of government by the King, Lords, and Commons.

A similar picture was drawn by Sir Frank Fox, an author and journalist with the *Morning Post*, in his book, *Parliamentary Government: A Failure?*, first published in 1930. 'The purpose of this book', he wrote:[64]

is to suggest that the grave, and quickly-growing, evils afflicting national administration in the United Kingdom threaten disaster; that they are implicit in, indeed the direct consequence of, our system of Parliamentary rule, and cannot be cured without such radical change of that system as to bring truly responsible government.

To some extent, the problem was one of 'inefficiency' created by 'administrative extravagance'.[65] But the fundamental problem was that the system had become 'corrupt', not just because of the way in which individual politicians or political parties behaved, but because the extension of the franchise had created a situation in which the balance of power rested with those who received more from the state in benefits and subsidies than they paid in taxes. Consequently, democracy had merely become a means by which 'the great majority of the voters help themselves out of the pockets of others', and 'social reform' had deteriorated into the grossest form of political bribery[66] (an old-fashioned argument that had been deployed by nineteenth-century anti-democrats such as Sir Henry Maine in his work on *Popular Government* published in 1885). One logical solution was to re-establish the minimal state on the lines proposed by Herbert Spencer,[67] but for two reasons this was impractical since, in the first place one could not ignore people's expectations, and in the second, a degree of collectivism was considered essential if Britain was to maintain her position in the world.[68] More appealing was the model provided by Mussolini. 'The example of Italy' (as Fox entitled one of his chapters) was a lesson of the utmost importance, especially as parliamentary democracy was beyond reform,[69] and this raised a question to which Fox had a ready answer: 'Should we, then, set out to imitate Italy? In principle, yes. In method, not necessarily.'[70]

What this meant, in practice, was again an interesting mixture. In the short-term, the dole was to be 'abolished completely'; housing subsidies, rent restrictions and so on were to be 'swept away'; non-contributory pensions were to disappear; education was to be made less extensive and more vocational; a policy of Empire migration was to be introduced; the land re-populated; industry safeguarded; strikes eliminated (the Italian system being 'worthy of almost exact imitation'); taxation reduced; and the bureaucracy minimised.[71] However, once this starkly competitive socio-economic system had been created constitutional changes would also be required. Thus, in the long-term, government would rest with *the King* who would work through a Prime Minister 'advised' by a Cabinet that 'consulted' the two Houses of Parliament, the most important of which would be a Senate 'nominated chiefly from the Peers of the Realm'. The Lower House was to be chosen by the people, preferably on a 'functional' basis.[72] In short, an entrepreneurial economy was married to an aristocratic state and the Tory philosophy of 'crown and country' revived as a creed of 'King and capital' in which the state was little more than 'the managing committee of the affairs of the bourgeoisie'.

Conclusions

As the introduction to this chapter suggested, right-wing attacks upon parliamentary democracy could usually be reduced to two charges: inefficiency and corruption. But the arguments that supported these assertions were neither static nor obviously compatible. The charge of inefficiency took two forms. The first was an attack upon the parliamentary system on the grounds that it was over-burdened, bureaucratic and indecisive. The second was an attack upon the democratic process (especially in so far as the existing parties were instrumental in its operation) on the grounds that this prevented 'leaders' from leading and encouraged them to support policies which were popular rather than prudent. Prior to 1918 the emphasis was more often on the former than the latter; after 1918 the position was reversed. The charge of corruption also took two forms, and again the emphasis shifted in the period after 1918. Prior to the extension of the franchise the argument had usually been that it was individual politicians or party organisations which were corrupt and that this led to the domination of politics by irresponsible interests. These were variously identified as pluto-crats, aliens, and press barons, and this was all the more worrying after the Parliament Act of 1911 had restricted the countervailing powers of the Lords. After 1918 the argument tended to take a different form, namely that the political system itself was corrupt because the competition between parties for votes had been reduced to a form of political bribery in which support was purchased through expenditure on welfare. Social reform was simply 'mass corruption'.

These analyses naturally suggested different solutions, and these solutions often appeared to be incompatible. To the extent that the system was 'inefficient' the remedy was to tighten control at the top; to the extent that it was 'corrupt' the best strategy was to circumvent the system altogether. At first sight, it appeared that the First World War and the subsequent extension of the franchise had merely deepened the divisions that Searle has argued already existed prior to 1914 between the populists and the elitists on the Right and that this division gradually resolved itself into a battle between those who favoured democracy and those who wanted dic-tatorship.[73] But this analysis is misleading, not only because there was no simple correlation between elitism and dictatorship or between populism and democracy, nor even because the distinction between democrats and putative dictators was and remains difficult to draw, but also because the demands for 'control' and 'circum-vention' usually went hand in hand. They were not regarded as con-flicting, but as complementary strategies, the first of which was desirable once power had been transferred to the 'right' people, the second of which was necessary so long as it remained in the 'wrong' hands.[74]

However, the Right disagreed about who should exercise control. In the years between the Boer War and the First World War when, as we suggested in the Introduction, the Right first assumed a recognisable shape, the first concern was to create a state strong enough to defend Britain's interests against external aggression but 'open' enough to prevent the aristocracy being swamped by the middle classes on the one hand and the working classes from estab-lishing independent political organisations on the other. This attitude could still be found after 1918. The Duke of Northumber-land, for example, in the days before he became an ardent supporter of capitalism, complained that parliamentary democracy 'resulted in the control of government not by the people, but by the capitalists, the monied classes, by the bourgeoisie; it is an organised deception of the people'.[75]

After 1918 the emphasis shifted. Faced with a near-universal franchise, and a 'socialist' party capable of forming a government, the Right were less enthusiastic about popular participation and more circumspect in their demands for a 'strong' state.[76] They were also less hostile towards capitalism and the middle classes. Consequently, they became less concerned to *avert* 'class politics' than to ensure that those with established interests to protect (including the middle classes) should not be swamped by those without. The state was, therefore, to be 'strong' but not indiscriminately so; the system was to be geared towards a perpetuation of the *status quo*; and if 'class' could not be disentangled from 'politics', then 'politics' would have to be disentangled from 'economics'. Yet in practice, these two conceptions of the state did not exist in complete isolation from each other because defensive aristocratic beliefs and aggressive capitalist ones were often fused.[77] Consequently, the line of division was usually a practical one. The crucial question was whether or not right-wingers continued to regard the Conservative Party as a suitable vehicle for their ideologies. But even this failed to bring order from the chaos, since those on the Right who supported the party often did so *despite* rather than because of their beliefs. They were rarely more 'democratic' than those who did not, and they were almost always at odds with conventional, 'moderate' Conservatives.

Notes

1. J. R. Jones, 'England' in H. Rogger and E. Weber (eds.), *The European Right* (London, 1965), pp. 29–70. Quote, p. 35.
2. G. R. Searle, 'Critics of Edwardian Society: the Case of the Radical Right' in A. O'Day (ed.), *The Edwardian Age* (London, 1979), esp. pp. 85–7.
3. G. R. Searle, 'The Revolt from the Right in Edwardian Britain' in P. Kennedy and A. Nicholls (eds.), *Nationalist and Racialist Movements in Britain and Germany Before 1914* (London, 1981), esp. pp. 32–3.
4. A. Sykes, 'The Radical Right and the Crisis of Conservatism Before the First World War', *HJ*, vol. 26 (1983), pp. 661–76.
5. G. D. Phillips, *The Diehards* (Cambridge, Mass., 1979).

6. G. R. Searle, *The Quest for National Efficiency* (Oxford, 1971).

7. See e.g. D. Jerrold, 'Current Comments', *ER*, Jan. 1934, p. 12: 'an appeal to principle is the only kind of appeal which can unite a people'.

8. N. Webster, *The Surrender of an Empire* (London, 1931), p. 273.

9. Dorothy Crisp, *The Rebirth of Conservatism* (London, 1931), p. 93; see also the *Morning Post*, 16.11.32, Editorial, p. 10, 'The War Front of Ideas'; and (for a contemporary example of the same phenomenon) the introduction to R. Scruton, *The Meaning of Conservatism* (Harmondsworth, 1980).

10. E.g. L. S. Amery to Worthington Evans, Oct. 1918, quoted in L. S. Amery, *My Political Life*, vol. II (London, 1953−5), p. 173 *n*4; see also vol. I (1953), p. 255 a 'party of mere negative *laissez-faire* anti-Socialism . . . was bound to be voted down by sheer numbers in the end'.

11. See e.g. Salisbury to Selborne, 18.3.29, 2nd Earl Selborne MS. 1/7/203−5: 'They [the party leaders] are of course anti-socialists . . . but . . . I am bothered if any of them know why they are Conservatives'.

12. Northumberland, *The Patriot*, 26.9.29.

13. *Morning Post*, 1.7.22.

14. See chs 2 and 3; also G. Peele, 'Revolt over India' in G. Peele and C. Cook (eds.), *The Politics of Reappraisal, 1918−1939* (London, 1975), ch. 5.

15. 'Baldwin and Baldwinism', *Morning Post*, 31.3.33, pp. 11 and 13.

16. Searle, 'Critics of Edwardian Society', pp. 79−96.

17. F. S. Oliver MS Box 98; The National Party, *A Statement of Policy* (1917), p. 5.

18. *National Opinion*, Mar. 1919.

19. Refer to ch. 2.

20. Thus John Gretton wrote to Croft on 4.2.24: 'It would be fatal to abandon Baldwin; for any alternative at the present time would split the party. If this is true the reason is sufficient.' CRFT 1/12.

21. J. Morell, 'The Life and Opinions of A. S. Leese', M.A., Univ. of Sheffield, 1974; British Fascists, *Manifesto* (1931); and *Action* esp. c. 1935.

22. *Blackshirt*, 22.11.35, p. 1.

23. *Blackshirt*, 8.11.35, p. 1.

24. O. Mosley, *Fascism, 100 Questions* (London, 1936), no. 9.

25. O. Mosley, *The Greater Britain* (London, 1932 and 1934).

26. N. Nugent, 'The ideas of the BUF' in N. Nugent and R. King (eds.), *The British Right* (Farnborough, 1977), ch. 6.

27. *Dictatorship* (London, 1933), p. 8.

28. Morell, 'A. S. Leese'; and J. S. Barnes, esp. *The Universal Aspects of Fascism* (London, 1925), and Fascism (London, 1931).

29. Quoted in J. E. Wrench, *Francis Yeats-Brown, 1886−1944* (London, 1948), p. 171. See also F. Yeats-Brown, *European Jungle* (London, 1939), p. 15; and cf. W. H. Mallock, *The Nation as a Business Firm. An Attempt to Cut a Path Through Jungle* (Alan and Charles Black, London, 1910).

30. C. F. Adam, *Life of Lord Lloyd* (London, 1948), p. 48. Likewise E. T. Raymond (pseudonym) on Viscount Milner in *Uncensored Celebrities* (Unwin, London, 1919), p. 124: 'His dislike of democracy is simply, in the ultimate analysis, the dislike of a civil servant for . . . that public which impudently insists on questioning and criticising when it should be content with paying taxes and being managed.'

31. 1939 pamphlet.

32. *The Forward View* (London, 1935), pp. 442−4; nevertheless Amery was an admirer of Mussolini.

33. Ibid., p. 444 ff.; L. S. Amery, *Thoughts on the Constitution* (London, 1953); and cf. Churchill's 'Overlords' experiment. Sentiments of this kind had, of course,

been a notable feature of the National Efficiency movement in the early 1900s.

34. A. M. Ludovici, *A Defence of Aristocracy. A Textbook for Tories* (London, 1933 edn), pp. 293–4; also 'Hitler and Nietzsche', *ER*, Jan./Feb. 1937; and Barnes, *Fascism* (1934 edn), p. 39.

35. A. M. Ludovici, *A Defence of Conservatism* (London, 1927), p. 207. House of Lords reform was also a special interest of the *Nineteenth Century and After* in the mid-1920s.

36. *Ich Dien, the Tory Path* (London, 1931), ch. 2. 'The Machinery of our National Survival'.

37. *Monarchy* (London, 1933), p. 300.

38. H. Vivian, *Kings in Waiting* (London, 1933), p. 295.

39. *Saturday Review*, 6.6.36.

40. British Fascists, *Summary of Policy and Practice* (1931); see also *British Fascism*, Oct. 1932.

41. C. Cross, *The Fascists in Britain* (London, 1961), p. 165.

42. O. Boulton, *The Way Out* (London, 1934), pp. 99–100.

43. *100 Questions*, no. 13 ff.

44. Ibid., no. 21.

45. Ibid., no. 11.

46. Ibid., no. 25 ff.

47. See esp. *The Greater Britain*, p. 100. For similarities with Marxism refer to W. E. D. Allen, 'The Fascist Idea in Britain', *Quarterly Review*, Oct. 1933; and R. Skidelsky, *Oswald Mosley* (London, 1981 edn), ch. 15.

48. E.g. Sir C. Petrie, *Chapters of Life* (London, 1950), p. 147; E. M. Roe, 'Fascism and Parliament', *British Fascism*, April 1931, p. 6; C. H. Sutherland to Salisbury, 22.11.29, Salisbury MS. S(4) 132/61.

49. *England* (London, 1926), p. 248; 'Our Present Discontents' in *Outspoken Essays* (London, 1921 edn), p. 11.

50. *England*, Preface, p. ix. Organised religion was also incapable of providing a political solution (*Outspoken Essays*, p. 30).

51. *England*, p. 269; 'Eugenics' in *Outspoken Essays II* (London, 1933 edn), p. 271. Undesirable types were those dependent upon state support.

52. O. A. Merritt-Hawkes, 'How shall we get democracy?', *English Review*, Mar. 1930, pp. 305–12.

53. *The Forward View* (London, 1935), esp. pp. 450–1. Amery actually believed economic questions to be inherently political. See e.g. *My Political Life*, vol. I, p. 308, where he describes imperial preference as 'simply the principle of Imperial unity in its economic aspect'; and *The Fundamental Fallacies of Free Trade* (London, 1906). The idea of a 'House of Industry' was quite common. It was supported (e.g.) by Inchcape, Macara, Milner, the Webbs, and Churchill. Refer to M. Gilbert, *W. S. Churchill*, vol. V, Companion. Documents 1929–1935 (London, 1981), pp. 163 and 324–5.

54. *ER*, Dec. 1930, 'The Twilight of Reason'; June 1931, 'What is Conservatism?'

55. Ibid., Dec. 1933, 'Current Comments'; Mar. 1934, 'The Future of Conservativism'.

56. Ibid., Dec. 1933 and Jan. 1934, 'Current Comments'. A similar argument was presented by the *Patriot* Leader, 28.10.37, p. 359: 'Democracy, as we have it, is no longer the destroyer of tyranny, but has become the tyrant itself, and without knowing it the country is enduring a dictatorship which is infinitely more dangerous to its existence than any could be in the hands of an individual.' Refer also to n. 24 above and cf. modern parallels in Scruton, *The Meaning of Conservatism*; and R. Moss, *The Collapse of Democracy* (Temple Smith, London, 1975).

57. Published 1938.

58. Quoted in *Georgian Adventure* (London, 1937; Right Book Club edn, London, 1938), p. 340. Written June 1933.

59. Letter, *Morning Post*, 7.10.31. See also an anonymous article in the same paper, 'The People vs. The Politicians', 17.7.22, p. 8.

60. Selborne to Salisbury, 20.12.09, Selborne MS. 1/6/31–2. See also V. Bogdanor, *The People and the Party System. The Referendum and Electoral Reform in British Politics* (Cambridge University Press, 1981), parts I–III; and D. Woods, 'The Walsall Referendum of 1911', *West Midlands Studies* (1981), pp. 27–31.

61. Selborne had not dissented from the extension of the franchise in 1918 though he believed that men and women over 25 would have provided a more 'stable' electorate. Selborne to Salisbury, 29.8.16, Selborne MS. 1/6/174–6.

62. Selborne to Salisbury, 17.6.18, Selborne MS. 7, fols. 33–40. On the idea of federalism refer especially J. E. Kendle, 'The Round Table Movement and Home Rule All Round', *HJ* (1968), pp. 332–53. There was also a 'racial' aspect to federalism, i.e. that it would allow for the English to be ruled by Englishmen. Refer to Selborne to Salisbury, 17.6.18, Selborne MS. 7, fols. 33–40; Lord Selborne, 'English Rule for England', *English Race*, spring/summer 1920, p. 7; and the columns of the *Englishman*.

63. Crisp, *Conservatism*, p. 75.

64. F. Fox, *Parliamentary Government: A Failure?* (London, 1930), p. 11.

65. Ibid., p. 113.

66. Ibid., p. 51.

67. Ibid., p. 115.

68. Ibid., p. 116.

69. Ibid., p. 148 (ch. VII).

70. Ibid., p. 149.

71. Ibid., p. 158ff.

72. Ibid., p. 170ff.

73. Searle, 'Critics of Edwardian Society', and 'Revolt from the Right'; R. Griffiths, *Fellow Travellers of the Right* (London, 1983 edn), esp. ch. 1, 'Weariness of Democracy and Admiration for Dictators'. There is even some evidence to support the claim (though very little). See e.g. Lady Bathurst to Leo Maxse, 12.6.18, Maxse MS. 475: 'It is curious how events affect different people. You become more democratic. I become more in favour of autocracy.'

74. Refer also R. Barker, *Political Ideas in Modern Britain* (London, 1978), p. 125.

75. *The History of World Revolution* (Hayes, 1954), p. 9. Written c. 1921. See also W. Sanderson, *Statecraft* (London, 1927): 'Democracy means, and has always meant, government by middle class intellectuals.' (p. 113).

76. The *Daily Mail* of 4.10.22 published a poem entitled 'State Enterprise' by Touchstone which neatly captured the changing attitude of the Right to the state:

In former days my reverence was great
For that mysterious entity, the State,
Which rules us dullards of the common herd,
And generally plays the part of fate . . .

But when the State explored a realm unknown
And ventured into business on its own,
I found my lofty notions of its powers
Were shattered and my idols overthrown . . .

And still in serried ranks there cling today
As limpets in their thousands crying, 'Pay!',
Like to old warriors they never die
But lack the decency to fade away.

77. Cf. the beliefs of capitalist anti-statists on the Right (ch. 5 above). The mixture of ancient and modern was exemplified by writers such as Crisp and Fox cited in the text, but see also the *Morning Post*, 18–24 July 1932, which ran a series of articles supposedly written by 'new' members of the House of Commons under the heading 'Is Parliament Up To Its Job?' This began with the ludicrous suggestion of knocking Parliament down and re-building it on a more spacious basis (with a gym!) and then moved on to serious issues: an industrial parliament (an idea borrowed from Churchill); an attack upon the 'Tyranny of the Party System' (19.7.32); a restriction on the powers of cabinets by limiting the PM's right of dissolution to 'crucial' matters and by allowing for the possibility of referenda (20.7.32); and protection of the powers of the House of Lords, which was held to be a better organ for single chamber government than the Commons (21.7.32).

7 THE OUTSIDE WORLD

Worried that society was being 'subverted' and in danger of disintegration, the Right sought ways of re-establishing the 'integrity' they supposed it once to have had. Sometimes, as previous chapters have shown, this involved the exploitation of 'unifying myths' that tapped Britain's rural, religious and cultural heritage. Sometimes it involved a consideration of economic or political reforms. Most commonly, however, the search for social unity centred around the two themes of nationalism and imperialism. The intended function of nationalism, though this was rarely stated so crudely, was to provide a focus of loyalty that transcended the attachment to class;[1] but this was not always easy to achieve and in the years from 1935 to 1940 the reality of nationalist politics was very different. Instead of providing a basis for social unity the catch-phrases of nationalism and imperialism merely provided the framework within which the Right themselves developed their internal disagreements.

However, the way in which this happened was complicated. In essence three schools of right-wing thought about international relations can be identified: 'militarism', 'imperial isolationism', and 'right-wing supra-nationalism'. Despite their differences all were broadly agreed on the need to maintain and strengthen the Empire but they differed in their responses to a possible threat from Germany, not only between, but also within these three groups. The militarists were in theory the most belligerent right-wingers, but in practice they supported the peace campaign at the end of the 1930s because they sympathised with Nazism. And these pro-Nazis were joined by the supra-nationalists, although the Catholics within this group were ambivalent in their attitudes towards Hitler. Meanwhile, the imperial isolationists were torn apart by the need to weigh their imperialism *against* their isolationism (at least in relation to the former German colonies), and by their need to specify the 'national interests' that they considered to be 'vital'. Consequently, while some imperial isolationists became prominent anti-appeasers, most remained confused and undecided, sometimes swayed by their admiration for the dictators, sometimes content to support Neville Chamberlain and hope for the best. As a result, the Right ceased to appear as a coherent or even as a distinct political group by the time that war was declared, and this created yet another paradox: from the turn of the century to the middle of the thirties, attitudes to the outside world had helped to keep the Right together; from the middle of the thirties to the outbreak of the Second World War they proved equally effective in pulling the Right apart.

Militarism

Militarists assumed that organised and armed conflict between nations was both inevitable and ultimately desirable, and this view of international relations was usually tied to a romantic conception of the nation itself that often deteriorated into a crude form of racism. Attitudes of this kind were rarely found in Britain. Although *The Englishman* argued that the nation was 'one and indivisible with an individuality and a soul, vital and sacred, which differentiate[d] it from every other nation',[2] such ideas sounded incongruous on the lips of men whose country had enjoyed a long and stable existence free from military defeat, invasion or annexation since the eleventh century,[3] and in general, sentiments of this kind were expressed most forcibly by men who had *not* been born in Britain.

The unpopularity of militarism was clear from the history of the ex-servicemen's movement. In the years after 1918 when such movements provided a focus for political discontent abroad, the only organisation of importance to emerge in Britain was the Royal British Legion which, if it was not entirely apolitical, at least had no corporate political identity.[4] Ex-servicemen's journals such as *The Veteran* (later entitled *The Veteran and Briton* and finally just *The Briton*) which did try to tap ex-service sentiments for political reasons were forced to abandon the distinctiveness of their appeal as they broadened their ideological commitments.[5] Likewise, although British Fascist movements attracted a disproportionate number of ex-servicemen into their ranks they were never able to establish any special claim to the allegiance of this group as a whole, despite the fact that Fascism gained a reputation as the 'soldiers' socialism' and that the para-military organisation of the BUF was itself taken as a model of the future Fascist state (i.e. a community based upon distinctions of rank rather than divisions of class).⁶ Other groups which attempted to capitalise upon the spirit of 'comradeship' during and after the First World War did not survive for long either. The National Party, for instance, which was created in 1917, was practically defunct by 1922.

Nevertheless, there did exist a small number of militarists in Britain, most of whom had been born abroad, made a living from writing and idealised violence. The best known was Francis Yeats-Brown, the author of *Bengal Lancer* (1930), the assistant-editor from 1926 to 1931 of the *Spectator*, and the editor, for a short time in 1933, of *Everyman*. Yeats-Brown was a man for whom violence held a peculiar attraction, and as a result he felt able both to deplore *and* to idealise war. For whilst there was nothing heroic in dying for an intellectual abstraction such as 'civilisation' or (worse still) 'democracy', it was, he argued, altogether different to fight for the supposed 'reality' of one's country. As Yeats-Brown put it in 1932:

> To fight is not the most terrible thing that can happen to a man or a nation . . . for the desire of nationhood is the germ of life itself. Perfect and perpetual peace seems to me to lead to stagnation, sterility, and psychic suicide.

Anthony Ludovici argued a similar case. It was characteristic of a healthy race, he believed, that it should have a high birth-rate, but childbearing constituted a form of 'reproductive violence' against the community.⁸ Consequently, in order to avert internal difficulties such as civil war or revolution it was necessary to 'distribute the burden of sacrifices over inferior races abroad' (and, he added without explanation, 'inferior human products in all classes at home').⁹ Thus imperial expansion and colonisation were regarded as necessary, desirable and justified. For Ludovici, as for Arnold Leese of the IFL and William Joyce of the BUF, war and imperialism were the ultimate expressions of national identity against which there could be no valid objections and inevitably this provided the basis for a considerable volume of self-righteous cant. Ludovici's 1927 claim was typical of the genre:¹⁰

> if the acquisition of the British Empire has been right, the Empire cannot now be abandoned without converting it into a wrong; and if it has been wrong, the best way to redeem that wrong, since it cannot now be undone, is to continue to

administer the Empire in such a manner as to make it a boon and not a bane to the world at large.

Militaristic beliefs also had consequences that went beyond international relations, and these were often unpleasant. Sometimes, for example, militarism helped to justify the hostility harboured by many of its exponents towards immigrants in general and Jews in particular on the grounds that these groups diluted the 'purity of the race' and so weakened the nation. On other occasions these racial aspects of militarism merely resulted in bizarre justifications for otherwise reasonable policies (Viscount Lymington, for example, supported tariff reform as a means of preventing racial 'contamination').[11] However, during the 1930s militarism was most notable for its failure to address the problems posed by the growing threat from Nazi Germany. Since British militarists were amongst Hitler's greatest admirers, the international difficulties of the late 1930s merely served to expose the internal inconsistencies of their arguments. For it now became clear that the concept of race which some of them liked to employ bore little relation to that of the nation which they used to justify their theories, and that the idea of a healthy war in which all of them professed to believe did not extend to the one conflict that seemed most likely to erupt.

Imperial Isolationism

Like the militarists, imperial isolationists assumed that war was a likely consequence of the inescapable tensions that existed between nations; but unlike them, they refused to believe that armed conflict was strictly inevitable or positively desirable. Adequate preparations for war were vital, but these were intended (if possible) to avert conflict and this outcome was thought to demand the co-existence of stable and complementary power blocs which, from the British point of view, implied a consolidation of imperial ties together with a renunciation of expansionist desires.

This was always the dominant strand of thought on the Right, but it was not, of course, exclusively right-wing, and the assumptions that the imperial isolationists shared tended to promote as much disagreement as they did unity since both the identification of 'national interests' and the stipulation of a priority amongst them were inclined to reduce themselves to questions of personal,

business or class interest. It was difficult, for example, to disentangle 'sectional' from 'national' interests when issues such as
tariff reform and India arose, and the question of trade with Russia
found businessmen such as Patrick Hannon who favoured the nor-
malisation of trade relations with the Soviet Union directly at odds
with those whose distrust of Bolshevism was unaffected by calcula-
tions of profit. Nevertheless, the Right were largely agreed upon
the policy of imperial isolation until the mid-1930s.

For the Right, this policy had two facets: one negative, one
positive, but both essentially defensive. The negative aspect of
imperial isolation was that nationalism sometimes came to mean
little more than opposition to 'internationalism'. Ideologically this
followed from a right-wing distrust of liberal individualism and
'Bolshevism', both of which, in different ways, regarded the nation
as a transient and unhealthy political phenomenon. Practically it
implied a marked hostility towards the League of Nations, and an
over-riding fear of the Soviet Union.[12] At the same time, and for
the same reasons, it also encouraged the demand for an improvement in defence capabilities (especially in the air), which sometimes
(but rarely until 1939) shaded off into something akin to militarism, as it had done before 1914.[13] These negative aspects represented a determination to defend established assets and to resist the
intrusion of supra-national bodies in the process of national
decision-making.

More positively, the policy demanded a strengthening of imperial
ties since 'splendid isolation' seemed possible only so long as the
Empire remained united, and this conviction most often found
expression as support for tariffs. Yet the policy of tariff reform was
no more coherent in the inter-war years than it had been in the
Edwardian era. For two decades or so after Joseph Chamberlain's
campaign of 1903, advocates of tariff reform provided a bewilder-
ing array of justifications for the policy. Tariffs were urged from
self-interest, national interest and imperial interest; they were
supposed to provide the basis for the functional integration of the
Empire as well as providing the means for penalising enemies and
rewarding allies; they were intended to appeal to landowners as well
as industrialists, to employers as well as employees and above all to
establish an alternative to class-based politics by promising to make
foreigners pay for social reform, increased defence expenditure and
just about anything else that came to mind. In short, tariffs were
supposed to provide a way not only of having one's cake and eating

it but of making somebody else pay for it as well.[14]

However, once the electoral defeat of 1923 proved that tariffs were a vote-loser, tariff reformers tended to rely more heavily upon arguments that stressed the economic necessity of protection.[15] This much was uncontroversial: the McKenna duties of 1915 had already imposed a 33⅓ per cent duty on a number of 'luxury' items, and this principle was extended after the war by the Safe-guarding of Industries Act (1921) which imposed an identical duty on a range of goods, most of which came from Germany. But right-wingers continued to see tariffs as something more than an economic shield and sanction. They also saw it as a means of con-solidating the Empire despite the fact that this argument was increasingly unconvincing. For while Britain was certainly becom-ing more dependent upon the Empire, the Empire was becoming less dependent upon Britain, and the dominions at least were openly hostile to anything resembling 'Empire free trade'.[16]

The policy of tariff reform was portrayed by its supporters as 'scientific'. More often it was a simple rationalisation of patriotic sentiment. It was also of limited political value to the Right. Quite apart from its own internal weaknesses, the policy of tariff reform was neither exclusive to the Right nor universally accepted within its ranks. Baldwin himself saw the need for some kind of tariff at least as early as 1923 (though the Right characteristically blamed him for bringing the policy into disrepute), whilst a handful of individuals otherwise identified with the Right were free-traders, the most notable example being Lord Salisbury. In fact, although tariffs provided a focus for much right-wing agitation prior to 1932 (and a degree of continuity with the traditions of Conservative dissent established before the First World War), they were probably less important in maintaining the unity of the Right after 1923 than the sentiments aroused by the Irish Settlement of 1921 and the India Act of 1935.[17]

In resisting what Nesta Webster referred to as *The Surrender of an Empire*, the Right were naturally inclined to indulge in rhetoric that smacked more of 'romanticism' than it did of practicality. Yet, in the circumstances, it was surprising that so few resorted to the language of those like General Blakeney (of the British Fascists) who defended British imperialism in terms of 'divine providence'.[18] There *was*, of course, an altruistic side to right-wing imperialism. The idea of the 'white man's burden' (the doctrine of *Noblesse Oblige* writ large) was often employed by the Right,[19] and it was by no means uncommon to find the gradual abdication of imperial 'responsibilities' represented as a *moral* as well as a practical failure.[20] Nevertheless, alongside and usually underlying these concerns there was almost always a hard-headed appreciation of the economic and strategic advantages of imperialism.

This was less true of Ireland than it was of India, but it remained true of both despite differences of emphasis. Though Ireland could not be regarded as an economic asset, its fate after 1918 was linked directly by the Right with the future of India and of Egypt where nationalist movements were already beginning to press for independence.[21] And a firm hand in India was assumed to be vital at least to the cotton industry in Lancashire. Of course, there were numerous other arguments deployed by the Right in their attempt to prevent an extension of democratic control in India. It was sometimes argued that religious cleavages, the caste system and widespread illiteracy would make democratic institutions in India a sham. At other times the Right stressed the fact that it was only a small and unrepresentative clique of Westernised intellectuals and Indian cotton manufacturers who wanted self-government at all. And some of these criticisms were indeed perceptive. But these considerations were hardly central to the right-wing case since, as was noted in the previous chapter, most right-wingers had serious misgivings about democracy even in Britain.[22]

In most cases the crucial issue was British self-interest. As Nesta Webster stated the matter in a passage that was unrepresentative only in its brevity: 'The British are not in India for purely philanthropic reasons; they are there . . . for their own interests, and these interests they have every right to defend.'[23] The *Morning Post* was more explicit still. As an editorial of 3 February 1933 put it:[24]

> The British Empire . . . was built up with the idea of giving a market for British goods . . . yet to mention it in political circles is like telling a broad story to a clergyman; . . . transferring the control of those rich countries to the very people who are trying to shut out British goods . . . may, or may not, be magnificent; but it accords ill either with the interests of this country or with the dictates of common sense.

It need hardly be stated that *all* Conservatives believed themselves to be acting in the interests of Britain, nor that some of those on the Right (most notably Amery) disagreed with the imperial fundamentalism of their erstwhile colleagues. It was nevertheless significant that the vast majority of the Right accepted the logic of imperial isolation and that their interpretation of it was so belligerent. For the fact that imperialism had once again become a 'dirty' word during the 1920s[25] and that the Right opposed the tactical concessions that Conservative Party leaders were prepared to make to nationalist movements within the Empire was of considerable importance in maintaining the political distinctiveness of the Right; whilst the fact that isolationism became an increasingly impractical policy option during the 1930s was of equal importance in destroying its political unity.

Right-wing Supra-nationalism

Right-wing supra-nationalists assumed that under certain circumstances war was permanently avoidable since the claims of the nation were ultimately subject to the prior claims of a universal ideal. But this position was more distinctive in theory than it was in fact. There were two variants upon the theme, one of which centred upon Catholicism, the other (more strangely) upon Fascism. Both were in some ways similar to 'liberal idealism', and most of those who can be identified as right-wing supra-nationalists had, in fact, originally come from the Left. But just as in domestic affairs their dislike of class inequity was now expressed as a desire for hierarchy rather than equality, so in foreign affairs their plans for peace involved a settled pattern of 'leadership' amongst nations rather than a vague notion of 'understanding' between them. International justice was considered meaningless without international 'order'.

The Catholic variant found expression in the columns of the *New English Weekly* which, though it was neither exclusively Catholic nor exclusively right wing, was heir to the tradition of anti-imperialism associated with Chesterton and Belloc. The journal, which was founded in 1932 by the former Guild Socialist, A. R. Orage, and, from the time of Orage's death in 1934, edited by Philip Mairet, promoted the ideas of the 'Social Credit' movement and identified imperialism as a mask for the interests of international financiers. Much of this reflected the spirit of Edwardian *liberalism* with which many of the journal's contributors had been

associated. But in the post-1918 period the attachment to Catholicism and Social Credit propelled them to the Right as they became
enthusiasts for (but not uncritical supporters of) Fascism in Italy.

During the early thirties contributors to the journal included
Hilaire Belloc, Major Douglas, Ezra Pound, Maurice B. Reckitt,
the Marquis of Tavistock, Viscount Lymington, Anthony Ludovici,
and William Sanderson — a list which was itself an indication of the
New English Weekly's eclecticism. By the latter part of the 1930s the
contradictions of its position were clear. The journal believed that
peace was attainable through the application of economic reforms
within and of Christian principles of conduct between different
countries, but it had nothing of practical value to suggest. The
journal continued to harbour a sneaking but, except in the correspondence columns, circumspect admiration for Mussolini,
though it was openly hostile to the Nazis. It opposed German expan-
sionism but its support for British re-armament was muted by its
belief that the arms industry worked to the advantage of special
financial interests, and by 1938 the journal had little that was
relevant to say about foreign policy. Subsequently contributors
began to drift into the 'alternative' (i.e. non-liberal) peace movement. Tavistock formed the British Peoples' Party; Lymington
established the *New Pioneer*; Mairet was associated with both.

However, the *New English Weekly* was an unusual journal with a
poorly defined corporate identity. The personal philosophy of
Douglas Jerrold was more coherent and therefore more interesting.
Jerrold, who was, of course, a liberal prior to the First World War,
believed along with many radicals that war was neither desirable
nor inevitable: 'War is a disease of civilisation, not an external
threat to civilisation.'[26] His theory of war was intimately related to
his belief in the need for religious values to determine the social and
economic priorities of a nation and for the ownership of property
to be widely dispersed. As Jerrold put it in 1936:[27]

> Secularism is so dissatisfying to the heirs of Christian civilisation
> that it leads directly and necessarily to the concentration of the
> religious impulse on the worship of the State, while socialization
> [i.e. the 'socialization' of property], denying to man the material
> basis of a free personality, will produce an insistent demand for
> State action on a wide and ruthless scale . . .

In theory peace could be secured through Catholicism, but for as long as the individual remained 'at war with himself, his neighbour, and his God' there was no alternative but to prepare for the worst (Jerrold regarded the League of Nations as a misguided and dangerous experiment). In practice, therefore, Jerrold adopted an attitude much like any other right-winger.[28] He, too, was an 'imperial isolationist', but even more than most, his beliefs appeared to resemble a patchwork of apparently contradictory arguments. Thus, although war was on the one hand a 'disease of civilisation', it was also seen as an essential mechanism of social integration:[29]

> With the end of war will come the end of society, not because war is good, or because society is evil, but because the desire for a private life is itself fundamentally anti-social and society will not survive any generalised expression of that desire.

Yet, whilst war might have its benefits, Jerrold believed that conflict with the European dictators was undesirable and in October 1938 he appeared as a signatory of the famous 'Link' letter to *The Times*.[30]

Mosley's position was somewhat similar. According to the 1932 edition of *The Greater Britain*, which was the Bible of the BUF, perfect and perpetual peace was possible if corporate economic structures were established throughout the world.[31] This would remove the economic motives for war by laying the basis for the 'rationalisation' of the world economy, and once this had been achieved rational co-operation would replace international competition; the 'technician' would replace the politician; and political animosities would become to all intents and purposes an irrelevance. The millennium could begin. However, whilst the claims of the nation were in this way only 'provisional', the existing international order rendered them in practice absolute, and as a result the central Fascist policy was simply that of imperial isolation sustained by re-armament and economic 'autarky'. Mosley liked to refer to the policy as one of 'Britain first'. But this was not a static policy as Mosley tried to suggest, since the simple slogan masked a number of different policy recommendations.

The first change related to the League of Nations. Prior to the Italian invasion of Abyssinia in 1935 Mosley contended that the League was a potentially valuable organisation which required only a revision of its constitution.[32] After 1936 it was definitely rejected as incapable of reform. The second important modification was the introduction of the argument that Britain and Germany had different 'missions' in the world. In 1932 Mosley's vision had been of a rationalised *world* economy emerging from the transitional medium and example of a corporate British Empire. By 1936 Mosley was talking of Britain and Germany as the *twin pillars* of world order, who would guarantee peace only on the basis of the 'profound differences of national objective between the British Empire and the New Germany'.[33] The final shift of emphasis concerned the role of the Jews. In 1932 Mosley located the cause of war primarily in the competition between nations for markets, raw materials and areas of investment. Increasingly, however, the argument was put forward that war would be brought about by Jews seeking to punish Germany for striking a blow at their interests (although this line of attack was often integrated with earlier arguments concerning the role of finance).[34] Such modifications of his position make it difficult to take seriously Mosley's claim to have been consistent, although they are insufficient to support the counter-claim that his foreign policy was merely designed to satisfy a continental audience.[35] They do, however, demonstrate the degree to which right-wing attitudes towards questions of foreign policy varied and shifted during the 1930s, and this was to be of increasing importance in the years after 1935.

1935–1940

After 1935 the Right appeared to divide into three competing factions, but these factions were not simple reflections of differences in principle. At the one extreme were a small group of anti-appeasers most of whom were imperial isolationists. At the other were an equally small group of 'pro-Germans', most of whom were supra-nationalists or militarists. But between the two were a large number of individuals with a wide variety of beliefs who were unwilling or unable to commit themselves to either position. Existing accounts of the period have, not unnaturally, concentrated upon the extremes.[36] But the indecision of the 'centre' was no less important, and possibly more so.

   As Neville Thompson has already shown, Conservative opposition to appeasement was a matter of 'sporadic and discontinuous dissent, of individual critics and small cliques but no cohesive group'.[37] The leading rebels were Churchill, Eden and Amery, and although of the three, Churchill and Eden were the more important, Amery is for us the more interesting. Despite the fact that his support of the government's Indian policy makes him a somewhat unusual case, Amery was in other respects clearly a man of the Right.[38] Moreover, until 1937 he shared the assumptions of the imperial isolationists and was by no means unfriendly towards the European dictators (A. L. Rowse's claim that Amery was 'consistently opposed to appeasement' is patently false).[39]

As early as 1918, Amery believed that the only viable alternative to the League was the creation of a number of more-or-less equal power blocs. Britain's place was with the Empire whilst continental Europe constituted a separate, if only embryonic, political unit.[40] He rejected the idea of entering into any treaties with European powers beyond Locarno (and later events suggested that he did not even take this too seriously), and he opposed the establishment of a formal alliance even between Britain and America. European entanglements had drawn Britain into the First World War, and this was a mistake that should not be made twice. Besides, since Europe was (he argued in 1935) in a state of 'natural balance', imperial isolation was practical politics. France posed no threat to Britain because she was preoccupied with the threat from Germany and:[41]

> Germany in her turn, though once more formidable in arms, has, I believe, learnt enough to abandon her dreams of overseas empire, and her aims, ambitious as they are, would seem to be confined to the expansion of Germany to the South and East within the confines of Europe.

Britain's major worry was a possible Russian expansion in Central Asia which might threaten India. Consequently, the logical policy was one of good will towards Japan which would keep Russia's attention focused in the East. In Europe Amery urged Britain to remain independent of continental powers, encouraging (but not participating in) any movement towards European unity.[42]

Though Amery disliked the idea of German domination in Europe, his policy was nevertheless one of accommodation and appeasement in relation to the dictators. Thus, for example, he applauded the Italian invasion of Abyssinia as a blow against the League of Nations and won praise from the BUF for his outspoken refusal 'to send a single Birmingham lad to his death' for the sake of the Abyssinians.[43] But he remained convinced of the need for improved defence capabilities and in the autumn of 1936 became Chairman of the newly-created Army League (which was later resurrected as the Citizen Service League).

However, by the beginning of 1937, Amery had begun to abandon his conception of 'Fortress Britannica', and what had changed his mind was the German claim for the restoration of the mandated colonies which the League of Nations had placed under British administration after the First World War. The Colonial issue did not come to the fore in Britain until October 1937 (some time after Amery had become concerned about the issue) when a vast correspondence in *The Times* was followed by a flurry of books in 1938 and 1939.[44] Importantly, however, this was an issue that tended to cut across the usual political divisions, and those who opposed the claim did so for a number of different reasons. Some were old-fashioned anti-Germans. Others were specifically anti-Nazi. Others still considered the rights of self-determination which belonged to the colonies. But the strongest opponents were Conservative imperialists such as Amery and Croft who believed that returning the mandated territories would undermine imperial defence. Even the *Patriot* (which was vaguely pro-Nazi) and the Imperial Fascist League (which was openly so) opposed the return of the former German colonies.[45]

The significance of these events was two-fold. In the first place they divided the Right. In the second they robbed them of a distinctive position. Some, like Wolmer and Lloyd, followed Amery in their support of Churchill (and to a lesser extent, Eden).[46] But by 1938 Churchill's 'Arms and the Covenant' campaign had attracted a following quite unlike that which he had acquired during the Indian agitation. His new allies included not only Amery, Wolmer and Lloyd, but Bracken, Cecil, Grigg, Boothby, Macmillan, Horne and Nicolson.[47] The divisions between 'progressives' and 'Diehards' no longer appeared to make much sense.

This sense of confusion was still more evident at the other extreme, though here the contrasts were starker. One or two of the unrepentant appeasers of 1939 were clearly pro-Nazi. Arnold Leese of the IFL, for example, despite his objection to the German colonial demand, had supported Hitler since 1933 and was one of the few individuals who continued to defend the 'final solution' after 1945.[48] Likewise, William Joyce (who had left the BUF in

1937 and subsequently formed the National Socialist League in association with the ex-ILPer, John Beckett) worked for the Nazis during the war and was later hanged for treason.[49]

Many others opposed the war on anti-Semitic grounds. George Lane-Fox Pitt-Rivers, for example, a veteran anti-Semite of the 1920s, re-appeared towards the end of the 1930s urging the British to fight 'not against Germany . . . but against the enemy in our midst'.[50] Individuals such as Admiral Sir Barry Domvile (of the Link) and Captain Ramsay MP (of the Right Club), though they had not become anti-Semitic until the 1930s, followed the same pattern.[51] Similarly, Viscount Lymington, much influenced by Col. A. H. Lane's book, *The Alien Menace* (1928), established the *New Pioneer* in December 1938 which attracted a wide range of contributors (including many ex-BUF members) who were more anti-Semitic than they were directly pro-Nazi.[52] Yet another example was the British Peoples' Party which was founded by the Social Crediter and Christian Pacifist, the Marquis of Tavistock, in May 1939 and which attracted many anti-Semites who had originally come from the Left. Ostensibly the party held war to be the work of financiers (who were not necessarily Jewish). However, since John Beckett was the editor of the party's journal, the *Peoples' Post*, such fine distinctions were scarcely relevant, and at a local level it was difficult to disentangle hatred of the Jews, admiration for the Nazis and genuine sentiments of 'pacifism'.[53] Consequently, by the time Mosley tried to rally a 'Peace Front' (in the wake of the Czech crisis) the anti-war lobby was a combination more curious even than the anti-appeasement lobby. It included, amongst others, the *Catholic Times*, the *Catholic Herald*, the Peace Pledge Union, Lord Elton, Lord Alfred Douglas, Sir Thomas Jones, Lord Ponsonby, the Marquess of Tavistock, Francis Yeats-Brown, Dean Inge and Hugh Ross Williamson.[54] The conventional distinctions of Left and Right suddenly seemed irrelevant.

However, whilst many of the Right were polarised between these extreme positions by 1939, many more stood somewhere between the two, either because they positively supported Chamberlain's policy or (more often) because they were unable to decide between competing loyalties. Lord Rothermere, the proprietor of the *Daily Mail*, was a classic example.[55] Intensely anti-Bolshevik, he was sympathetic to the European dictatorships; but intensely patriotic, he was also fearful of a re-armed Germany. Consequently, he was, like Mosley, both an arch-appeaser *and* a staunch re-armer, though, unlike Mosley, his faith in appeasement did not survive the German invasion of Czechoslovakia in March 1939.[56] But it would be misleading to suggest that the Czech crisis sent everyone on the Right scurrying to one or other of the two extremes. Often it did little more than increase their sense of confusion and anxiety.

The events of March 1939 were obviously important in under-mining support for the policy of appeasement. The seizure of Prague not only violated the Munich agreement of September 1938, but also made it clear that Hitler was prepared to occupy non-German territory and consequently undermined the argument that he was only interested in reversing the injustices of Versailles. But although Henry Page Croft, for instance, subsequently described the events as the 'turning point of our times',[57] the Czech crisis was not *always* as critical as existing accounts of the period suggest. Furthermore, the effects of the crisis on the Right were difficult to predict and remain difficult to analyse. The Fascist and pro-German groups within the 'peace movement' *continued* to grow in spite (or perhaps because) of the crisis. And few of those on the Right who were not *already* prominent 'anti-appeasers' subse-quently became so.[58] One of the examples that Griffiths gives of the way in which Czechoslovakia is supposed to have destroyed beliefs in appeasement typifies the difficulty of generalising about the issue. Thus, although it was true that the book which Francis Yeats-Brown published in May 1939 entitled *European Jungle* began by lamenting the fact that 'recent hopes of disarmament and reconciliation lie shattered beyond the possibility of quick repair',[59] the fact that appeasement had 'for the moment failed'[60] did not significantly affect his position, and he remained active in the 'peace' movement until at least July 1939 (though he ceased to trust Mosley).[61] In fact, it had *always* been clear that if one was forced to choose between 'John Bull and the Foreigners'[62] the priority was, to use the Fascist slogan, 'Britain first'. Yeats-Brown nevertheless regarded it as a 'pity' that the choice might have to be made, and his attitude towards Germany remained one of distrustful admira-tion. Whilst he was appalled at the German treatment of the Jews and disappointed with German foreign policy he nevertheless remained anti-Semitic, anti-liberal, anti-capitalist, anti-Com-munist, anti-democratic, anti-pacifist, anti-internationalist and broadly pro-Nazi.[63]

The whole confusing picture was exemplified by the indecision of the *Patriot* (the journal which the Duke of Northumberland had created in 1922). It was anti-Semitic and in general sympathetic to Nazism, but it was also anti-German and worried by the 'socialism' of Nazi economic policy.[64] Prior to 1933, *The Patriot* believed that the world's problems were the result of a German-Jewish conspiracy, but after 1933 they were faced with an anti-Jewish German state towards which they had no fixed attitude. Consequently, the usual pattern of opinion during the years from 1936 to 1939 was for the journal to praise Hitler between crises and criticise him during them until, eventually, the Nazi-Soviet pact made such equivocation impossible.[65]

Conclusion

Right-wing attitudes towards the outside world were never as simple as the (more-or-less) united opposition to imperial retreat suggested. There were three different schools of thought about international relations and these were tied to corresponding theories of man and society. The militarists viewed the nation as a community of 'real' interests and believed the propensity for conflict to be an ineradicable aspect of human nature. The imperial isolationists saw the nation (and the Empire) as a conjunction of actual interests (mostly economic) and regarded man as insufficiently good to desist from war without the threat of retaliation, but insufficiently evil to sanction war in favour of negotiation. Right-wing supra-nationalists professed to believe differently. Like many liberals and socialists, they regarded the nation as a transient phenomenon that would eventually be superseded, if not by a truly international, at least by a trans-national or supra-national ideal. Similarly, they spoke of human nature as if it were capable, if not of perfection, at least of improvement.

However, all of these ideas suffered from logical defects that bred inconsistency. The militarists assumed that man possessed a fixed and permanent 'human nature' which impelled him towards war, but they also believed that successful attempts to avoid conflict perverted human nature (which was an admission that it could *not* be fixed and permanent), or alienated man from his 'real' feelings (which was an admission that instincts did *not* necessarily determine behaviour). Similarly, they argued that war was an inevitable result of the division of the world into nations, but they also regarded war as beneficial because it sustained this division (which demonstrated that their analysis was *prescriptive* rather than descriptive). The imperial isolationists were also plagued by difficulties, although their problems were common to most Conservatives (and to many non-Conservatives as well). Until the latter part of the 1930s they tended to assume that national interests were self-evident, but once they were faced with a possible threat from Germany they were forced to admit that the identification of national interests was a matter of *judgement*. Moreover, the judgements that they made depended upon a variety of factors, many of which (anti-Semitism, pro-Germanism, religious affiliation and so forth) were tangential to the question of security. The same was true of right-wing supra-nationalists. Their prescriptions for peace rested upon circular arguments that assumed a non-existent premiss (i.e. that most if not all nations *already* believed in a given doctrine). Confronted with the reality of German aggression they merely appeared to be what many of them were — apologists and fellow-travellers.

Consequently, when the Right split over questions of European foreign policy it was difficult to perceive a logical pattern. As one would expect, most of the Fascists (especially those who had originally come from the Left) opposed the war, but this fact was somewhat difficult to interpret since the Fascist movement of 1939 was in many respects *unlike* the movement in earlier years.[66] Nor was it easy to understand the differences that emerged amongst the Conservative Right. 'Simon Haxey', in his contemporary (and partisan) work, *Tory MP* (1939), suggested that the crucial division between those Conservatives who favoured and those who opposed appeasement was an economic one. The anti-appeasers, he argued, consisted predominantly of businessmen 'with a stake in the Empire' whilst the pro-appeasement lobby had interests in 'large scale industry and finance'.[67] But even though anti-appeasers such as Amery and Croft had links with companies in British Africa whilst the Anglo-German Fellowship received a disproportionate amount of support from banks and insurance companies, Haxey's economic categories were by no means mutually exclusive, and at least amongst the anti-war lobby, arguments from economic self-interest often rubbed shoulders with those that were openly hostile to the interests of 'middle-class trader[s] and manufacturer[s]'.[68] The divisions made most sense in relation to (but not as straightforward reflections of) differences of belief, but even then the reality was messy. Some right-wingers (who were imperial isolationists) were associated with the critics of appeasement. Others (drawn from the ranks of the supra-nationalists *and* the militarists) were linked with the peace movement. But most right-wingers trailed in the wake of the government, more through indecision than conviction. As a result, the picture that emerged was above all one of confusion. But this confusion was not without significance. For it disrupted an established pattern of right-wing politics that had persisted for twenty years or more, and in so doing it helped to facilitate a gradual realignment of right-wing forces thereafter.

Notes

1. Northumberland, 'The Curse of Internationalism', *The Patriot*, 8.2.23.
2. H. Ogle, 'What We Stand For', *The Englishman*, vol. 1, no. 1, 7.2.20.
3. H. Kohn, 'The Origins of English Nationalism', *Journal of the History of Ideas* (1940), pp. 69–94, argues that because English nationalism was shaped by seventeenth-century struggles against ecclesiastical and civil authority it was predominantly 'liberal' in tone.
4. G. Woolton, 'Ex-Servicemen in Politics', *PQ* (1958), pp. 28–39. At the time less attention was paid to the Right than the Left. Refer to S. R. Ward, 'Intelligence Surveillance of British Ex-Servicemen, 1918–20', *HJ* (March 1973), pp. 179–88.
5. *The Veteran* was established in Feb. 1921. In May 1922 it changed its title to *The Veteran and Briton*. In Nov. 1922 it became *The Briton*. It became the official journal of the British Legion in Scotland and described itself as 'a non-political organ . . . that . . . will have no dealings with individuals who follow the red flag' (July 1921, no. 6, p. 1). Its fate after Jan 1925 is unknown.
6. O. Mosley. *My Life* (London, 1968), p. 305.
7. 'Why I believe in War', *Spectator*, 30.12.32.
8. A. M. Ludovici, *Violence, Sacrifice and War* (London, 1934), p. 10. Ludovici believed that, by increasing the competition for resources, childbearing constituted 'a peaceful invasion of the community' (p. 6).
9. Ibid., p. 15.
10. *A Defence of Conservatism* (London, 1927), p. 253. Refer also to 'Are we Pacifists?', *New Pioneer*, Dec. 1938. On Joyce see *Fascism and India* (n.d.). On Leese refer to J. E. Morell, 'The Life and Opinions of A. S. Leese', M. A., Univ. of Sheffield, 1974, ch. 3.
11. *Ich Dien, the Tory Path* (London, 1931), ch. III, 'The Meaning of Protection'.
12. Anti-Bolshevism was common, but see in particular Collinson Owen, 'Smash it! Or it will Smash us', *Daily Mail*, 2.7.31. Owen was a member of the selection committee of the Right Book Club (on which refer to G. C. Webber, 'Patterns of Membership and Support for the BUF', *JCH* (Oct. 1984), pp. 592–3 and the Appendix).
13. See e.g. 'Lest we Forget', *Citizen Service*, April 1939.
14. On tariff reform in general refer to A. Sykes, *Tariff Reform in British Politics, 1903–1913* (Oxford, 1979); and B. Semmel, *Imperialism and Social Reform* (Allen and Unwin, London, 1960). Note that after 1923 these claims were usually toned down in favour of arguments from economic necessity.

15. Many tariff reformers blamed Rothermere who urged the readers of his newspapers to support the Liberals in 1923. This was yet another reason for his unpopularity on the Right. See e.g. N. Webster, *The Surrender of an Empire* (London, 1931), pp. 204–7.

16. R. Skidelsky, *Politicians and the Slump* (London, 1967), p. 250.

17. Although, with these issues, as with tariff reform, there were examples of 'right-wingers' being on the 'wrong' side, e.g. Hannon in 1921 and Amery in the early 30s.

18. R. Blakeney, 'British Fascism', *Nineteenth Century and After*, Jan. 1925, pp. 132–41.

19. Refer A. P. Thornton, *The Imperial Idea and its Enemies* (London, 1959), pp. 68–75.

20. See e.g. *The Daily Mail Blue Book on the Indian Crisis* (London, 1931).

21. This sometimes took the form of a conspiracy theory. See e.g. Northumberland *et al.*, *Conspiracy against the British Empire* (London, 1921).

22. See in particular the writings of Lord Sydenham and Sir Michael O'Dwyer (who had been Governor of the Punjab at the time of the Amritsar massacre). Refer also to the *Indian Empire Review*. On the question of democracy see e.g. W. A. Le Rossignol, 'Why Try Democracy?', *IER* (April 1933) and 'Tiresias', *IER* (May 1934). Here the objection to self-government in India is rooted in an attack upon democracy in general: 'Democracy is bankrupt. It has been superseded for incompetence in Italy and Germany; America is the most criminal country in the world and is swayed by gangs of criminals . . . Democracy spells corruption; the elected bribe the electors, and the electors blackmail the elected. That is the precise situation today in France.' (p. 206). Refer also to the previous chapter.

23. Webster, *The Surrender of an Empire*, p. 314. This book was serialised in weekly instalments by the *Saturday Review* from June 1933 and for about a year thereafter!

24. 'Losing the Latchkey', Editorial, *Morning Post*, 3.2.33.

25. Thornton, *The Imperial Idea*, p. 190ff.

26. D. Jerrold, *They That Take the Sword, the future of the League of nations* (London, 1936), p. 21.

27. Ibid., pp. 20–1.

28. For a summary of Jerrold's position see *England* (first published London, 1935; Introduction to 2nd edn, 1936), p. xxxi.

29. *Georgian Adventure* (London, 1937; Right Book Club edn, 1938), p. 105.

30. R. Griffiths, *Fellow Travellers of the Right* (London, 1983 edn), p. 330.

31. O. Mosley, *The Greater Britain* (London, 1932), esp. p. 140ff. The BUF did try to create a common Fascist front within the Empire, the New Empire Union (est. July 1933; refer to the *Blackshirt*, 8–14 July 1933), but even this attempt at Fascist internationalism was a failure.

32. See e.g. O. Mosley, 'Eden and Ethiopia', *Blackshirt*, 7.6.35, p. 1; and O. Mosley, *Fascism 100 Questions Asked and Answered* (London, 1936), no. 92.

33. 'The World Alternative', *Fascist Quarterly*, July 1936, pp. 383–4.

34. See e.g. *Action*, 3.9.38, and as far back as *Blackshirt*, 4–10 Nov. 1933. Refer also to N. Nugent, 'The Ideas of the BUF' in N. Nugent and R. King (eds.), *The British Right* (Farnborough, 1977), p. 159.

35. Mosley, *My Life*, pp. 377–97.

36. Griffiths, *Fellow Travellers*; and N. Thompson, *The Anti-Appeasers, Conservative Opposition to Appeasement in the 1930s* (Oxford, 1971).

37. Thompson, *The Anti-Appeasers*, p. 2.

38. (Churchill was not.) J. Gunther, *Inside Europe* (London, 1936), p. 281, places Amery on the 'extreme Right', a view which was not unreasonable in the light of Amery's *The Forward View* (London, 1935).

39. A. L. Rowse, *All Souls and Appeasement. A Contribution to Contemporary History* (Macmillan, London, 1961), p. 1.

40. L. S. Amery, *My Political Life*, vol. II (London, 1954), p. 162, Amery to Reading, Oct. 1918.

41. *The Forward View*, p. 278.

42. After 1945 Amery favoured an anti-Soviet European bloc that *included* Britain. Hence his involvement with the United Europe Committee (established 1947). Refer to L. S. Amery, *The British Commonwealth in World Affairs* (Longmans, London, 1948).

43. Speech delivered in Birmingham 8.10.35, reported in *Blackshirt*, 18.10.35, p. 1.

44. Amongst which was Amery's *The German Colonial Claim* (London, 1939).

45. 'Mandated Territories', *The Patriot*, 23.7.36; 'The German Claim to her Former Colonies', *The Fascist*, May 1939, p. 3.

46. See also ch. 3, esp. notes 46 and 47. Wolmer's draft memoirs stated: 'Chapter III of Eden's autobiography is entitled 'The Eden Group', of which I had never heard before, and I find myself mentioned in it as a member. As far as I was concerned there never had been an Eden Group. I had been supporting the line Winston Churchill had taken.' 3rd Earl Selborne MS., Eng. Hist., c. 1017, fol. 128.

47. M. Cowling, *The Impact of Hitler* (Cambridge, 1975; 1977 edn), p. 244.

48. A. S. Leese, *Out of Step* (Guildford, 1951).

49. J. A. Cole, *Lord Haw-Haw — and William Joyce* (London, 1964).

50. G. L-F. Pitt-Rivers, *The Czech Conspiracy* (London, 1938), pp. 87–8.

51. B. Domvile, *From Admiral to Cabin Boy* (London, 1947); A. H. M. Ramsay, *The Nameless War* (London, 1952). Both signed the 'Link Letter' to *The Times*, 12.10.38.

52. Viscount Lymington, *Famine in England* (London, 1938). The *New Pioneer* attracted Right *and* Left, but the former predominated. Contributors included A. K. Chesterton, P. C. Loftus MP, Sir Arnold Wilson, A. Ludovici, Rolf Gardiner, John Beckett, Sir Louis Stuart (editor of the *Indian Empire Review*), Maj. J. F. C. Fuller, Ben Greene, Francis Yeats-Brown, Compton Mackenzie and Philip Mairet.

53. Philby MS, St. Anthony's Coll., Oxford, File 'British Politics', esp. D. Duff to Philby, 4.8.39.

54. R. Skidelsky, *Oswald Mosley* (London, 1975; 1981 edn), p. 439.

55. P. Addison, 'Patriotism Under Pressure. Lord Rothermere and British Foreign Policy' in G. Peele and C. Cook (eds.); *The Politics of Reappraisal, 1918–1939* (London, 1975), ch. 8.

56. 'Words Don't Count Any More', *Daily Mail*, 18.3.39.

57. H. P. Croft, *My Life of Strife* (London, 1948), p. 294.

58. M. Ceadel, *Pacifism in Britain, 1914–1945* (Clarendon Press, Oxford, 1980); Webber, 'Patterns of Membership', pp. 587–98. This contradicts the general assumption made by Griffiths, *Fellow Travellers*.

59. June 1939 edition, p. 11. Also quoted by Griffiths, *Fellow Travellers*, p. 347. Griffiths is aware of the difficulty himself and returns to Yeats-Brown on p. 356.

60. Ibid., p. 13.

61. Skidelsky, *Mosley*, pp. 440–1.

62. Title, ch. XII of *European Jungle* (London, 1939).

63. Ibid., esp. chs I, VI and XII. Other examples of the need to treat Griffiths's comments about this period with care include G. Ward Price (see e.g. his 1936 article, 'Negotiate — But Arm', *Daily Mail*, 16.6.36) and Sir Arnold Wilson (see e.g. *Walks and Talks Abroad* (London, 1936), p. 283ff). In both cases the undeniable disillusion that sets in after March 1939 appears less dramatic when seen in the context of the works quoted.

64. See esp. 'Nazi Policies', *The Patriot*, 23.6.32.

65. Even then the *Patriot* was schizophrenic. The Leader of 31.8.39 suggested that Hitler had been consistent but that Stalin had suddenly abandoned Communism. However, William Faulkner (one of the contributors to the anonymous book, *The Cause of the World Unrest* (1920). Introduction by H. A. Gwynne), called the pact 'the most cynical piece of secret diplomacy ever recorded', and this was the line that the journal subsequently took.

66. Webber, 'Patterns of Membership', pp. 575–606.

67. S. Haxey, *Tory MP* (London, 1939), p. 230.

68. A. P. Laurie, 'Where Democracy has Failed', *Anglo-German Review* (April 1939), p. 144. The *AGR* was edited by C. E. Carroll, formerly editor of the British Legion's paper, and later arrested under defence regulation 18B.

8 CONCLUSION

It often appeared as if those on the Right disagreed more with one another than they did with their political opponents (socialists, liberals, and 'liberal Conservatives'). There was, as we have seen, no single right-wing attitude towards society, the economy, the state or the outside world, and it was symptomatic of this heterogeneity that the Right could be represented by so many different symbols — the aristocratic 'backwoodsman', the retired colonel, the big industrialist, and the sinister dictator. In addition there was an institutional cleavage between those who supported the Conservative Party and those who joined other movements such as the Fascists. As the Right had emerged, so they continued to exist: as a loose coalition of individuals and movements whose fears, interests, objectives and personnel imperfectly overlapped.

It might be objected that these considerations preclude a clear definition of the subject matter, but this criticism makes sense only if we expect too much of social-scientific 'definitions'. As Ian Gilmour noted in 1977, 'right-wingery' is a strange phenomenon: it 'cannot be exactly defined but it is, like the elephant, easily recognised when seen'.[1] Many writers have attempted to list the 'essential' features of the Right by drawing up a kind of ideological 'shopping list' of right-wing beliefs, each item of which can be ticked off as it is discovered in the speeches or writings of particular groups or individuals,[2] but this approach has several defects. Stipulative definitions of this kind tend to be far too narrow. Empirical definitions tend to be insufficiently distinctive. Moreover, both assume (quite wrongly) that ideologies may be regarded as a series of static propositions, whereas the crucial feature of all systems of belief is the *relationship* that exists between one proposition and another. However, it need not be concluded that *all* forms of 'definition' are, therefore, impossible. Indeed, what this study has attempted to do has been to clarify the concept of 'the Right' by describing a series of 'family resemblances'. This approach cannot, of course, dispense with the problem of 'indeterminacy' in the way that formal definitions (supposedly) do, but rigorous boundaries do not exist in the real world and the notion of 'family resemblances' provides us with an organising concept which does not require us to pretend that they do.

In this respect, two features of the British Right need to be emphasised. First, that the Right were united more by shared anxieties than they were by shared aspirations; and secondly that they drew their support from social groups that appeared to have little in common. Both factors made the Right seem oddly disunited, but both were crucial to the development of right-wing ideas, and these ideas played an important part in shaping the struggle for power within (and on the fringes of) the Conservative Party between the wars.

Sociologically, the Right appeared to represent a diverse collection of 'interests'. It was suggested in the Introduction that the Conservative Party might usefully be considered as an institution, the success of which has depended upon its ability to represent the interests of rising *and* of declining elites whilst also attracting the support of many who belong to neither. Within this perspective the Right can be understood as those at the extremes of this sociological constellation who believe the Conservative Party to be unwilling or unable to defend their interests properly. Thus, the British Right between the wars attracted old-fashioned landed aristocrats and individuals (particularly writers) whose occupational status appeared peripheral to (and perhaps threatened by) the dominant cleavage of 'class'; businessmen anxious to consolidate their power and prestige by weakening 'insurgent' interests below and 'entrenched' interests above them; and, when the Right attracted support from non-elites (as the Fascist movement did), the young, the unemployed and the non-unionised sections of the working class. Yet these groups rarely opposed one another directly despite the fact that their 'objective' interests sometimes appeared to conflict. More often they united in an effort to challenge those things which they felt were inimical to the interests that they held in common.

In Britain, this conjunction of disparate forces assumed its distinctive form slowly and imperfectly as changes in the pattern of late nineteenth- and early twentieth-century British politics pushed a number of different groups beyond the limits of the political 'consensus' spanned by the major parties. Gradually these individuals were distanced both from the Liberals *and* from mainstream Conservatives by fears of imperial decline, social disintegration, constitutional imbalance, and economic change (though here in particular profound disagreements existed between those who thought that the process was proceeding too rapidly and those who believed it was not proceeding rapidly enough). Disillusion with 'the system' was usually incremental, but sometimes specific events, such as the passage of the Parliament Act in 1911, were sufficient to disrupt traditional loyalties. Indeed, it is tempting to assume (as Alan Sykes does)[3] that the Right could not have survived further internal diversification after 1911, but the assumption is false. The Right had not disintegrated before 1914, and after 1918 the bloc was held together not only by the common concerns of the Edwardian Age but also by the new fears that arose from the extension of the franchise and the rise of the Labour Party.

The most striking feature of the Right was consequently its opposition to others, and this 'negative' emphasis was paralleled in the realm of ideas. In general, the Right were opposed to liberalism and, to a lesser extent, socialism (in some cases, most notably in the case of the Fascist movement, right- and left-wingers *shared* sentiments of anti-liberalism). In particular, the Right rejected liberal theories of 'rationalism' and 'progress'. The individual was regarded not as a freely-contracting agent but as someone who was indivisible from his social group and who was consequently obliged (when necessary) to subordinate his 'individual rights' to his 'social duties' since, as William Sanderson put it, a right was merely 'the passive aspect of a relationship of which duty is the active principle'.[4] Furthermore, though it was agreed that man had the capacity for rational thought and action, 'reason' itself was treated with scepticism and distrust. At best it was considered an insufficient condition of political wisdom; at worst it was thought to be destructive of 'racial instinct'. Moreover, 'reason' could not be considered as a guarantee of 'progress'. If history had any pattern those on the Right usually believed it to be cyclical rather than linear and to reflect the *continuities* (rather than to suggest the perfectibility) of human nature.[5]

However, the Right were not devoid of positive proposals. Indeed, their favourite criticism of the Conservative Party was precisely that it had abandoned its 'principles' and deteriorated into a party of 'mere' anti-socialism. Principally, the Right sought ways of creating or, if they were less pessimistic, of stabilising a society in which the competition between groups for political power was isolated from the struggle between classes for economic power. Unlike the liberals, the Right nevertheless believed that the general pattern of economic organisation should be strictly circumscribed. Unlike the socialists, they stressed the value of inequality and believed that conflicts of interest could be reconciled, if not by the inculcation of shared values, at least by the creation of hierarchical institutions which would render society 'vertically integrated' rather than 'horizontally divided'. However, unlike mainstream Conservatives, the Right believed that these goals could not be achieved by a party committed to the 'pragmatic' recognition of changes already implicit in society, since existing social, economic and political trends appeared detrimental to the unity and strength of the nation. Consequently, those on the right argued that Conservative values could only be defended by a party that was committed to positive *principles*, and resolute *leadership*.

But, of course, the diversity of interests represented by the Right meant that agreements in principle were often only the prelude to disagreements in practice, not only about the tactics that should be employed (i.e. whether they should work with or against the Conservative Party), but also about the ends that should be pursued. Thus, at one extreme were individuals who wanted to restrict access to the machinery of government and restore the power of a landed aristocracy; at the other, those who sought to incorporate all social and economic groups within the state and fortify the institution of capitalism. Besides, the kaleidoscopic nature of the right inevitably generated exceptions to every rule. Mosley, for example, having come from the Left, did not straightforwardly reject his liberal inheritance. He limited his faith in 'reason' to the field of 'technocratic expertise', combined it with elements of romanticism, and used it to attack the concept of democracy. Likewise, many of the 'capitalist anti-statists' on the Right accepted certain tenets of classical liberalism (though they did so for non-liberal reasons) and combined a belief in *laissez-faire* economics with a distrust of utilitarian politics. However, what was remarkable about the British Right between the wars was that the different strands within it rarely existed independently of each other and were usually *combined* in the most curious ways.

Why, then, was the British right so weak? In part this was simply because the Conservative Party was so strong. The Right were most active when the Conservatives were (or appeared to be) least successful, but the party was only in trouble on a few occasions. Prior to 1914, when the party seemed incapable of winning elections, the Right were instrumental in removing Balfour from the

leadership. After 1918, when it was feared that coalition government might weaken the challenge to Labour, the Right played a
prominent part in toppling Austen Chamberlain. After 1929, when
Baldwin led the party first to defeat and then into an apparently
unnecessary coalition, the Right once again challenged the party's
leader, and the Fascists appeared (briefly) to benefit from the
disruption. But the dissidents were in an awkward position. The
electoral success of the Conservative Party after 1922 calmed many
of the fears that had initially driven Conservatives to the Right, and
in the years that followed it was difficult to see what practical
alternative to conservatism there might be. The relative solidity of
the middle-class Conservative vote meant that those within the
party were unwilling to break away from it, whilst those outside the
party (the Fascists) were practically unable to challenge it. Despite
the growth of the Fascist movement in the early part of 1934
relatively few Conservatives were lost to the BUF. Most leading
right-wingers distrusted Mosley, and many potential Fascists were
worried by the violence that was associated with the movement (but
not, it seems, by the anti-Semitism).[6] As a result, most of those on
the Right continued to support the Conservative Party, but they did
so *despite* rather than because of its leaders and its policies.

However, it is important to remember that the Right were not as
insignificant a force within the Conservative Party as is usually
assumed. As we saw in Chapters 2 and 3, although it is conventional to regard the Conservative Party as an organisation characterised by 'tendencies' rather than 'factions', and to explain the
triumph of moderation within it as a natural outcome of political
'pragmatism' and 'deference' to the party leader, these descriptions
of Conservative Party politics are misleading.[7] In the inter-war
years (as at other times) the Conservative Party was very definitely
afflicted by factional struggles in which the Right played an
important part. It was true that at the *parliamentary* level the Right
were poorly represented, but within the party *as a whole* they
attracted considerable (sometimes majority) support, and came
close to undermining Baldwin's position on several occasions in the
early 1930s. What was more, these divisions (although they tapped
general sentiments of dissatisfaction with Baldwin) centred upon
fundamental questions of Conservative *ideology*, and the victory of
'Baldwinian pragmatism' can hardly be accounted for in terms of
the supposed 'deference' of party members since the further down
the Conservative hierarchy one looks the *less* prepared the

followers were to trust their leaders.

Nevertheless, the Right failed to capture the party in the early thirties and subsequently found themselves unable to mount a serious challenge to the established party chiefs. In part, this failure was a reflection of the fact that although the Right spoke endlessly about the need for 'leadership', they were quite incapable of providing it themselves. Indeed, their internal disagreements were such that the Right were constrained to accept the ostensible leadership of men such as Salisbury, Rothermere, Beaverbrook and Churchill whenever they tried to rally behind a single cause, even though the interests and intentions of these men were often at odds with those of their 'supporters'. Besides, after 1935 the Right were in an increasingly difficult position. Once the India Act was passed into law and attention turned to questions of European foreign policy, the Right began to divide and were soon in a state of intellectual and organisational chaos. The issues that had previously united them no longer appeared to be salient, and the problems that now faced them were the subject of sharp internal disagreements. These weaknesses, however, were far from new.

'Salience' had been a constant problem. Of all the issues with which the Right were asociated tariff reform had probably been the most practical, but this had never been an exclusively right-wing policy, and once the economic crisis of 1931 had prompted the government to introduce the Import Duties Act and conclude the Ottawa agreements, the general principle was no longer in dispute. The question of 'imperial retreat' was similarly defused, first by the negotiation of the Irish Settlement in 1921 and later by the passage of the Government of India Act in 1935 which (despite providing a focus for discontent) presented the Right with a *fait accompli*. Notwithstanding the enthusiasm of Conservative Party conferences for constitutional reform, this too seemed irrelevant: it was increasingly anachronistic to decry the Parliament Act of 1911 and wholly unnecessary to abandon the traditional system of parliamentary democracy. Likewise, though most Conservatives were determined to resist socialism, the 'anti-Bolshevik' crusades associated with the Right seemed quite out of place once the industrial militancy of the immediate post-war years had subsided. Besides, the Trades Disputes Act of 1927 (which followed the collapse of the General Strike in 1926) allayed many of the fears even of the most belligerent Tories. Other issues were more marginal still. Anti-Semitism, for example, was academic unless one lived in East London or Leeds, and notwithstanding the attention that this subject has received in scholarly books and articles, it was never the only and rarely the most important aspect of right-wing ideologies. The glorification of Britain's rural, cultural, and religious heritage was also incapable of generating political enthusiasm — and in so far as such appeals could be made to serve any political purpose, Baldwin had already laid claim to them. As with English nationalism, the values themselves were not in dispute but the philosophies that right-wing zealots derived from them were esoteric and usually impractical. Disregarding the economic reactionaries who opposed capitalism, the Right made most sense when they considered questions of broad economic strategy, but those who opposed the interference of the state in the operation of the market had little to say during the 1930s when a policy of financial management and industrial non-intervention was being pursued, and those who proposed to extend and formalise governmental control were in no position to influence policy.[8]

The second weakness (implicit in the first) was that right-wing beliefs often ran contrary rather than parallel to one another, and one of the important consequences of this was that it created specific *ideological* barriers to the growth of Fascism in Britain.[9] To achieve success, the Fascist movement needed to attract disillusioned Conservatives into its ranks, but those who were most inclined to support the Fascists were least receptive to the official ideology of the BUF. Mosley was an economic 'moderniser'; most of the old-fashioned Tories who were sympathetic to Fascism were economic reactionaries. Nor were these as numerous as one might have expected. Landed aristocrats in Britain were rarely unwilling to diversify their economic interests beyond land, and many of the richest channelled their wealth into finance.[10] Naturally, this made it unlikely that such men would support a movement that was hostile to 'financiers' as a group or accept the idea that the only important ones were evil-minded Jews. Similarly, many of those who admired dictatorships remained distrustful of Germany as a nation and, as a result, were increasingly wary of the British Union of Fascists and National Socialists (as the movement became known after 1936). Besides, most dissident Conservatives (even though they accepted the case for tariffs) were *opposed* to government intervention in the domestic economy — and this was one of the central tenets of BUF policy.

Such cross-cutting patterns of belief were not peculiar to the

Fascists and those who sympathised with them. They were also mirrored amongst loyal right-wing Conservatives. Yet the different ideological elements within the Right were rarely divided according to the logic of their positions, and when at the end of the thirties the Right split, the result appeared mainly to be confusion. But this confusion was not without significance. The events of the years from 1935 to 1940, by confronting the Right with problems that exposed the internal contradictions of their beliefs, robbed them of their foreign policy 'consensus', and in the process destroyed the illusion of unity by disturbing established patterns of co-operation. This in turn helped to facilitate a gradual re-alignment of right-wing forces. Prior to the 1930s the identity of the Right was related to (and to some extent determined by) shared anxieties about imperial decline that masked profound differences of belief in economic matters, but this uneasy alliance was shattered by the events of the thirties, and subsequently it was *economic* rather than nationalistic issues that gradually came to dictate the pattern of right-wing politics. For although the negative bonds of imperialism were never entirely broken until the Empire itself had been relinquished, this was one of the critical junctures at which those on the Right were forced to re-assess their political identity. And even though the events of the late 1930s were not to be the final shock,[11] they nevertheless represented an important stage in the bifurcation of right-wing forces between the 'neo-Fascists' and the 'New Right' of the late 1960s — two groups divided by positive, but mutually antagonistic proposals for social and economic reform.

Notes

1. I. Gilmour, *Inside Right. Conservatism, Policies and the People* (London, 1977; London, 1978 Quartet edn) note, p. 12.
2. See e.g. W. Pickles, 'Left and Right' in J. Gould and W. L. Kolb (eds.), *Dictionary of Social Sciences* (UNESCO, 1964). R. Bennett, R. King and N. Nugent, 'Introduction: the Concept of the Right' in N. Nugent and R. King (eds.), *The British Right* (Farnborough, 1977). H. Rogger and E. Weber (eds.), *The European Right* (London, 1965), first and last chapters.
3. A. Sykes, 'The Radical Right and the Crisis of Conservatism before the First World War', *HJ* (1983), pp. 661–76. Sykes concludes that the realignment of right-wing forces between 1909 and 1911 created a situation in which 'the Radical Right was all but swamped in a sea of traditional Conservatives defending traditional causes . . . by 1914 the "crisis of Conservatism" was over' (p. 676). In fact, as we saw in Chapters 2 and 3, men such as Salisbury and Selborne who had moved to the Right after 1911 (and remained there after 1918) were *themselves* swamped by 'radicals'.

4. W. Sanderson, *Statecraft* (London, 1927), p. 37.

5. See, e.g., the works of Northumberland cited in the Bibliography. Usually assumptions of this kind were implicitly accepted rather than explicitly defended.

6. G. C. Webber, 'Patterns of Membership and Support for the BUF', *JCH* (Oct. 1984), pp. 596–7. See also Petrie quoted in C. Cross, *The Fascists in Britain* (London, 1961), p. 101. What worried him (it seems) were the *implications* of anti-Semitism rather than the anti-Semitism itself, even though he disliked the kind of religious persecution practised in Germany.

7. R. Rose, 'Parties, Factions and Tendencies in Britain', *PS* (1964), pp. 33–46. S. Finer, H. Berrington and D. Bartholomew, *Backbench Opinion in the House of Commons, 1955–1959* (Pergamon Press, Oxford, 1961). R. T. McKenzie, *British Political Parties* (London, 1963 edn).

8. This was true across the political spectrum. Mosley was discredited by his Fascism; Amery had been kept out of office since 1929 because of his belligerent protectionism; Macmillan was not yet influential enough (the Next Five Years Group was not established until 1935, *The Middle Way* was not published until 1938, and Macmillan was not given a position of responsibility until 1940 when he became Parliamentary Secretary at the Ministry of Supply); Lloyd George was supported by a weak and divided party; Keynes suffered from his association with Lloyd George; the ILP had been disaffiliated by the Labour Party in 1932, and the Socialist League (which took its place) was distrusted by the Labour Party leaders. Meanwhile, the Exchequer was controlled by Philip Snowden (1929–31); Neville Chamberlain (1931–7); and Sir John Simon (1937–40).

9. This is *not* meant to be a mono-causal explanation of Fascist failure. For alternative and complementary perspectives see esp. R. Benewick, *Political Violence and Public Order* (London, 1969); and R. Skidelsky, *Oswald Mosley* (London, 1975).

10. W. D. Rubinstein, *Men of Property. The Very Wealthy in Britain Since the Industrial Revolution* (London, 1981).

11. The Suez Crisis of 1956 and the events in Rhodesia in 1965 both provoked traditional imperialist revolts.

APPENDIX

This appendix contains information related to lesser-known individuals and organisations referred to in, or relevant to, the study.
An asterisk denotes a separate entry.

Acworth, Capt. Bernard

A naval officer who ran the anti-Semitic Evolution Protest Movement; signed the Link* letter of Oct. 1938; and founded the Liberty Restoration League.*

Air League

Initially estd. 1909 as the Aerial League of the British Empire. Changed name to the Air League of the British Empire in 1920. Chairman, Lord Mottistone (a friend of Ribbentrop); Sec.-Gen., Air Commodore J. A. Chamier (a member of the January Club*); Sec., Col. N. Thwaites.* Also included Lord Sempill,* later on the council of Link.*

Amery, Leopold S. (1873–1955)

Born in India. Educated Harrow and Balliol, Oxford. Con. MP Birmingham South, 1911–18; Birmingham Sparkbrook, 1918–45. Parliamentary Under-Sec., Colonies 1919–21; Parliamentary and Financial Sec., Admiralty 1922–4; Sec. of State, Dominions, 1925–9; for India, 1940–5. A tariff reformer closely associated with Lord Milner* and the British Covenanters prior to 1914. Linked with numerous ginger groups including the EIA,* EEU,* Army League,* Colonial League,* and Citizen Service League.*

Ampthill, 2nd Baron (1869–1935)

Arthur Olivier Villiers Russell. Private Sec. to Joseph Chamberlain at the Colonial Office after 1895; Gov. of Madras, 1899–1906; Acting Viceroy and Gov. Gen. of India, 1904. A Diehard of 1911 associated with the National Service League prior to WW1, elected Pres. of the National Party* in 1919.

Anglo-German Fellowship (Estd 1935)

A pro-German organisation estd. partly at the behest of Ribbentrop via E. W. D. Tennant* and attracting considerable support from businessmen. Chairman, Lord Mount Temple.* Members included Lords Londonderry,* Sempill,* and Wellington,* Admiral Sir Barry Domvile,* and Lt. Col. Sir Thomas Moore, MP.*

Anti-Socialist Union

Initially estd. 1908 with the Duke of Devonshire as titular Pres. and Walter Long as Vice-Pres. but operating after WW1 as the Reconstruction Society and officially known thereafter as the Anti-Socialist and Anti-Communist Union. Chairman, Lord Mount Temple.* Members included R. D. Blumenfeld (editor of the *Daily Express*), Lady Askwith,* and Sir Harry Brittain, MP (later a member of the IDL* and the AGF*).

Army League (Estd Autumn 1936)

Chairman, L. S. Amery.* The organisation was committed to the improvement of defence capabilities. It was effectively superseded by the Army and Home and Empire Defence League in 1938 which was in turn superseded by the Citizen Service League* in 1939.

Ashley, Wilfred MP

Refer to Lord Mount Temple.

Askwith, Lady

Wife of the industrial relations expert, Lord Askwith (Pres. of the Middle Classes Union*). Lady Askwith was a member of the ASU,* the MCU,* the NCA* and the Eugenics Society* and was also linked with the National Association of Merchants and Manufacturers.

Balfour, George (1872–1941)

Con. MP Hampstead, 1918–41. Businessman with major interests in the electrical supply industry. Also a director of the Commercial Bank of Scotland. A persistent dissident who was a Diehard of 1921/2 and a member of the Council of the IDL* in the early 1930s.

Banbury, 1st Baron (1850–1936)

Sir Frederick Banbury. Con. MP Peckham, 1892–1906; City of London, 1906–24. Associated with the Unionist War Committee* during WW1; signed the Diehard Manifesto of March 1922. A director of the *Morning Post* from 1924.

Barnes, Maj. James Strachey (b. 1892)

Cousin to St Loe Strachey (ed. of the *Spectator*). Journalist and writer. Born in India; raised in Italy; converted to Roman Catholicism in 1914; served in France and Italy during WW1; attended Peace Conference as a supernumerary expert on Italian affairs. Became a member of the Italian Fascist Party and a friend of Mussolini. Sec.-Gen. of CINEF* from 1927. Reuter's correspondent with the Italian forces during the Abyssinian war. A member of the Royal Institute of International Affairs and a Fellow of the Royal Geographical Society. Last mentioned in *Who's Who* in 1943.

Beamish, Henry Hamilton (d. 1948)

Founder member of the Britons* who fled to Southern Africa soon after WW1 in order to avoid prosecution for libel and subsequently became associated with both Mussolini and Hitler (as early as 1923). Died in Rhodesia, leaving a large sum of money to Arnold Leese.*

Beaumont, Michael (1903–58)

Con. MP Aylesbury, 1929–38. Spoke in support of the BUF* after Olympia. Later a member of the English Mistery* and the English Array.*

Beazley, Prof. Sir (Charles) Raymond (b. 1868)

Hon. Vice-Pres. of the Royal Historical Society. Prof. of History, University of Birmingham, 1909–33. Expert on Russia who travelled and lectured extensively in Germany during the 1930s. Member of both the AGF* and Link.*

Beckett, John (1894–1964)

Lab. MP Gateshead, 1924–9; Peckham, 1929–31. ILP socialist who became a leading member of the BUF.* Left 1937. Founder member (with William Joyce*) of the National Socialist League,* also associated with the BCAEC,* the *New Pioneer*, and the BPP.*

Bedford, 11th Duke (1858–1940)

Herbrand Arthur Russell. Educated Balliol, Oxford. Succeeded to title in 1893. Refused office under Lord Salisbury in 1900 and subsequently declined a Colonial appointment. Chiefly interested in his estates and in science. Pres. of the Zoological Society from 1899; FRS, 1908. A Diehard of 1911 and a prominent member (with Willoughby de Broke) of the British League for the Support of Ulster and the Union (estd. 1913). A trustee of the *Morning Post*'s Diehard Fund in 1922.

Bedford, 12th Duke

Refer to Marquis of Tavistock.

Bellairs, Carlyon (1871–1955)

MP (Lib. later Con.) Kings Lynn, 1906–Jan. 1910; Maidstone, 1915–31. Associated with the National Efficiency Movement before WW1. An enthusiast for 'streamlined' government. Officially joined the BUF* in June 1934.

Benn, Sir Ernest (1875–1954)

Publisher and author. Estd. Ernest Benn Ltd. in 1923. Founder of the Society of Individualists and the Individualist Bookshop, 1926. A Liberal until 1929 (he was the son of the Lib. MP, Sir John Williams Benn), but subsequently a right-wing 'libertarian'.

Blakeney, Brig. Gen. Robert B.D. (b. 1872)

Entered army 1891. Fought in S. Africa and Egypt. Gen. Manager, Egyptian State Railway, 1919–23. Pres. of the British Fascists* from 1924 until 1926 when he and Rotha Lintorn-Orman* split over the attitude that they should adopt during the General Strike. Subsequently a member of the Nordic League,* the IFL* and the BUF.*

Boswell Press

An important right-wing publishing company created by the Duke of Northumberland* in 1921 and later controlled by Lady Houston.* Boswell published works by many right-wing activists including Oscar Boulton,* Dorothy Crisp, Admiral Domvile,* George Lane-Fox Pitt-Rivers,* Lord Sydenham* and Nesta Webster.*

Boulton, Lt. Col. Oscar

Educated Harrow and Oxford. An industrialist and author who established the Unity Band.*

British Commonwealth Union

Originally estd. c. 1915 as the Anti-German Union, then as the British Empire Union. Its titular heads after WW1 were Lord Derby and the Duke of Northumberland,* but its chief organiser was Patrick Hannon.* This was an 'anti-Bolshevik' organisation funded by industry. It gave birth to the Economic League* and in 1926 appeared to merge with the EIA.*

British Council Against European Commitments (Estd 1938)

Pres., Vt. Lymington.* Vice-Pres., William Joyce.* Hon. Sec., John Beckett.* An anti-(2nd World) war group linked with the *New Pioneer* which attracted support from many anti-Semites and ex-BUF* activists. Members included G. Lane-Fox Pitt-Rivers,* Capt. A. H. Ramsay,* Maj. J. F. C. Fuller* and A. K. Chesterton.*

British Council for Christian Settlement

A crypto-Fascist organisation associated with the BPP.* Sec. (1940), John Beckett.*

British Empire Union

Refer to BCU.

British Fascists (1923–35)

Initially known as the British Fascisti and after 1924 formally called the British Fascists Ltd. This was the first organisation in Britain to call itself Fascist (although a group known as the Loyalty League, estd. Oct. 1922, had already called for 'the fascisti in England'). Created by Rotha Lintorn-Orman,* the BFs attracted at one time or another, R. G. D. Blakeney,* Arnold Leese,* William Joyce* and others later to join the BUF* including E. G. Mandeville Roe and Neil Francis-Hawkins. In 1924 or '25 a breakaway organisation known as the National Fascisti* was established.

British Peoples' Party (Estd May 1939)

An 'anti-war' Party. Pres., Marquis of Tavistock* (later 12th Duke of Bedford), an ex-socialist Christian and Social Crediter. Gen. Sec., John Beckett.* Treasurer, Ben Greene, JP. Members included Vt. Lymington,* Anthony Ludovici,* Philip Mairet* and John Scanlon (ex-ILP). In July 1939 H. St. John Philby* represented the BPP at a by-election in Hythe, Kent. He was supported by a number of prominent pro-Germans and Fascists including Lady Pearson (sister to Henry Page Croft*) who was prospective parliamentary candidate for the BUF* in Canterbury.

British Union of Fascists (1932–40)

The major Fascist organisation in Britain. Estd. and led by Sir Oswald Mosley.* In 1936 it officially changed its title to the British Union of Fascists and National Socialists but referred to itself simply as the British Union.

British Workers' League (1919–c. 1925)

A 'patriotic labour' movement. Initially estd. as the British Workers' National League in March 1916. This organisation grew from Victor Fisher's anti-pacifist Socialist National Defence Committee (created 1915) but also attracted prominent Conservatives such as Lord Milner* and Waldorf Astor MP. In 1918 the BWL estd. the National Democratic and Labour Party which returned 10 MPs, but the movement was practically dead by 1922 and in 1925 the organisation changed its name to the Empire Citizens' League after which it became increasingly orthodox in its conservatism. Published the *Empire Citizen*.

Britons (Estd July 1919)

Founded by H. H. Beamish.* Vice-Chairman, Dr John Henry Clarke (chief consulting physician at the London Homeopathic Hospital). Members included Lord Sydenham,* Lt. Col. A. H. Lane,* Victor Marsden* and George P. Mudge (a lecturer at the London Medical School who had been a founding member of the Eugenics Society* and the Order of the Red Rose*). The Britons was an explicitly anti-Semitic organisation. From 1922 onwards its activities were mainly confined to the publication of anti-Semitic books.

Carlyle Club (Estd 1939)

An off-shoot of the National Socialist League* created by William Joyce* in order to attract 'respectable' support for pro-Nazi policies.

Carson, Sir Edward, 1st Bt. (1854–1935)

Con. MP Dublin University, 1892–1918; Belfast Duncairn, 1918–21; 1st Lord Admiralty, 1916–17; Minister without portfolio, 1917–18. Awarded a Judicial Life Peerage in 1921. Southern Irish leader of the Ulster Unionists until 1921. Associated with the anti-Semitic movement after WW1 (refer to Northumberland* *et al.*, Bibliography); signed the Diehard Manifesto in 1922; a Vice-Pres. of the IDL* in the early 1930s.

Chandos Group (Estd May 1926)

Established in the wake of the General Strike by the Social Crediter, W. T. Symons to promote ideas that would favour 'hierarchy' without destroying a sense of 'community'. The group was influenced by the ideas of the psychologist, Alfred Adler, by a Jugoslavian 'pan-humanist' called D. Mitrinovic, by the economic teachings of Maj. C. H. Douglas,* by ancient Indian and Greek cultures and by orthodox Christian doctrine. The movement attracted many of those later associated with the *New English Weekly*, including its editor, Philip Mairet* and (occasionally) T. S. Eliot.

Chesterton, A. K. (b. 1899)

Journalist. Cousin to G. K. Chesterton. Born in S. Africa where he lived until the early 1920s. Joined the BUF* in 1933; edited *Action*; left the BUF in March 1938. Subsequently associated with Vt. Lymington* and the *New Pioneer* circle. After WW2 he created the League of Empire Loyalists (1954) which fed into the National Front.

CINEF (Estd 1927)

Centre International d'Etudes sur la Fascisme. Created by the Swiss (Catholic) historian, H. de Vries de Heekelingen. It was intended to facilitate the study of Fascism and dispel the idea that Fascism and Catholicism were incompatible. J. S. Barnes* (Gen. Sec.) was the main representative of CINEF in Britain, but Lord Sydenham,* Prof. Edmund Gardner (a scholar of Italian literature) and Prof. Walter Starkie (a Spanish expert at Trinity College, Dublin) were also members of the Governing Body. In addition, Arnold Leese* was an occasional 'correspondent'.

Citizen Service League (Estd Jan. 1939)

Heir to the Army League* and a conscious imitation of the National Service League (estd. 1902 and led by Lord Roberts from 1905). Titular leaders: Lords Iliffe, Willingdon and Salisbury.* Actual leader (Chairman of Executive Committee) L. S. Amery.*

Colonial League (Estd 1937)

Urged resistance to the German demand for the return of the mandated territories. Pres., Lord Lugard (former colonial administrator; member, Permanent Mandates Commission of the League of Nations, 1922–35). Chairman, L. S. Amery.*

Colvin, Ian D. (1877–1938)

Scottish journalist and author. Worked as a journalist in India and S. Africa from 1900 to 1907. Became leader writer with the *Morning Post*, 1909. 'Honorary Editor' of the *Patriot* in 1922 and contributor to the anti-Semitic pot-boiler, *The Cause of the World Unrest* (1920, intro. H. A. Gwynne*).

Conservative and Unionist Movement (Estd June 1922)

Created by Lord Salisbury* as an anti-Coalition 'ginger group', but used as an alternative name for the Diehard movement in general after Salisbury was given nominal control of the *Morning Post*'s 'Diehard Fund' in July 1922. It was increasingly distant from Salisbury's own 'moderate' position. After the Carlton Club meeting Salisbury sought to disband the movement, but the members rejected this course of action on the advice of Edward Carson.* Fate thereafter unknown.

Cooper, Richard, 2nd Bt. (1874–1946)

Independent Unionist MP Walsall, 1910–22. Represented the National Party* after 1918.

Croft, Henry Page, 1st Bt. (1881–1947)

Con. MP Christchurch, Jan. 1910–18; Bournemouth, 1918–40. Parliamentary Under-Sec., War, 1940–5. A tariff reformer who created the National Party* in 1917 and was associated with almost every dissident Conservative organisation thereafter, including the EIA,* the Imperial Economic Unity Group,* the IDL* and the anti-appeasement lobby. He was also a director of the *Morning Post* after 1924 and Chancellor of the Primrose League, 1928–9. His sister, Lady Pearson, was prospective parliamentary candidate for the BUF* in Canterbury. Croft was described by E. T. Raymond as 'most impressive on first acquaintance . . . [and] . . . better heard only once' (*Outlook*, 31.1.20).

Domvile, Admiral Sir Barry (b. 1878)

Entered RN, 1892; Asst. Sec. CID, 1912–14; Naval Commander, 1914–19; Director, Plans Division, Admiralty, 1920–2; Chief of Staff, Mediterranean, 1922–5; Commander HMS Royal Sovereign, 1925–6; Director, Naval Intelligence, 1927–30; Commander 3rd Cruiser Squadron, Mediterranean, 1931–2; Pres. Royal Naval College, Greenwich, 1932–4. Knighted, 1932. Retired, 1936. Member AGF.* Established the Link* in 1937. Arrested under defence regulation 18B in 1940.

Dorman-Smith, Col. Sir Reginald (b. 1899)

Con. MP Petersfield, 1935–41; Min. of Agriculture and Fisheries, 1939–40; Gov. of Burma, 1941–6. Member of the English Mistery* and the English Array.*

Douglas, Lord Alfred (1870–1945)

Son of 8th Marquis of Queensberry and one-time lover of Oscar Wilde. In or around 1912 converted to Roman Catholicism. Proprietor and editor of the anti-Semitic journals, *Plain English* (1920–2) and, in association with H. Moore Pim (real name, A. Newman, an Ulster Protestant converted to Catholicism and violently opposed to Sinn Fein), *Plain Speech* (1922). Later associated with the pre-WW2 peace campaign.

Douglas, Maj. C. H. (1879–1952)

Engineer and manager who reached rank of Major in the Royal Flying Corps and RAF during WW1. Founding father of the Social Credit movement asociated with the Guild Socialist, A. R. Orage. Principal reconstruction adviser to the Govt. of Alberta (Canada), 1935–6. An anti-democrat who believed in a conspiracy of 'world Jewry, Freemasonry, International finance, Bolshevism and Nazism' (*DNB 1951–60*, p. 307).

Drage, Geoffrey (1860–1955)

Con. MP Derby, 1895–1900. Publicist and writer. Chairman, Finance Committee of the OMS.*

Economic League (Estd 1926)

Until 1926 the Economic Study Club of the BCU.* In April 1926 John Baker White, an acquaintance of Nesta Webster,* later a Con. MP for Canterbury (1945–53), was appointed Director. By the late 1930s it was closely associated with the Conservative Research Department but in 1937 linked briefly with the United Christian Front Committee.* The League was mostly run and supported by businessmen such as Sir Vincent Caillard (Director, Vickers Ltd.) who wanted to 'drop politics' from 'economic' questions. It still survives today, compiling blacklists of political and trade union activists for various employers.

Empire Economic Union (Estd July 1929)

Created by L. S. Amery* and 1st Baron Melchett (Alfred Mond, head of ICI, a former free-trade liberal by this time a protectionist Conservative). The organisation was a 'research and propaganda' unit for the tariff reform lobby. Chairman: Lord Lloyd.*

Empire Industries Association (Estd 1925)

A tariff reform 'ginger group' that was not exclusively right-wing but was dominated by its right-wing members. Practically subsumed the BCU* in 1926; gave birth to the Imperial Economic Unity Group* in 1930. Initially the EIA attracted Milner* (who died in 1925) and Neville Chamberlain. But by 1931 (when Chamberlain was at the Exchequer) the major activists were Croft,* Lord Lloyd,* L. S. Amery,* Patrick Hannon* and Herbert Williams MP (Parl. Sec., Board of Trade, 1928–9; later associated with the IDL*).

English Array (Estd 1936)

A ruralist organisation created by Vt. Lymington* after breaking with William Sanderson* and the English Mistery.* Most members of the Mistery appeared to join the Array.

English Mistery (Estd mid-1931)

An anti-democratic back-to-the-land organisation. Forerunner to the English Array* which saw itself as a 'school for leadership' and sought to promote the ideas presented in William Sanderson's* book, *Statecraft* (1927). Members included Vt. Lymington,* Anthony Ludovici,* Michael Beaumont* and Reginald Dorman-Smith.* Vt. Wolmer* and Lord Lloyd* were also sent English Mistery circulars although it is not clear that they asked for them.

Eugenics Society

First established in 1907 as the Eugenics Education Society. Adopted present title in 1926. A propaganda organisation in favour of voluntary sterilisation of the 'unfit'. During the inter-war period it attracted a variety of members with dissimilar political beliefs. Council members included right-wingers such as Lady Askwith,* Dean Inge* and Capt. G. Lane-Fox Pitt-Rivers,* but also included 'progressives' such as the scientists, J. B. S. Haldane and Julian Huxley. Internal disagreements and (perhaps) the rise of Nazism weakened the movement during the 1930s.

Finlay, 1st Vt. (1842–1929)

Sir Robert Bannatyne Finlay. Scottish MP who began life as a Liberal, became a Liberal Unionist and then a Conservative. Elevated to the Lords, 1916 (as Lord Chancellor). Signed the Diehard Manifesto of March 1922.

Fox, Sir Frank (b. 1874)

Journalist and author. Born in Australia and active during the 1890s in the Australian Labour Party. Came to England in 1909 and subsequently joined the *Morning Post*. Served with the Royal Field Artillery during WW1. Wounded twice in the Battle of the Somme. Refer to Bibliography.

Fuller, Maj. Gen. John F. C. (1878–1966)

Known as 'Boney' Fuller. Served in S. Africa and India prior to 1914; in France during 1915; and by the end of 1916 was Chief of Staff of the Tank Corps. After WW1 supported modernisation of the Army. Retired by the War Office in 1933. Joined BUF* in 1934. Associated with Lymington* and the *New Pioneer* after 1938 and regarded by the Nazis as a possible 'Quisling'. Fuller was a respected military strategist and an admirer of the mystic, Aleister Crowley.

Glasgow, 8th Earl (1874–1963)

Patrick James Boyle, DSO. Entered RN, 1888; Lieut., 1897; Commander RN, 1914–18 who was in Vladivostock in 1917. Landowner with estates in Ayr, Fife, Renfrew, Bute and Dumbarton. Member of the BFs* in the 1920s, linked with the BUF* and AGF* in the 1930s.

Gretton, Col. John, 1st Bt. (1867–1947)

Con. MP Derbyshire S., 1895–1906; Rutland, 1907–18; Burton, 1918–43. Director Bass (the brewers) and an exceptionally wealthy businessman. A leading Conservative rebel throughout the inter-war period associated with the Unionist Reconstruction Committee,* the Diehards of 1921/2, the OMS,* the IDL,* and the tariff agitation. He destroyed his papers before his death.

Gwynne, Howell Arthur (1865–1950)

Journalist. Organiser, Reuter's war service, Boer War. Editor of the *Standard*, 1904–11; editor of the *Morning Post*, 1911–37. This newspaper was closely associated with the Conservative Right and after 1924 was owned by right-wing Conservatives. In 1937 it was incorporated within the *Daily Telegraph*.

Gwynne, Rupert (1873–1924)

Con. MP Eastbourne, 1910–24. A prominent Diehard of 1921/2. Became a director of the *Morning Post* in the year that he died but not (it appears) related to H. A. Gwynne.*

Hall, Admiral Sir (William) Reginald (1870–1943)

Known as 'Blinker' Hall. Director, Naval Intelligence during WW1. Subsequently associated with covert anti-socialist organisations such as the National Security Union* and National Propaganda (refer to Liberty League*). Con. MP Liverpool W. Derby, 1919–23; Eastbourne, 1925–9. Trustee of the *Morning Post*'s Diehard Fund in 1922; made Principal Agent of the Conservative Party, 1923; implicated in the 'Zinoviev Letter' affair of 1924; appointed as the Organising Manager of the *British Gazette* during the General Strike.

Hannon, Patrick (1874–1963)

Irish businessman and Con. MP Birmingham Moseley, 1921–50. Associated with the BCU* and the EIA.* Vice-Pres. of the Federation of British Industries from 1925. Later a council member of the IDL.*

Houston, Lady Lucy (d. 1936)

Eccentric millionairess who owned and edited the *Saturday Review* from 1933 to 1936 and controlled the Boswell Press,* at least after the death of the Duke of Northumberland* in 1930. Between c. 1924 and 1936 she was also responsible for publishing the *Patriot*.

Imperial Economic Unity Group (Estd July 1930)

An off-shoot of the EIA.* Chairman: H. P. Croft.* Hon. Secs.: Henry Mond (2nd Baron Melchett) and Vt. Lymington.*

Imperial Fascist League (Estd 1929)

Run by Arnold Leese,* the IFL survived the creation of the BUF* in 1932 and preached an explicitly racist and anti-Semitic form of Nazism unlike all other Fascist groups except the National Workers' Party (estd. 1933 and run by Lt. Col. G. S. Hutchinson, a former Liberal). Members included R. B. D. Blakeney* (who came to the movement via the Nordic League*), Arthur Kitson,* Col. A. H. Lane* and William Sanderson.* Leese opposed the German demand for former colonies at the end of the 1930s but supported extermination of the Jews even after 1945. Leese was detained during the war but he and his wife later re-organised the movement as the National Socialist League with the help of money received from H. H. Beamish.* This organisation was run by Colin Jordan (later of the National Front).

Imperial Policy Group (Estd Dec. 1934)

Chairman: Vt. Wolmer.* Intended to channel discontent over India into an attack upon the imperial policy of the National Government and the leadership and organisation of the Conservative Party.

India Defence Committee

Founded by Henry Page Croft* in the early 1930s as a focus of opposition to the Government of India Bill in the House of Commons. Subsumed by the IDL* in 1933.

India Defence League (Estd 1933)

A confederation of the IDC* and the IES.* Pres., Lord Sumner;* Principal Vice-Pres., Lord Lloyd;* Chairman Exec. Committee, Vt. Wolmer;* Treasurer, Col. J. Gretton.* Full list of members, *Morning Post*, 2.6.33.

Indian Empire Society (Estd 1930)

The brainchild of Lord Sydenham,* sanctioned by Lord Salisbury.* Pres., Lord Sumner;* Sec., Sir Louis Stuart,* editor of the official journal of the IES (and later the IDL*), the *Indian Empire Review*.

Inge, William Ralph (1860–1954)

Eldest son of William Inge, Provost, Worcester College, Oxford. Educated Eton and Kings College, Cambridge. Elected Fellow and Tutor, Hertford College, Oxford, 1888. Dean of St Paul's Cathedral from 1911. Author and regular contributor to the *Evening Standard* (1921–46). His wooden features and pessimistic, anti-democratic, Tory views earned him the nickname of the 'Gloomy Dean'. A member of the Eugenics Society* (despite being physically defective, i.e. deaf), associated with the anti-war campaign of 1939.

January Club (Estd Jan. 1934)

A BUF* front organisation designed to attract 'respectable' support for Fascism. The first Chairman was Sir John Squire (editor of the *London Mercury*) but subsequently the organisation was run by Col. N. G. Thwaites* and Francis Yeats-Brown.* It attracted a wide range of supporters including Sir Charles Petrie,* G. Ward Price* and Lord Lloyd* (although he did not want his interest to be known).

Jerrold, Douglas (1893–1964)

Author and publisher. Educated Westminster and New College, Oxford but left to fight in WW1. Severely wounded during the Battle of the Somme. Civil servant, 1918–23. With Benn Bros. (publishers), 1923–8. Director, later Chairman of Eyre and Spottiswoode after 1929. Editor of the *English Review*, 1930–6. A Liberal prior to 1914, Jerrold was a staunch Catholic Conservative after 1918; an opponent of the India Act; an advocate of corporatism; a supporter of Franco; and a signatory of the Link* letter to *The Times*, 12.10.38. His associates included Petrie,* Lloyd* and Amery.* He was described by Wyndham Lewis as 'the brains of the Right' (*Blasting and Bombardiering* (Eyre and Spottiswoode, London, 1937), p. 306).

Joyce, William (1906–46)

Better known as Lord Haw-Haw (the Nazi broadcaster). Born in New York of a naturalised American father and an Irish mother. Moved to Ireland, 1909. Educated at Catholic schools although his mother was a Protestant and he was intensely pro-British. Moved to England, 1921. Attended Birkbeck College, London, 1923–7. Pres. of the Conservative Society. Obtained 1st class degree in English Literature. Joined the BFs* in 1923; subsequently associated with the National Fascisti.* Joined the BUF* in 1932. Formed the National Socialist League* in 1937 (with John Beckett*) and the Carlyle Club* in 1939. Member of the Right Club* after 1938 and the BCAEC.* Moved to Germany, August 1939. Hanged for treason by the British Government in 1946, although he was not a British citizen.

Kitson, Arthur (1859–1937)

A British engineer, inventor and currency reformer associated with the Left prior to 1914. In 1918 Kitson stood as a 'National' candidate for Nottingham Central. Subsequently he was associated with the Britons,* the New Constitutional Party,* the Social Credit movement and Arnold Leese* of the IFL.* He was also a friend of, and collaborator with, the German anti-Semite, Col. Fleischhauer who published the *Weltdienst*.

Knox, Maj. Gen. Sir Alfred (1870–1964)

British Military Attaché on the Russian front at the time of the revolution. Con. MP Wycombe, 1924–45. Member of the Exec. Committee of the IDL.* Later associated with the AGF.*

Lane, Col. Arthur H.

Served with Kitchener in Egypt, then with Milner* in S. Africa. Member of the Britons;* Chairman, National Citizens' Union* in 1927; author of *The Alien Menace* (1928); founder of the Militant Christian Patriots* c. 1928/9 which later published the *Free Press*; and one of the earliest members of the Unity Band.*

Leese, Arnold (1878–1956)

A vet who specialised in camels. Prior to WW1 worked in Africa and India. During WW1, volunteered for the Royal Army Veterinary Corps. After 1918 worked as a vet in Stamford. Retired 1928. Established the IFL* in 1929. Also linked with CINEF,* Arthur Kitson* and H. H. Beamish.* After WW2 Leese became 'the high priest of post-War neo-Nazism' (G. Thayer, *The British Political Fringe. A Profile* (Anthony Blond, London, 1965, 1968 edn), p. 15) and was closely associated with Colin Jordan (later of the National Front).

Liberty League (Estd March 1920)

An 'anti-Bolshevik' organisation headed by H. Rider Haggard (author of *King Solomon's Mines* etc.), Rudyard Kipling and Lord Sydenham.* It collapsed within a year because the treasurer ran off with the money. It was subsequently incorporated within National Propaganda which was run by Admiral Hall.*

Liberty Restoration League

Founded by Capt. Bernard Acworth.* Pres., Duke of Wellington.* Associated in 1937 with the United Christian Front Committee.*

Link (Estd Sept. 1937)

Chairman: Admiral Sir Barry Domvile.* The Link was a distinctly anti-Semitic counterpart to the AGF* which was famous for organising the 'Link letter' to *The Times*, 12.10.38, and which took over the *Anglo-German Review* in 1939. The editor of this journal, C. E. Carroll, was a member of Link and the AGF, and had formerly been the editor of the British Legion's newspaper. He and Domvile were both arrested in 1940.

Linlithgow, 2nd Marquis (1887–1952)

Victor Alexander John Hope. Civil Lord of the Admiralty, 1922–4; Viceroy and Gov. Gen. India, 1936–43. Signed the Diehard Manifesto, March 1922.

Appendix 155

Lintorn-Orman, Rotha (1895–1935)

Founder of the BFs.* Military background; Girl Guide leader before 1914; an ambulance driver during WW1; invalided home suffering from malaria, 1917; subsequently joined the British Red Cross Society. Thought (by the Special Branch) to have become an alcoholic after the creation of the BUF* undermined support for the BFs. Died at the age of 40.

Lloyd, 1st Bt. (1879–1941)

Sir George Ambrose Lloyd. Grandson of Thomas Lloyd (Director of Lloyd's Bank). Educated Eton and Trinity, Cambridge. Con. MP Staffordshire W., Jan. 1910–23; Governor of Bombay, 1918–23; Con. MP Eastbourne, 1924–5; High Commissioner, Egypt and the Sudan, 1925–9; Sec. of State for Colonies and Leader of the House of Lords, 1940–1. Chairman, EEU;* Principal Vice-Pres., IDL;* associated with Douglas Jerrold* and the January Club.* Said (by the Special Branch) to have offered to join the BUF* in January 1935, but later associated with the anti-appeasement lobby.

Londonderry, 7th Marquis (1878–1949)

Charles Stewart Henry Vane-Tempest-Stewart, Vt. Castlereagh. An Ulsterman. Con. MP Maidstone, 1906–15; Parl. Under-Sec. for Air, 1920–1; signed the Diehard Manifesto, 1922; Sec. of State for Air, 1931–5; met with and befriended Hitler, 1936; associated with the peace campaign of 1938/9 (refer to Bibliography).

Ludovici, Capt. Anthony Mario (1882–1971)

Journalist and author of more than 30 published works. Presumably of Italian abstraction, but born in London. One-time secretary to the sculptor, Rodin; translated Nietzsche into English; member Royal Field Artillery; fought in France during WW1; attached to intelligence staff, War Office, April 1917; editor of *Air*; member of English Mistery* and English Array;* closely associated with Vt. Lymington* and the *New Pioneer* (1938–40); author of *Jews and the Jews in England* (1938) under the pseudonym of Cobbett; also a member of the Selection Committee of the Right Book Club.*

Lymington, Vt. (b. 1898)

Gerald Wallop, later 9th Earl Portsmouth. Born in Chicago; raised in Wyoming; educated Winchester and Balliol, Oxford; served as Lieut. 2nd Life Guards and Guards Machine Gun regiment during WW1; became Viscount in 1926 when his childless uncle died. Con. MP Basingstoke, 1929–34. Hon. Sec., IEUG;* founder member of the English Mistery,* English Array,* BCAEC* and the *New Pioneer*. Despite his anti-(2nd World) war stance, he later became chairman of the Navy League.

Mairet, Philip (1886–1975)

Full name, Phillipe Auguste Mairet. Son of a Swiss watchmaker who lived and worked in Britain as a draughtsman, stained-glass craftsman, author and journalist. Associated with the Chandos Group;* editor of the *New English Weekly* after 1934; linked in the late 1930s with Vt. Lymington's* *New Pioneer* and with the BPP.*

Marsden, Victor

Foreign correspondent with the *Morning Post* who translated the *Protocols of the Learned Elders of Zion* into English. A member of the Britons.*

Maxse, Leopold (1864–1932)

Proprietor and editor of the *National Review* of great importance to the Right before 1914 but less influential after 1918. Brother-in-law to Lord Milner* after 1921.

McNeill, Ronald (Lord Cushenden) (1861–1934)

Con. MP St Augustine's, Kent, 1911–18; Canterbury, 1918–27. Parliamentary Under-Sec., F.O., 1922–4 and 1924–5; Financial Sec., Treasury, 1925–7; Chancellor of the Duchy of Lancaster, 1927–9. A member of the Ulster Unionist Council's Provisional Government of 1914; joint head of the Unionist War Committee* after 1916; and a prominent Diehard of 1921/2 associated with Salisbury.* A 'moderate' Conservative by the mid-1920s.

Middle Classes Union (Estd 1919)

Pres., Lord Askwith. Founded 'to withstand the rapacity of the manual worker and profiteer' (*The Times*, 7.3.19) and to provide essential services during a general strike. In 1921 it became the National Citizens' Council and by 1926 this had become the National Citizens' Union.*

Militant Christian Patriots (Estd c. 1928/29)

Created by Col. A. H. Lane* as an anti-liberal, anti-pacifist and anti-Semitic organisation dedicated to the principles of 'muscular' (Conservative) Christianity. From 1935 to 1940 the MCPs published the *Free Press* which thought of the Conservative Party as 'Fabian' and was particularly concerned about the organisation known as Political and Economic Planning. The MCPs attracted both A. K. Chesterton* and Joseph Banister (a member of the Britons*).

Milner, Lord Alfred (1854–1925)

High Commissioner, S. Africa, 1897–1905; Min. without Portfolio, 1916–18; Sec. of State for War, 1918–19; for Colonies, 1919–21. A leading Social Imperialist associated with the National Efficiency movement. Estd. Round Table, 1910; a

Diehard of 1911; estd. the British Covenanters, 1914; Chairman of National Service League, 1915; linked with the BWL* in 1918. A hero of the Right before 1914, of less influence after 1918. In 1921 he married the sister of Leopold Maxse* who took over the editorship of the *National Review* after her brother's death in 1932.

Moore, Lt. Col. Sir Thomas, 1st Bt. (1886–1971)

Con. MP Ayr Burghs, 1925–50; Ayr, 1950–64. Spoke in support of the BUF* in 1934; opposed the Government of India Bill, but only until Feb. 1935; later associated with the *Anglo-German Review* (Aug. 1937), the journal of the AGF* and Link.*

Mosley, Sir Oswald, 6th Bt. (1896–1980)

Con. MP Harrow, 1918–22; Independent MP Harrow, 1922–4; Lab. MP Smethwick, 1926–31; Chancellor of the Duchy of Lancaster, 1929–30. Created New Party Feb. 1931 and the BUF* in Oct. 1932.

Mount Temple, Lord (1867–1939)

(William) Wilfred Ashley. Con. MP Blackpool, 1906–18; Fylde, 1918–22; New Forest, 1922–32. Chairman of the ASU;* a Diehard MP of 1921/2; later Chairman of the AGF.*

National Air League (Estd c. 1934)

Founded by Lord Rothermere* with the help of Lady Houston* (proprietor of the *Saturday Review*) in order to publicise the threat from the air.

National Citizens' Union (Estd c. 1926)

Superseded the MCU* but was organised more on a local than a national basis. In 1927 Col. A. H. Lane* became the NCU's Chairman. In 1937 it was associated with the United Christian Front Committee.*

National Constitutional Association (Estd 1921)

Successor to the National Party* after it was officially disbanded in Jan. 1921 (although the name was not adopted until April). Headed by Lord Ampthill* and including Lady Askwith.* The NCA was amalgamated with the Conservative and Unionist Movement* in Oct. 1922.

National Fascisti (Estd 1924 or 1925)

A splinter group that broke from the BFs* because they considered the organisation to be insufficiently radical. William Joyce* was at one time a member. Described by Colin Cross as a mixture of 'Ku Klux Klan and Undergraduate rag' (*The Fascists in Britain* (London, 1961), p. 61).

National Party (Estd 1917)

Founded by Henry Page Croft* with Richard Cooper* and Lord Ampthill* (elected President in 1919). An ultra-Conservative organisation designed to appeal to 'patriotic labour'. Manifesto written by F. S. Oliver.* The party was a flop. It originally took eight MPs from the Unionist Party but two resigned early, one died before the 1918 election, another was too ill to stand, a fifth member returned to the Conservative Party, and a sixth withdrew in the face of Conservative opposition. The party eventually fielded 27 candidates in 1918. Eleven lost their deposit and only Croft and Cooper (the two remaining MPs) were returned — both without Conservative opposition. The party was disbanded in Jan. 1921 and reconstituted as the NCA.* Croft and Cooper re-joined the Conservative Party in April 1921.

National Security Union (Estd 1919)

An 'anti-Bolshevik' organisation closely related to the Unionist Reconstruction Committee.* Members included Henry Page Croft* and Admiral Hall.*

National Socialist League (Estd 1937)

Founded by William Joyce*, John Beckett* and John Angus McNab in March 1937 after they had been dismissed from the staff of the BUF.* Joyce later established an associated 'front' organisation known as the Carlyle Club.* The NSL was linked with Count Potocki* and financed (it appears) by A. C. Scrimgeour, a stockbroker who had previously donated large amounts of money to the BUF.*

New Constitutional Party (Estd Dec. 1926)

Intended to unite 'seasoned members of the Conservative Party' and to establish 'a Party within a Party'. Headed by William Marshall Freeman and including (by 1929) Arthur Kitson.*

Nordic League (Estd 1933)

A racialist organisation that attracted both R. B. D. Blakeney* and Capt. A. H. Ramsay* but was absorbed by the IFL* shortly after its creation.

Northumberland, 8th Duke (1880–1930)

Alan Ian Percy. Educated Eton and Christ Church, Oxford. Joined Grenadier Guards, 1900; served in S. Africa (1901–2) and Egypt (1907–10); retired with rank of Major in 1912. Worked for the intelligence dept. of the War Office during WW1. Succeeded to title in 1918. Played a prominent part in the Diehard Revolt of 1921/2, founded the Boswell Press* in 1921 and in Feb. 1922 founded the anti-Semitic journal, the *Patriot*. (After 1924 the *Patriot* was published by Lady Houston* who also took control of the Boswell Press.) A major landowner and coal owner who was Chairman of the Board of Directors of the *Morning Post* after 1924. Highly religious, although (like other members of the Percy family) he belonged to a sect known as the Catholic Apostolic Church. J. G. Lockhart and Lady Craik, writing as 'Janitor', said of the Duke that he 'was not quite a tiger, but he had at least the appearance and the ferocity of a large and articulate ferret' (*The Feet of the Young Men. Some Candid Comments on the Rising Generation* (Duckworth, London, 1928), p. 131).

O'Dwyer, Sir Michael (1864–1940)

Indian administrator. Lieut. Gov. of the Punjab, 1912–19 (which encompassed the Amritsar Massacre of 1919). O'Dwyer supported General Dyer; subsequently became a member of Lord Esher's committee on the organisation of the Indian Army, 1919–20. An anti-Semite of the early 1920s associated with Northumberland.* A prominent member of the Exec. Committee of the IDL* in the 1930s. Shot dead in London by an Indian nationalist.

Oliver, Frederick Scott (1864–1934)

A Scottish businessman (who made Debenham's famous) and author interested in federalism (especially at the time of the Ulster Crisis). A Social Imperialist associated with Milner* and the Round Table movement but also with Carson,* Amery* and the National Party* (whose manifesto he wrote). He identified briefly with the Right but lost sympathy with the Diehards after 1922.

Order of the Red Rose (Estd 1917)

A patriotic 'Bond Burning' organisation that was anti-Semitic and hostile to finance capitalism. Founding members included William Sanderson,* George Mudge (of the Britons*), and Arthur Gray (Master of Jesus College, Cambridge).

Organisation for the Maintenance of Supplies (Estd Sept. 1925)

A government-inspired but independently run organisation designed to facilitate the maintenance of essential supplies during a general strike. It was not a right-wing 'ginger group' although Col. Gretton was treasurer (for a while), the President of the OMS was Lord Hardinge of Penshurst (a former Viceroy of India who later signed the Link* letter), and one of its leading members, Sir James Rennell Rodd, was later linked with the January Club.* The OMS was used by William Joynson-Hicks in an attempt to destroy the BFs* during the General Strike of May 1926 (refer to Ch. 2, n. 36).

Petrie, Sir Charles (1895–1977)

Irish Baronet (3rd Bt. Carrowcarden). Prolific historian and journalist. Catholic pro-Fascist but anti-Nazi. Educated privately and at Corpus Christi, Oxford. Served with RGA, 1915–19; attached War Cabinet Office, 1918–19; foreign editor of the *English Review*, 1931–7; editor of the *Fascist Review* in 1934 also associated with the January Club.* An enthusiastic corporatist and monarchist.

Philby, Harry St John Bridger (1885–1960)

Educated Westminster and Trinity Coll., Cambridge (1st in Modern Languages). Joined Indian Civil Service, 1907. Worked as a linguist in Mesopotamia during WW1. Chief British representative in Trans-Jordania, 1921–4 (in succession to T. E. Lawrence). Subsequently became unofficial adviser to King Saud of Arabia and embraced the Moslem faith. An ex-socialist, Philby returned to Britain in 1939 and stood as parliamentary candidate for the BPP* at the Hythe by-election, July 1939. In 1940 he was arrested (in India) and detained (in England) under defence regulation 18B. After the war he returned to Arabia.

Pitt-Rivers, Capt. George Lane-Fox (1890–1966)

Grandson of the famous General. West Country landowner; owner-director of the Pitt-Rivers Museum, Oxford. Life member of the Eugenics Society;* a social anthropologist who was Gen. Sec. of the International Union for the Scientific Investigation of Population. An anti-Semite associated with the BCAEC* who signed the Link* letter to *The Times* in Oct. 1938.

Potocki, Count of Montalk (b. 1903)

Geoffrey Wladislas Vaile. Born in New Zealand. He believed himself to be heir to the throne of Poland and declared himself King Wladislaw V in Dec. 1939. He lived in France and in London where he published the *Right Review*. He modelled himself on Lord Byron, was imprisoned for six months in 1932 for publishing obscene poetry, and was regarded by the police as 'a sexual pervert'. In 1937 he was linked with the National Socialist League* and was thought (by John Beckett*) to be an intimate friend of Bryan Guinness (formerly married to Diana Mosley) from whom the National Socialist League hoped to attract funds. After WW2 Potocki remained 'moderately pro-Fascist' and became a Hindu.

Price, George Ward (b. 1886)

Journalist and director of Associated Newspapers Ltd. Educated St Catherine's College, Cambridge. Joined *Daily Mail* in 1909; press correspondent at the Dardanelles during WW1; subsequently a European specialist much-impressed by Mussolini and Hitler. Linked with the January Club* in 1934. A prominent pro-German until March 1939.

Ramsay, Capt. Archibald H. (1894–1955)

Scottish. Educated Eton and Sandhurst. Invalided out of the army during WW1. Con. MP Peebles, 1931–45. Member of the Nordic League* who established the United Christian Front Committee* and the Right Club.* Arrested under defence regulation 18B in 1940.

Reconstruction Society (Estd 1919)

An alternative title for the ASU.*

Right Book Club (Estd 1937)

A counterpart to the Left Book Club run by W. and G. Foyles Ltd. The Selection Committee consisted of: Lt. Col. N. G. Thwaites* (also Chairman of the January Club*); Capt. Anthony Ludovici* (of the English Mistery* etc.); Trevor Blakemore (a poet); Derek Walker-Smith (editor of the *English Review* from July 1936, the indirect successor to Douglas Jerrold*); and Collinson Owen (a fanatical anti-Bolshevik who occasionally contributed to the *Daily Mail* see, e.g., 2.7.31).

Right Club (Estd May 1939)

Founded by Capt. A. H. Ramsay MP.* A pro-Nazi, anti-war organisation. Members included William Joyce* and the Duke of Wellington.*

Rothermere, Vt. (1868–1940)

Harold Sidney Harmsworth, younger brother of Northcliffe. Baron, 1914. Viscount, 1919. Sec. of State for Air, 1917–18. Proprietor of the *Daily Mail* (which supported the BUF* for the first six months of 1934). Instrumental in the creation of the National Air League,* and the UEP.* Described by L. S. Amery as a 'perfect specimen of the plutocrat cad' (*Diary*, 8.11.18).

Royalist International (Estd May 1929)

Founded by Herbert Vivian* to oppose Bolshevism and restore monarchy but in practice pro-Fascist. Published the *Royalist International Herald*.

Salisbury, 4th Marquis (1861–1947)

James E. H. G. Cecil. Eldest son of the famous Lord Salisbury. Educated Eton and University College, Oxford. Con. MP Darwen, 1885–92; Rochester, 1893–1903; succeeded to Peerage, 1903 and appointed Lord Privy Seal. Pres. of the Board of Trade until 1905. A Diehard of 1911 and supposed 'leader' of the Diehards in 1921/2 (refer to Conservative and Unionist Movement*). Made Leader of the House of Lords in 1925; resigned post in 1931. Subsequently a leading opponent of the Government of India Act (1935) and instrumental in the creation of the IES.* Inactive in the foreign policy disputes of the late 1930s. Salisbury was widely respected within the Conservative Party but was less of a 'pragmatist' than the party leaders and less of a 'radical' than most Conservative dissidents.

Sanderson, William

Freemason and author. Associated with the Order of the Red Rose,* the English Mistery* and the IFL.*

Selborne, 2nd Earl (1859–1942)

William Waldegrave Palmer. Liberal Unionist Chief Whip; Under-Sec. of State for the Colonies, 1895–1900; First Lord of the Admiralty, 1900–1905; High Commissioner and Gov. Gen. S. Africa, 1905–10; Pres. Board of Agriculture, 1915–16. A Diehard of 1911 closely associated with Lord Salisbury* during the inter-war period.

Selborne, 3rd Earl

Refer to Vt. Wolmer.

Sempill, 19th Baron (1893–1965)

Col. William Francis Forbes-Sempill. Scottish Peer, engineer, author and airman. A Diehard of 1911; a council member of the Air League;* Chairman of the Royal Aeronautical Society in 1926 and Pres., 1927–30; Chairman, London Chamber of Commerce, 1931–5. A pro-Fascist who was associated with the BUF* via Geoffrey Dorman (editor of *Action* and sub-editor of the *Aeroplane*). A friend of Ribbentrop from 1933; later a council member of Link.*

Stuart, Sir Louis (1859–1949)

Member of the judicial branch of the Indian Civil Service. Sec. to the IES.* Council member of the IDL.* Editor of the *Indian Empire Review*, later associated with Lymington's* *New Pioneer*.

Sumner, 1st Vt. (1859–1934)

John Andrew Hamilton. Life Peer, 1913. Viscount, 1927. Judge. Educated at Balliol College, Oxford; later a Prize Fellow of Magdalen College, Oxford (1882–9). Signed the Diehard Manifesto in March 1922. President of the IES* and the IDL.*

Sydenham of Combe, Lord (1848–1933)

Sir George Sydenham Clarke. Sec. Colonial Defence Committee, War Office, 1885–92; Member Committee on War Office Re-organisation, 1900–1; Gov. Victoria, 1901–4; Member War Office Reconstruction Committee, 1904; Sec. Committee of Imperial Defence, 1904–7; Gov. Bombay, 1907–13. Member of the Liberty League,* the Britons,* CINEF* and the IES.* Also associated with the Duke of Northumberland's* journal, the *Patriot*. His wife ran the BF's* Children's Club.

Tavistock, Marquis of (1885–1953)

Hastings, W. S. Russell, later 12th Duke of Bedford. A socialist and Christian pacifist who established the BPP* in 1939.

Tennant, Ernest W. D.

Merchant banker and cousin to Margot Asquith. Befriended Ribbentrop in the early thirties and was instrumental in the formation and financing of the AGF.*

Thwaites, Col Norman (b. 1872)

Served in Boer War with the S. African Light Horse Regiment and in WW1 with the Royal Irish Dragoon Guards. Stood (unsuccessfully) as Con. Candidate, Hillsborough, Sheffield, 1924. A friend of Francis Yeats-Brown;* member (later Chairman) of the January Club*; Sec. of the Air League*; editor of the Journal, *Air*; Hon. Sec. of the English Speaking Union; and a member of the Selection Committee of the Right Book Club.* Last listed in *Who's Who* in 1956.

Unionist Business Committee (Estd 1915)

A backbench pressure group headed by Walter Long, W. A. S. Hewins and Edward Carson* intended to act as a barometer of Conservative 'rank and file' sentiment during the war.

Unionist Reconstruction Committee (Estd c. 1918)

Successor to the Unionist War Committee.* Members included Carson* and Gretton.* Closely associated with the National Security Union.*

Unionist War Committee (Estd Jan. 1916)

Created in order to support a 'vigorous prosecution of the War'. Headed by Sir Frederick Banbury* and Ronald McNeill,* both of whom later signed the Diehard Manifesto of March 1922.

United Christian Front Committee (Estd Sept. 1937)

Chairman: Capt. A. H. Ramsay.* This organisation sought to present the 'true facts of the War in Spain' and was linked in 1937 with the National Citizens' Union,* the Liberty Restoration League,* and the British Empire League (which had been formed in 1891 as the London branch of the Imperial Federation League but was chaired for some time after 1913 by Lord Sydenham*). However, these other organisations were quickly repelled by Ramsay's blatant pro-Nazi anti-Semitism.

United Empire Party (Estd Feb. 1930)

Created by Beaverbrook and Rothermere* to press for tariffs and embarrass Baldwin.

Unity Band (Estd c. 1930)

Intended to provide a united right-wing Conservative/Fascist front. Committed to 'order in politics' and 'freedom in economics'. Led by Lt. Col. Oscar Boulton* and supported by Col. A. H. Lane.* The Unity Band published the *British Lion* which had been an official publication of the BFs* until 1929. It was later associated with the *Patriot* (estd. by the Duke of Northumberland*).

Vivian, Herbert (b. 1865)

Educated Harrow and Trinity College, Cambridge. A journalist with the *Morning Post* and the *Daily Express* who met Mussolini and D'Annunzio in 1920 and was subsequently a pro-Fascist as well as a monarchist. In 1929 he created the Royalist International.*

Webster, Nesta H.

Anti-Semitic author. Grand-daughter of Philip Nicholas Shuttleworth (Warden of New College, Oxford, later Bishop of Chichester) and daughter of R. C. L. Bevan (head of Barclay's Bank). She began writing as a hobby but became convinced that a Jewish world conspiracy existed after her book on the French Revolution (which argued a similar case for 1789) was badly received. She subsequently became the leading anti-Semite of the period; was closely linked with the *Patriot*; joined the BF's* in 1926; was favoured by the *Saturday Review* during the 1930s; and is still revered by the National Front today.

Wellington, 5th Duke (1876–1941)

Arthur Charles Wellesley. Succeeded father, 1934. Educated Eton and Trinity College, Cambridge. Fought for the Grenadier Guards in the Boer War (1900). Landowner. Pres. of the Liberty Restoration League.* Member of the Right Club* and the AGF.*

Wilson, Lt. Col. Sir Arnold (1884–1940)

Con. MP Hitchin, 1933–40. Editor of the *Nineteenth Century and After* from 1935. A prominent supporter of appeasement until March 1939.

Wolmer, Vt. (1877–1971)

Roundell Cecil Palmer, 3rd Earl Selborne, known as 'Top'. Con. MP Newton, Dec. 1910–18; Aldershot, 1918–40. Parliamentary Sec., Board of Trade, 1922–4; Asst. Postmaster General, 1924–9; Min. of Economic Warfare, 1942–5. A Diehard of 1921/2 in sympathy with Salisbury* but increasingly radical thereafter. Chairman Exec. Committee of the IDL;* vaguely associated with the English Mistery;* Chairman of the Imperial Policy Group;* later associated with Churchill and the anti-appeasers.

Yeats-Brown, Francis (1886–1944)

Author. Born in Genoa. Served with the Indian Army until 1924. Asst. Ed. *Spectator*, 1926–31; Editor *Everyman* 1933; famous for writing *Bengal Lancer* (1930). A pro-Fascist and pro-Nazi, linked with the January Club* and the peace movement of 1939 even after Czechoslovakia, but distrustful of Mosley and of Hitler.

SELECT BIBLIOGRAPHY

(A) Manuscript Sources

(i) Private Papers and Public Records

8th Duke of Northumberland, Alnwick Castle, Alnwick.
Austen Chamberlain, University Library, Birmingham.
Henry Page Croft, Churchill College, Cambridge.
Admiral Sir Reginald Hall, Churchill College, Cambridge.
David Margesson, Churchill College, Cambridge.
Stanley Baldwin, University Library, Cambridge.
Leopold Maxse, West Sussex Record Office, Chichester.
F. S. Oliver, National Library of Scotland, Edinburgh.
4th Marquis Salisbury, Hatfield House, Hatfield.
Lord Sydenham of Combe, British Library, London.
Patrick Hannon, House of Lords Record Office, London.
Labour Party Archives (Fascism), Labour Party HQ, London.
Home Office Files (Mosley), Public Record Office, London.
Conservative Party Archives, Bodleian Library, Oxford.
Geoffrey Dawson, Bodleian Library, Oxford.
H. A. Gwynne, Bodleian Library, Oxford.
2nd Earl Selborne, Bodleian Library, Oxford.
3rd Earl Selborne, Bodleian Library, Oxford.
Sir Louis Stuart, Bodleian Library, Oxford.
Geoffrey Drage, (OMS), Christ Church, Oxford.
H. St. J. Philby, Middle East Centre, St. Anthony's College, Oxford.

(ii) Unpublished Theses etc.

B. L. Farr, 'The Development and Impact of Right-wing Politics in Great Britain, 1903–1932', Ph.D., Univ. of Illinois at Chicago Circle, 1976.
D. M. Geiger, 'British Fascism as Revealed in the BUF's Press', Ph.D., New York Univ., 1963.
J. M. McEwen, 'Unionist and Conservative Members of Parliament, 1914–1939', Ph.D., Univ. of Lon., 1959.
J. Morell, 'The Life and Opinions of A. S. Leese', M.A., Univ. of Sheffield, 1974.
G. Peele, 'Dissent, Faction and Ideology in the Conservative Party; some Reflections on the Inter-war Period', paper prepared for the ECPR Joint Session on Conservatism, Brussels, 1979 (based upon 'The Conservative Party and Opposition to the Government of India Act, 1929–1935', B.Phil., Oxford, 1972).

(B) Printed Sources

(a) Published Papers and Diaries

Barnes, J. and Nicolson, D. (eds.), *The Leo Amery Diaries*, 2 vols. (Hutchinson, London, 1980–1)

Gilbert, M. (ed.) *W. S. Churchill*, vol. V, Companion. Documents, 1929–1935. (Heinemann, London, 1981)
Higgins, D. S. (ed.) *The Private Diaries of Sir Henry Rider Haggard, 1914–1925* (Cassell, London, 1980)
James, R. R. (ed.) *Memoirs of a Conservative, J. C. C. Davidson's Memoirs and Papers, 1910–1937* (Weidenfeld and Nicolson, London, 1969)
Nicolson, N. (ed.) *Harold Nicolson, Diaries and Letters*, 3 vols. (Collins, London, 1966–8)
Ramsden, J. (ed.) *Real Old Tory Politics. The Political Diaries of Robert Sanders, Lord Bayford, 1910–1935* (Historians Press, London, 1984)

(b) Newspapers and Journals

Dates of special interest and/or publication given where appropriate.

Action (1931)
Action (1936–40)
Aeroplane (1934–9)
Anglo-German News (1934)
Anglo-German Review (1936–9)
Blackshirt (1933–9)
British Fascism (1930–4)
British Fascist Bulletin (1924–5)
British Lion (1926–9; 1932–40)
British Union News (Bethnal Green edition, 1939)
British Union Quarterly (1937)
Briton (1922–5)
Citizen Service (1939)
Daily Express
Daily Mail
Enemy (1927–9)
Englishman (1919–20)
English Race (1918–36)
English Review (1931–7)
Everyman (1933)
Fascist (1929–39)
Fascist Quarterly (1935–6)
Free Press (1935–40)
G.K.'s Weekly (1925–38)
Hidden Hand (1920–4)
Indian Empire Review (1931–5)
Jewish Chronicle
Morning Post
National Opinion (1918–23)
National Review (1918–32)
Nationalist (1939)
New Britain (1934)
New English Weekly (1932–9)
New Pioneer (1938–40)
Nineteenth Century and After
Patriot (1922–40)
People's Post (1939–40)
Plain Dealer (1930–4)
Plain English (1920–2)

Plain Speech (1921)
Quarterly Gazette of the English Array (1937)
Right Review (1936—47)
Saturday Review (1933—6)
Spectator
The Times
Veteran (1921—2)
Veteran and Briton (1922)
Weekly Review (1938—40)

(c) Contemporary Books, Pamphlets and Articles (including Autobiographies etc. published after 1939)

Allen, W. E. D. (as James Drennan) *The BUF, Oswald Mosley and British Fascism* (Murray, London, 1934)
—— *Fascism in Relation to British History and Character* (BUF, London, 1936)
Amery, L. S. *National and Imperial Economics* (National Unionist Association, Westminster, 1924)
—— *The Empire in the New Era* (Arnold, London, 1928)
—— *Empire and Prosperity* (Faber, London, 1931)
—— *A Plan of Action* (Faber, London, 1932)
—— *The Forward View* (G. Bles, London, 1935)
—— *The German Colonial Claim* (Chambers, London, 1939)
—— *My Political Life*, 3 vols. (Hutchinson, London, 1953—5)
Anti-Socialist Union *The ASU Course in Anti-Socialism* (Westminster, 1926)
—— *The ASU Course in Elementary Economics* (Westminster, 1926)
—— *Booklets 1—3* (London, 1935—8)
Banister, J. *Our Judaeo-Irish Labour Party* (Britons, London, 1931)
Barnes, J. S. *The Universal Aspects of Fascism* (Williams and Norgate, London, 1928)
—— *Fascism* (Home University Library, London, 1931)
—— *Half a Life* (Eyre and Spottiswoode, London, 1933)
—— *Half a Life Left* (Eyre and Spottiswoode, London, 1937)
Beamish, H. H. *The Jew's Who's Who* (Britons, London, 1920)
Belloc, H. (and Chesterton, C.) *The Party System* (Swift, London, 1911)
—— *The Servile State* (Foulis, London, 1913)
—— *The Jews* (Constable, London, 1922)
—— 'Capitalism and Communism — the Hellish Twins', *English Review*, Feb. 1932
Benn, Sir. E. *The Confessions of a Capitalist* (Hutchinson, London, 1925)
—— *The Return to Laisser-Faire* (Benn, London, 1928)
—— *Account Rendered, 1900—1930* (Benn, London, 1931)
—— *Happier Days* (Benn, London, 1949)
—— *The State the Enemy* (Benn, London, 1953)
Birch, L. *Why They Join the Fascists* (People's Press, London, 1932)
Blakeney, R. 'British Fascism', *Nineteenth Century and After*, Jan. 1925
Boulton, O. *Fads and Phrases* (Boswell, London, 1930)
—— *The Way Out* (Boswell, London, 1934)
British Peoples' Party *The Truth About This War* (London, 1939)
British Union of Fascists *Red Violence and Blue Lies* (BUF, London, 1934)
—— *Notes for Speakers, No. 9. The Corporate State* (BUF, London, 1935)
—— *Cotton, India and You* (BUF, London, 1936)
Cardozo, H. *March of a Nation* (Right Book Club, London, 1937)

Catlin, Sir G. E.C. 'Fascist Stirrings in Great Britain', *Current History*, Feb. 1934
Chesterton, A. K. *Oswald Mosley: Portrait of a Leader* (Action Press, London, 1937)
────── *Why I Left Mosley* (London, 1938)
Chesterton, G. K. *What's Wrong with the World* (Cassell, London, 1910)
Churchill, W. S. *The Gathering Storm* (Cassell, London, 1948)
CINEF *A Survey of Fascism* (CINEF Yearbook, London, 1928)
Clarke, E. G. *The British Union and the Jews* (BUF, Westminster, 1938)
Clarke, Dr J. H. *England under the Heel of the Jews* (Britons, London, 1918)
────── *Democracy of Shylocracy?* (Britons, London, 1921)
Cobbett (Pseud. A. M. Ludovici) *Jews and the Jews in England* (Boswell, London, 1938)
Colvin, I. D. *The Germans in England* (National Review, London, 1915)
────── *The Unseen Hand in English History* (National Review, London, 1917)
────── *The Life of General Dyer* (Blackwood, Edinburgh, 1929)
────── *The Life of Lord Carson*, vols. 2 and 3 (Gollancz, London, 1932–6)
Conservative Party *Gleanings and Memoranda* (1918–33)
────── *Politics in Review* (1934–9)
Cooper, A. Duff *Old Men Forget* (Hart Davis, London, 1953)
Crisp, D. *The Rebirth of Conservatism* (Methuen, London, 1931)
────── *Christ is no Pacifist* (Boswell, London, 1937)
────── *England — Mightier Yet* (National Review, London, 1939)
Croft, H. P. *Towards a National Policy* (National Review, London, 1916)
────── *Spain, the Truth at Last* (Bournemouth, 1937)
────── *My Life of Strife* (Hutchinson, London, 1948)
Daily Mail *The Economic Crisis* (London, 1931)
────── *The Daily Mail Blue Book on the Indian Crisis* (London, 1931)
Demant, Rev. V. A. *God, Man and Society* (Student Christian Movement Press, London, 1933)
Domvile, Adm. Sir B. *By and Large* (Hutchinson, London, 1936)
────── *Look to Your Moat* (Hutchinson, London, 1937)
────── *From Admiral to Cabin Boy* (Boswell, London, 1947)
Driberg, T. *Mosley? No!* (W. H. Allen, London, n.d.)
Eliot, T. S. *The Idea of a Christian Society* (Faber, London, 1939)
────── *Notes Towards the Definition of Culture* (Faber, London, 1948)
Empire Economic Union *Tariffs and Treaties* (EEU, London, 1933)
────── *Future Fiscal Policy* (EEU, London, 1935)
────── *Further Considerations* (EEU, London, 1936)
────── *The British Colonial Empire and the German Claim* (EEU, London, 1937)
Engledown, J. *Holy War: The Menace of International Finance* (Birmingham, 1937)
Eugenics Society Annual Reports
────── *Who Are the Best People?* (London, 1936)
────── *Eugenics and Politics* (by H. Brewer, London, 1937)
────── *Aims and Objects of the Eugenics Society* (London, 1944)
Eyre-Todd, G. *Mobocracy, or towards the Abyss* (National Citizens' Union, Glasgow, 1922)
Fox, Sir F. *Parliamentary Government: A Failure?* (Stanley Paul, London, 1930)
Fry, M. *Hitler's Wonderland* (John Murray, London, 1934)
────── *Waters Flowing Eastwards* (London, 1953)
Fuller, J. F. C. *Memoirs of an Unconventional Soldier* (Nicolson and Watson, London, 1936)
────── *The First of the League Wars* (Eyre and Spottiswoode, London, 1936)
────── *What the British Union has to Offer* (BUF, London, 1937)

Grant, M. *The Passing of the Great Race, or The Racial Basis of European History* (G. Bell, London, 1917)

Gwynne, H. A. *The Cause of the World Unrest*, 'Introduction' (Morning Post, London, 1920)

—— *Controversy on Spain between H. A. Gwynne . . . and A. Pamos Oliveira* (United Editorial, London, 1938)

Haxey, S. *Tory MP* (Gollancz, London, 1939)

Hewins, W. A. S. *The Apologia of an Imperialist*, 2 vols. (Constable, London, 1929)

Heydon, J. K. *Fascism and Providence* (Sheed and Ward, London, 1937)

Hollis, M. C. *The Breakdown of Money* (Sheed and Ward, London, 1934)

—— *The Two Nations* (Routledge, London, 1935)

Imperial Fascist League *Mightier Yet (London, 1935)*

—— *Freemasonry* (London, 1935)

—— *Our Jewish Aristocracy* (London, 1936)

—— *Jewish Press Control* (London, 1937)

—— *Race and Politics* (London, n.d.)

—— *Agriculture Comes First* (London, n.d.)

Inge, W. R. *Outspoken Essays* (Longmans, London, 1919)

—— *Outspoken Essays II* (Longmans, London, 1922)

—— *England* (Benn, London, 1926)

—— *Vale* (Longmans, London, 1934)

Jenks, J. *The Land and the People* (BUF, London, n.d., c. 1934)

—— *Spring Comes Again: A Farmer's Philosophy* (Bookshelf, London, 1939)

Jerrold, D. *The Hawke Battalion* (Benn, London, 1925)

—— *England* (Arrowsmith, London, 1935)

—— *They That Take the Sword, the Future of The League of Nations* (Lane, London, 1936)

—— *Georgian Adventure* (Collins, London, 1937)

—— *Spain: Impressions and Reflections* (Nineteenth Century and After, 1937)

—— *The Necessity of Freedom* (Sheed and Ward, London, 1938)

Joyce, W. *Dictatorship* (BUF, London, 1933)

—— *Fascism and Jewry* (BUF, London, 1936)

—— *Fascism and India* (BUF, London, 1936)

—— *National Socialism Now* (NSL, London, 1937)

Kitson, A. *The Bankers' Conspiracy* (Elliot Stock, London, 1933)

Knight, G. E. O. *In Defence of Germany* (Golden Vista, London, 1933)

—— *Germany's Demand for Security* (Golden Eagle, London, 1934)

Labour Research Department *Who Backs Mosley?* (London, 1934)

—— *Mosley Fascism* (London, 1935)

Lane, A. H. *The Alien Menace* (King, London, 1928)

Leese, A.S. *My Irrelevant Defence* (IFL, London, 1938)

—— *Out of Step* (Leese, Guildford, 1951)

Lewis, Percy Wyndham *Hitler* (Chatto & Windus, London, 1931)

—— *Left-wings over Europe* (Cape, London, 1936)

—— *The Hitler Cult* (Dent, London, 1939)

Lintorn-Orman, R. *The Red Menace to British Children* (BF Publications, London, 1926)

Lloyd, 1st Baron *Leadership in Democracy* (Oxford University Press, London, 1939)

Londonderry, 7th Marquis *Ourselves and Germany* (Penguin, Harmondsworth, 1938)

Ludovici, A. M. *A Defence of Aristocracy. A Textbook for Tories* (Constable, London, 1915)

—— *The False Assumptions of Democracy* (Heath Cranton, London, 1921)

—— *A Defence of Conservatism* (Faber, London, 1927)

—— *Violence, Sacrifice and War* (English Mistery, London, 1933)

—— *Recovery: the Quest of Regenerate National Values* (English Mistery, London, 1935)

—— *English Liberalism* (English Mistery, London, 1939)

Lunn, A. *Spanish Rehearsal* (Hutchinson, London, 1937)

—— *The Unpopular Front* (London, 1937)

—— *Come What May, an Autobiography* (Eyre and Spottiswoode, London, 1940)

Lymington, Viscount *Ich Dien, the Tory Path* (Constable, London, 1931)

—— *Horn, Hoof and Corn* (Faber, London, 1932)

—— *Should Britain Fight? The British Position and Some Facts on the Sudeten Problem* (BCAEC, London, 1938)

—— *Famine in England* (Witherby, London, 1938)

—— *Alternative to Death* (Faber, London, 1943)

—— *A Knot of Roots: An Autobiography* (G. Bles, London, 1965)

Macara, C. W. *The Industrial Situation. Bolshevism. Conscription of Wealth.* (Sherratt and Hughes, Manchester, 1922)

Mairet, P. *Aristocracy and the Meaning of Class Rule* (Daniel, London, 1931)

—— *A. R. Orage. A Memoir* (with an Introduction by G. K. Chesterton) (Dent, London, 1936)

—— *Autobiographical and Other Papers* (ed. by C. H. Sisson) (Carcanet, Manchester, 1981)

Marsden, V. (translator) *Protocols of the Learned Elders of Zion* (Eyre and Spottiswoode, London, 1920)

—— *The Jews in Russia* (Britons, London, 1921)

Martin, K. *The British Public and the General Strike* (Hogarth, London, 1926)

—— 'Fascism and the Daily Mail', *Political Quarterly*, April 1934, pp. 273–6

Melville, C. F. *The Truth About the New Party* (Wishart and Co., London, 1931)

Mosley, O. *The Greater Britain* (BUF, London, 1932)

—— *Fascism, 100 Questions Asked and Answered* (BUF, London, 1936)

—— *Tomorrow We Live* (Greater Britain Publications, London, 1938)

—— *The Alternative* (Mosley Publications, Ramsbury, 1947)

—— *My Life* (Nelson, London, 1968)

Murchin, M. (Pseud.) *Britain's Jewish Problem* (Hurst and Blackett, London, 1939)

National Association of Merchants and Manufacturers *Speeches* (London, 1921)

National Party *National Opinion, a Pamphlet Setting Forth the Principles and Aims of the National Party* (London, 1917)

Northumberland, 8th Duke *International Revolutionary Propaganda* (Reconstruction Society, London, 1920)

—— *et al. Conspiracy against the British Empire* (London, 1921)

—— *The Passing of Liberalism* (Morning Post, London, 1925)

—— *The History of World Revolution* (The Society for the Advancement of Knowledge, Hayes, Middx., 1954)

Penty, A. J. *Distributism, a Manifesto* (Distributist League, London, 1937)

Percy, Lord Eustace *Some Memories* (Eyre and Spottiswoode, London, 1958)

Petrie, Sir C. *The History of Government* (Methuen, London, 1929)

—— *Mussolini* (Holme Press, London, 1931)

—— *Monarchy* (Eyre and Spottiswoode, London, 1933)

—— *The British Problem* (Nicholson and Watson, London, 1934)

—— *Lords of the Inland Sea* (Lovat Dickson, London, 1937)

—— *The Chamberlain Tradition* (Lovat Dickson, London, 1938)

—— *Chapters of Life* (Eyre and Spottiswoode, London, 1950)

Philby, H. St J. *Arabian Days, an Autobiography* (Hale, London, 1948)

Phillips, Sir P. *The Red Dragon and the Black Shirts* (Daily Mail, London, 1923)

Pitt-Rivers, G. L-F. *The World Significance of the Russian Revolution* (Blackwell, Oxford, 1920)

—— *The Czech Conspiracy* (Boswell, London, 1938)

Price, G. Ward *I Know These Dictators* (Harrap, London, 1937)

—— *Year of Reckoning* (Cassell, London, 1939)

Ragg, Rev. F. W. *Land Ownership and Magna Carta* (Patriot, London, 1925)

Ramsay, Capt. A. H. M. *The Nameless War* (Britons, London, 1952)

Reckitt, M. B. *As it Happened, an Autobiography* (Dent, London, 1941)

Reed, D. *Insanity Fair* (Cape, London, 1938)

Right Book Club *The Right Booklets*, nos. 1 and 2 (London, 1938)

Rothermere, Viscount *Solvency or Downfall?* (Daily Mail, London, 1921)

—— *Warnings and Predictions* (Eyre and Spottiswoode, London, 1939)

Round Table 'The Blackshirts', *Round Table*, Sept. 1934

Rudlin, W. A. *The Growth of Fascism in Great Britain* (Allen and Unwin, London, 1935)

Sanderson, W. *Statecraft* (Methuen, London, 1927)

—— *That Which Was Lost* (Constable, London, 1930)

Sarolea, Prof. C. *Daylight on Spain* (Hutchinson, London, 1938)

Sellon, H. *Democracy and Dictatorship* (Dickson, London, 1934)

Strachey, J. *The Menace of Fascism* (Gollancz, London, 1933)

Stutfield, H. E. *Priestcraft* (National Review, London, 1921)

—— *Mysticism and Catholicism* (Unwin, London, 1925)

Sydenham, 1st Baron *The Jewish World Problem* (Britons, London, 1921)

—— *My Working Life* (Murray, London, 1927)

—— *Studies of an Imperialist* (Chapman and Hall, London, 1928)

—— *A Perilous Election* (Boswell, London, 1929)

Tavistock, Marquis of (later 12th Duke of Bedford) *The Years of Transition* (Dakers, Edinburgh, 1949)

Templewood, Viscount (Sir Samuel Hoare) *Nine Troubled Years* (Collins, London, 1954)

Thomson, A. R. *The Coming Corporate State* (Greater Britain, London, 1937)

Varley, K. *The Unseen Hand in Britain* (Generation Press, London, 1917)

Vivian, H. *Myself Not Least* (London, 1925)

—— *Secret Societies Old and New* (Butterworth, London, 1927)

—— *Kings in Waiting* (Hamish Hamilton, London, 1933)

—— *Fascist Italy* (Melrose, London, 1936)

Waddell, Col. L. A. *The Makers of Civilisation in Race and History* (Luzac, London, 1929)

Webster, N. *World Revolution, the Plot Against Civilisation* (Constable, London, 1921)

—— *Secret Societies and Subversive Movements* (Boswell, London, 1924)

—— *The French Revolution* (Constable, London, 1926 edn)

—— *The Socialist Network* (Boswell, London, 1926)

—— *The Surrender of an Empire* (Boswell, London, 1931)

—— *Germany and England* (Boswell, London, 1939)

Wilson, Sir A. *Walks and Talks* (Oxford University Press, London, 1934)

—— *Walks and Talks Abroad* (Oxford University Press, London, 1936)

—— *Thoughts and Talks* (Longmans, London, 1938)

—— *Thoughts and Talks Abroad* (Longmans, London, 1939)

Yeats-Brown, F. *European Jungle* (Eyre and Spottiswoode, London, 1939)

(d) Secondary Sources

(Works of a general or comparative nature have been included only if they have been particularly useful.)

Adam, C. F. *Life of Lord Lloyd* (Macmillan, London, 1948)
Allen, H. Warner *Lucy Houston, DBE* (Constable, London, 1947)
Atholl, Duchess of, *Searchlight on Spain* (Penguin, Harmondsworth, 1938)
Barker, R. *Political Ideas in Modern Britain* (Methuen, London, 1978)
Benewick, R. J. *Political Violence and Public Order* (Allen Lane, London, 1969)
Bergonzi, B. 'Chesterton and/or Belloc', *Critical Quarterly*, vol. 1, no. 1 (1959), pp. 64–71
——— 'Roy Campbell: Outsider on the Right', *JCH* (1967), pp. 133–48
Blake, R. 'Baldwin and the Right' in J. Raymond (ed.) *The Baldwin Age* (Eyre and Spottiswoode, London, 1960)
——— *The Conservative Party from Peel to Churchill* (Eyre and Spottiswoode, London, 1970)
Bosworth, R. F. B. 'The British Press, the Conservatives and Mussolini, 1920–34', *JCH* (1970), pp. 163–82
Brewer, J. D. *Mosley's Men: The BUF in the West Midlands* (Gower, London, 1984)
Brittan, S. *Left or Right: The Bogus Dilemma* (Secker and Warburg, London, 1968)
Brown, K. D. (ed.) *Essays in Anti-Labour History* (Macmillan, London, 1974)
Butler, Lord (ed.) *The Conservatives* (Allen and Unwin, London, 1977)
Carpenter, L. P. 'Corporatism in Britain, 1930–45', *JCH* (1976), pp. 3–25
Cato (Pseud.) *Guilty Men* (Gollancz, London, 1940)
Chester, L. Fay, S. and Young, H. *The Zinoviev Letter* (Heinemann, London, 1967)
Close, D. 'Conservatives and Coalition After the First World War', *JMH* (1973), pp. 240–60
Cole, J. A. *Lord Haw-Haw — and William Joyce* (Faber, London, 1964)
Cowling, M. *The Impact of Labour, 1920–1924* (Cambridge University Press, Cambridge, 1971)
——— *The Impact of Hitler* (Cambridge University Press, Cambridge, 1975)
———(ed.) *Conservative Essays* (Cassell, London, 1978)
——— *Religion and Public Doctrine in Modern England* (Cambridge University Press, Cambridge, 1980)
Cross, C. *The Fascists in Britain* (Barrie and Rockliffe, London, 1961)
Douglas, R. 'The National Democratic Party and the British Workers' League', *HJ* (1972), pp. 533–52
Eatwell, R. 'Munich, Public Opinion and the Popular Front', *JCH* (1971), pp. 122–39
Eccleshall, R. 'English Conservatism as an Ideology', *PS* (1977), pp. 62–83
Feiling, K. *The Life of Neville Chamberlain* (Macmillan, London, 1946)
Finlay, J. L. 'John Hargrave, the Greenshirts and Social Credit', *JCH* (1970), pp. 53–71
Foot, M. (as Cassius) *Brendan and Beverley. An Extravaganza* (Gollancz, London, 1944)
Foot, P. *Immigration and Race in British Politics* (Penguin, Harmondsworth, 1965)
Gamble, A. *The Conservative Nation* (Routledge and Kegan Paul, London, 1974)
Gannon, F. R. *The British Press and Germany, 1936–1939* (Clarendon, Oxford 1971)
Garrard, J. A. *The English and Immigration* (Oxford University Press, London, 1971)

Ghosh, S. C. 'Decision making and Power in the British Conservative Party: a Case Study of the Indian Problem, 1929–34', *PS* (1965), pp. 198–212

Gilbert, M. *W. S. Churchill*, vol. V, Companion. Documents *1922–39* (Heinemann, London, 1976)

—— *Churchill's Political Philosophy* (Oxford University Press, London, 1981)

Glass, S. T. *The Responsible Society: The Ideas of Guild Socialism* (Longmans, London, 1966)

Glickman, H. 'The Toryness of English Conservatism', *JBS* (Nov. 1961), pp. 111–43.

Gollin, A. M. *Proconsuls in Politics: A Study of Lord Milner in Opposition and in Power* (Blond, London, 1964)

Green, E. H. 'Radical Conservatism and the Electoral Genesis of Tariff Reform', *HJ* (1985), pp. 667–92

Greenleaf, W. H. 'The Character of Modern British Conservatism' in R. Benewick, R. Berki and B. Parekh (eds.), *Knowledge and Belief in Politics* (St Martins Press, New York, 1973), pp. 177–212

Griffiths, R. *Fellow Travellers of the Right. British Enthusiasts for Nazi Germany, 1933–39* (Constable, London, 1980)

Hamilton, A. *The Appeal of Fascism. A Study of Intellectuals and Fascism, 1919–1945* (Blond, London, 1971)

Harris, N. *Competition and the Corporate Society* (Methuen, London, 1972)

Harrison, M. *The Reactionaries* (Gollancz, London, 1966)

Hayes, P. *Fascism* (Allen and Unwin, London, 1973)

Holmes, C. *Anti-Semitism in British Society, 1876–1939* (Edward Arnold, London, 1979)

Huntington, S. 'Conservatism as an Ideology', *APSR* (1957), pp. 454–73

Hurst, M. 'What is Fascism?', *HJ* (1968), pp. 165–85

Hynes, S. *The Edwardian Turn of Mind* (Princeton University Press, Princeton, 1968)

Jessop, R. D. *Traditionalism, Conservatism and British Political Culture* (Allen and Unwin, London, 1974)

Jones, Aubrey *The Pendulum of Politics* (Right Book Club, London, 1947)

Jones, A. and Bentley, M. 'Salisbury and Baldwin' in Cowling (ed.), *Conservative Essays*, pp. 25–40

Jones, G. 'Eugenics and Social Policy between the Wars', *HJ* (1982), pp. 717–28

Jones, J. R. 'England' in Rogger and Weber (eds.), *The European Right*, pp. 29–70

Kendle, J. E. 'The Round Table Movement and Home Rule All Round', *HJ* (1968), pp. 332–53

Kennedy, P. *The Rise of the Anglo-German Antagonism, 1860–1914* (Allen and Unwin, London, 1980)

—— and Nicholls, A. (eds.) *Nationalist and Racialist Movements in Britain and Germany Before 1914* (Macmillan, London, 1981)

Kirk, R. *The Conservative Mind* (Faber, London, 1954)

Kornhauser, W. *The Politics of Mass Society* (Free Press of Glencoe, Illinois, 1959)

Koss, S. E. *Lord Haldane: Scapegoat for Liberalism* (Columbia University Press, New York and London, 1969)

Laqueur, W. (ed.) *Fascism: a Reader's Guide* (Penguin, Harmondsworth, 1979)

Lasky, M. 'Who's Left, What's Right?' *Encounter*, Feb./Mar. 1977

Layton-Henry, Z. (ed.) *Conservative Party Politics* (Macmillan, London, 1980)

Lebzelter, G. C. *Political Anti-Semitism in England, 1918–1939* (Macmillan, London, 1978)

Levy, D. J. 'On Being Right', *Salisbury Review*, Autumn 1982

Lindsay, T. and Harrington, M. *The Conservative Party, 1918–1979* (Macmillan, London, 1979)

Lipset, S. M. and Raab, E. *The Politics of Unreason. Right-wing Extremism in America, 1790–1970* (Heinemann, London, 1971)
Lunn, K. and Thurlow, R. C. (eds.). *British Fascism. Essays on the Radical Right in Inter-war Britain* (Croom Helm, London, 1980)
Madge, C. E. and Harrison, T. *Britain By Mass Observation* (Penguin, Harmondsworth, 1939)
Mandle, W. F. 'The Leadership of the BUF', *Australian Journal of Politics and History* (1966), pp. 360–83
―――― *Anti-Semitism and the British Union of Fascists* (London, 1968)
McDowell, R. B. *British Conservatism, 1832–1914* (Faber, London, 1959)
McEwen, J. M. 'The Coupon Election of 1918 and Unionist MPs', *JMH* (1962), pp. 294–306
McKenzie, R. T. *British Political Parties* (Heinemann, London, 1955)
Middlemas, R. K. *Politics in Industrial Society* (Deutsch, London, 1979)
―――― and Barnes, J. *Baldwin. A Biography* (Wiedenfeld and Nicolson, London, 1969)
Monroe, E. *Philby of Arabia* (Faber, London, 1973)
Morgan, K. O. *Consensus and Disunity. The Lloyd George Coalition Government, 1918–1922* (Clarendon, Oxford, 1979)
Mosley, N. *Rules of the Game* (Secker and Warburg, London, 1982)
―――― *Beyond the Pale* (Secker and Warburg, London, 1983)
Mowat, C. L. *Britain Between the Wars, 1918–1940* (Methuen, London, 1955)
Mullally, F. *Fascism inside England* (Morris, London, 1946)
Norton, P. and Aughey, A. *Conservatives and Conservatism* (Temple Smith, London, 1981)
Nugent, N. and King R. (eds.) *The British Right* (Saxon House, Farnborough, 1977)
O'Day, A. (ed.) *The Edwardian Age* (Macmillan, London, 1979)
Orwell, G. *Collected Essays* (Secker and Warburg, London, 1961)
O'Sullivan, N. *Conservatism* (Dent, London, 1976)
Peele, G. and Cook, C. (eds.) *The Politics of Reappraisal, 1918–1939* (Macmillan, London, 1975)
Phillips, G. D. *The Diehards* (Harvard Univ. Press, Cambridge, Mass., 1979)
Pinto-Duschinsky, M. 'Central Office and "Power" in the Conservative Party', *PS* (1972), pp. 1–16
Pryce-Jones, D. *Unity Mitford. A Quest* (Wiedenfeld and Nicolson, London, 1976)
Pugh, M. *The Making of Modern British Politics, 1867–1939* (Blackwell, Oxford, 1982)
Ramsden, J. *The Age of Balfour and Baldwin, 1902–1940* (Longmans, London, 1978)
Renshaw, P. 'Anti-Labour Politics in Britain, 1918–27, *JCH* (1977), pp. 693–705
Rogger, H. and Weber, E. (eds.) *The European Right* (Wiedenfeld and Nicolson, London, 1965)
Rose, K. *The Later Cecils* (Wiedenfeld and Nicolson, London, 1975)
Rose, R. 'Parties, Factions and Tendencies in Britain', *PS* (1964), pp. 33–46
Rubinstein, W. D. 'Henry Page Croft and the National Party, 1918–22', *JCH* (1974), pp. 129–48
―――― *Men of Property. The Very Wealthy in Britain Since the Industrial Revolution* (Croom Helm, London, 1981)
―――― *The Left, the Right and the Jews* (Croom Helm, London, 1982)
Schmitter, P. C. 'Still the Century of Corporatism?', *Review of Politics* (1974), pp. 85–131
Schumann, H. G. 'The Problem of Conservatism: Some Notes on Methodology', *JCH* (1978), pp. 803–17

Scruton, R. *The Meaning of Conservatism* (Penguin, Harmondsworth, 1980)
Searle, G. R. *The Quest for National Efficiency* (Blackwell, Oxford, 1971)
———— 'Critics of Edwardian Society: the Case of the Radical Right' in O'Day (ed.), *The Edwardian Age*, ch. 4
———— 'Eugenics and Politics in Britain in the 1930s', *Annals of Science* (1979), pp. 159–69
———— 'The Revolt from the Right in Edwardian Britain' in Kennedy and Nicholls (eds.), *Nationalist and Racialist Movements in Britain and Germany Before 1914*, ch. 2.
Selver, P. *Orage and the New Age Circle* (Allen and Unwin, London, 1959)
Sharf, A. *The British Press and Jews under Nazi Rule* (Oxford University Press, London, 1964)
Skidelsky, R. 'Great Britain' in Woolf (ed.), *European Fascism*, ch. 11.
———— *Oswald Mosley* (Macmillan, London, 1975)
Stannage, T. *Baldwin Thwarts the Opposition* (Croom Helm, London, 1980)
Stevenson, J. *British Society, 1914–45* (Penguin, Harmondsworth, 1984)
———— and Cook, C. *The Slump* (Cape, London, 1977)
Sykes, A. *Tariff Reform in British Politics, 1903–1913* (Clarendon, Oxford, 1979)
———— 'The Radical Right and the Crisis of Conservatism before the First World War', *HJ* (1983), pp. 661–76
Taylor, A. J. P. *Politics in Wartime and Other Essays* (Hamish Hamilton, London, 1964)
———— *English History, 1914–1945* (Oxford University Press, Oxford, 1965)
Thompson, N. *The Anti-Appeasers, Conservative Opposition to Appeasement in the 1930s* (Clarendon, Oxford, 1971)
Thornton, A. P. *The Imperial Idea and its Enemies* (Macmillan, London, 1959)
Turner, J. A. 'The British Commonwealth Union and the General Election of 1918', *EHR* (1978), pp. 528–59
Waley, D. *British Public Opinion and the Abyssinian War, 1935–6* (Temple Smith, London, 1975)
Watkins, K. W. *Britain Divided. The Effect of the Spanish Civil War on British Public Opinion* (Nelson, London, 1963)
Webber, G. C. 'Patterns of Membership and Support for the BUF', *JCH* (1984), pp. 575–606
———— 'The British Isles' in D. Mühlberger (ed.), *The Social Base of European Fascist Movements* (forthcoming, 1987)
West, R. *The Meaning of Treason* (Macmillan, London, 1949)
Wiener, M. *English Culture and the Decline of the Industrial Spirit, 1850–1980* (Cambridge University Press, Cambridge, 1981)
Williams, R. *Culture and Society, 1780–1950* (Chatto and Windus, London, 1959)
Williams, P. 'Safety First: Baldwin, the Conservative Party, and the 1929 General Election', *HJ* (1982), pp. 385–409
Wise, L. *Arthur Kitson* (Holborn, London, 1946)
Woolf, S. J. (ed.) *European Fascism* (Wiedenfeld and Nicolson, London, 1968)
Woolton, G. 'Ex-Servicemen in Politics', *PQ* (1958), pp. 28–39
Wrench, J. E. *Francis Yeats-Brown, 1886–1944* (Eyre and Spottiswoode, London, 1948)
Young, G. M. *Stanley Baldwin* (Hart-Davis, London, 1952)
Zeman, Z. A. B. *Nazi Propaganda* (Oxford University Press, London, 1973)

(e) Reference Books

In addition to the usual works (*DNB*, *Who's Who*, *Burke*'s etc.) the following have been particularly helpful.

Block, G. D. M. *A Source Book of Conservatism* (CPC, London, 1964)
Cook, C. *Sources in British Political History, 1900–1950*, 5 vols. (Macmillan, London, 1975)
Craig, F. W. S. *Minor Parties at British Parliamentary Elections 1885–1974* (Macmillan, London, 1975)
Rees, P. *Fascism in Britain: An Annotated Bibliography* (Harvester Press, Hassocks, 1979)

INDEX

For additional references to and information about most of the individuals and organisations mentioned in the text and footnotes see the Appendix. The Appendix is cross-referenced and has not been indexed.